ICEMAN

THAWING OUT

Writer/**SINA GRACE**

ISSUES #1, #3 & #5
Artist/**ALESSANDRO VITTI**

ISSUES #2 & #4
Pencilers/**EDGAR SALAZAR**
with **IBRAIM ROBERSON** (#2)
Inkers/**ED TADEO**
with **IBRAIM ROBERSON** (#2)

Color Artist/**RACHELLE ROSENBERG**

Letterer/**VC's JOE SABINO**

Cover Artists/**KEVIN WADA** (#1-4)
& **MARCO D'ALFONSO** (#5)

Assistant Editor/**CHRIS ROBINSON**
Editors/**DANIEL KETCHUM** & **DARREN SHAN**
X-Men Group Editor/**MARK PANICCIA**

ICEMAN CREATED BY **STAN LEE** & **JACK KIRBY**

Collection Editor/**JENNIFER GRÜNWALD** • Assistant Editor/**CAITLIN O'CONNELL**
Associate Managing Editor/**KATERI WOODY** • Editor, Special Projects/**MARK D. BEAZLEY**
VP Production & Special Projects/**JEFF YOUNGQUIST** • SVP Print, Sales & Marketing/**DAVID GABRIEL**
Book Designer/**JAY BOWEN**

Editor in Chief/**AXEL ALONSO** • Chief Creative Officer/**JOE QUESADA**
President/**DAN BUCKLEY** • Executive Producer/**ALAN FINE**

ICEMAN VOL. 1: THAWING OUT. Contains material originally published in magazine form as ICEMAN #1-5. First printing 2017. ISBN# 978-1-302-90879-9. Published by MARVEL WORLDWIDE, INC., a subsidiary of MARVEL ENTERTAINMENT, LLC. OFFICE OF PUBLICATION: 135 West 50th Street, New York, NY 10020. **Printed in the U.S.A.** DAN BUCKLEY, President, Marvel Entertainment; JOE QUESADA, Chief Creative Officer; TOM BREVOORT, SVP of Publishing; DAVID BOGART, SVP of Business Affairs & Operations, Publishing & Partnership; C.B. CEBULSKI, VP of Brand Management & Development, Asia; DAVID GABRIEL, SVP of Sales & Marketing, Publishing; JEFF YOUNGQUIST, VP of Production & Special Projects; DAN CARR, Executive Director of Publishing Technology; ALEX MORALES, Director of Publishing Operations; SUSAN CRESPI, Production Manager; STAN LEE, Chairman Emeritus. For information regarding advertising in Marvel Comics or on Marvel.com, please contact Jonathan Parkhideh, VP of Digital Media & Marketing Solutions, at jparkhideh@marvel.com. For Marvel subscription inquiries, please call 888-511-5480. **Manufactured between 11/3/2017 and 12/4/2017 by LSC COMMUNICATIONS INC., KENDALLVILLE, IN, USA.**

10 9 8 7 6 5 4 3 2 1

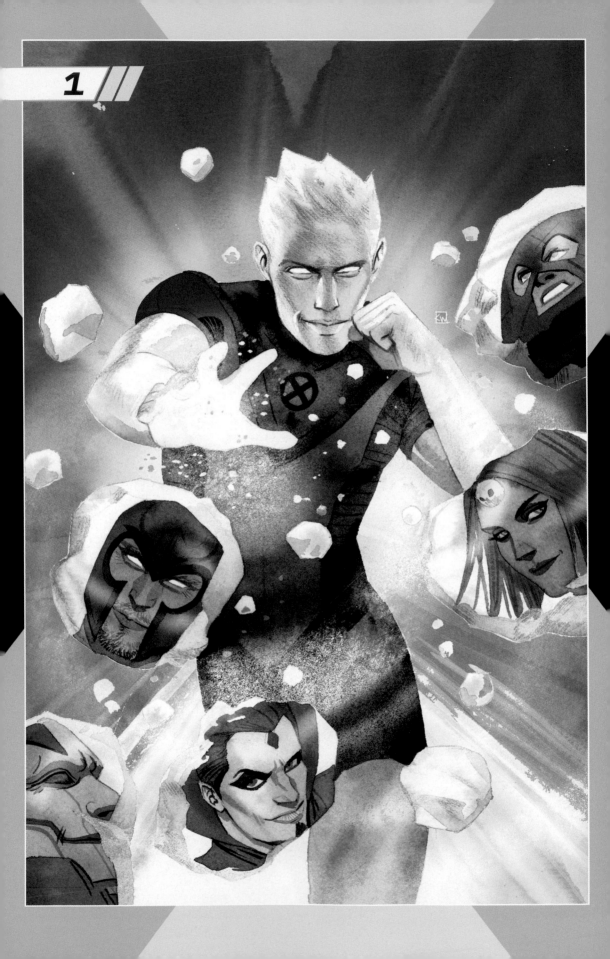

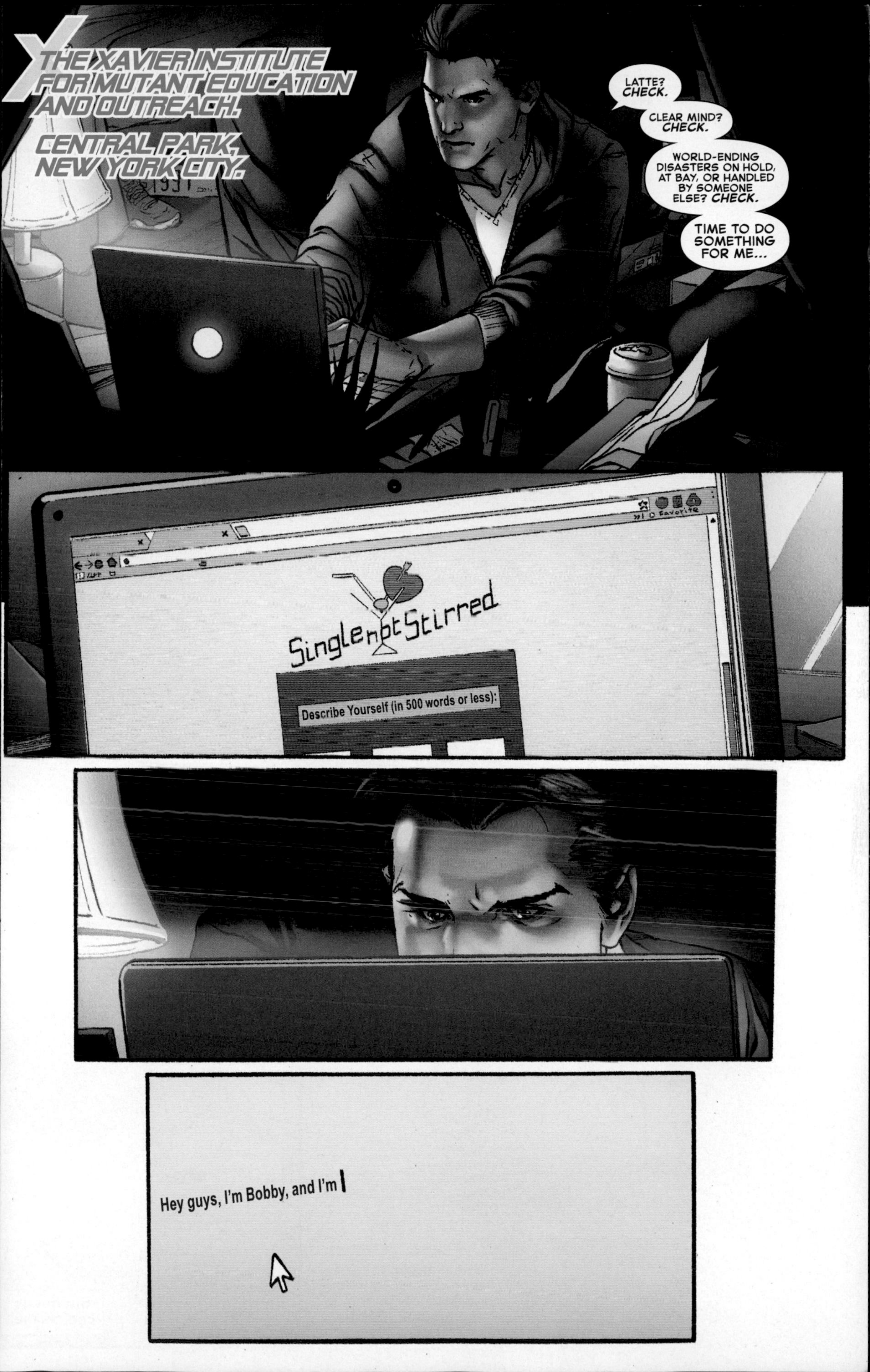
THE XAVIER INSTITUTE FOR MUTANT EDUCATION AND OUTREACH.
CENTRAL PARK, NEW YORK CITY.
LATTE? CHECK.
CLEAR MIND? CHECK.
WORLD-ENDING DISASTERS ON HOLD, AT BAY, OR HANDLED BY SOMEONE ELSE? CHECK.
TIME TO DO SOMETHING FOR ME...
Favorite
Single not Stirred
Describe Yourself (in 500 words or less):
Hey guys, I'm Bobby, and I'm

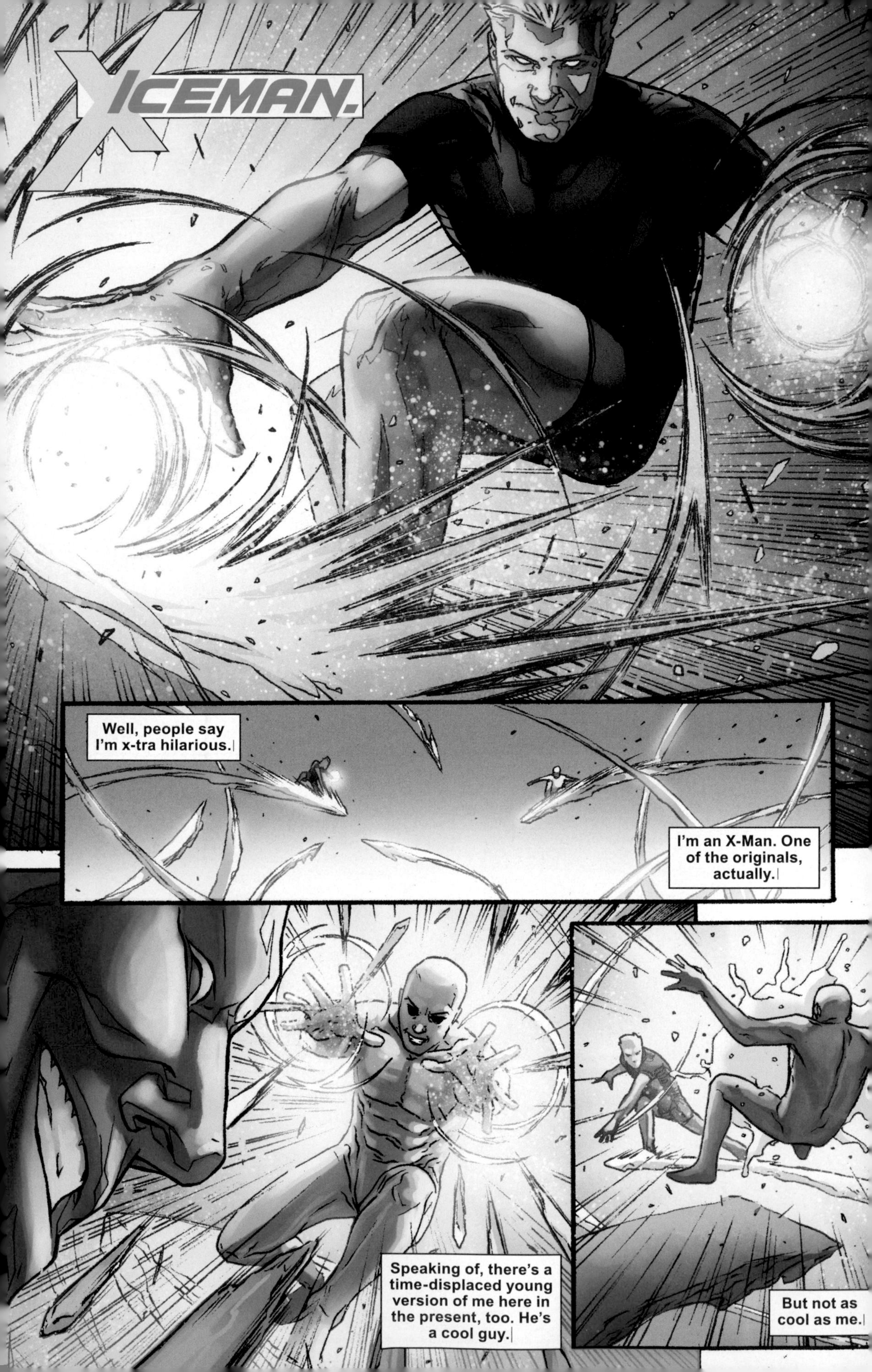
ICEMAN.
Well, people say I'm x-tra hilarious.
I'm an X-Man. One of the originals, actually.
Speaking of, there's a time-displaced young version of me here in the present, too. He's a cool guy.
But not as cool as me.

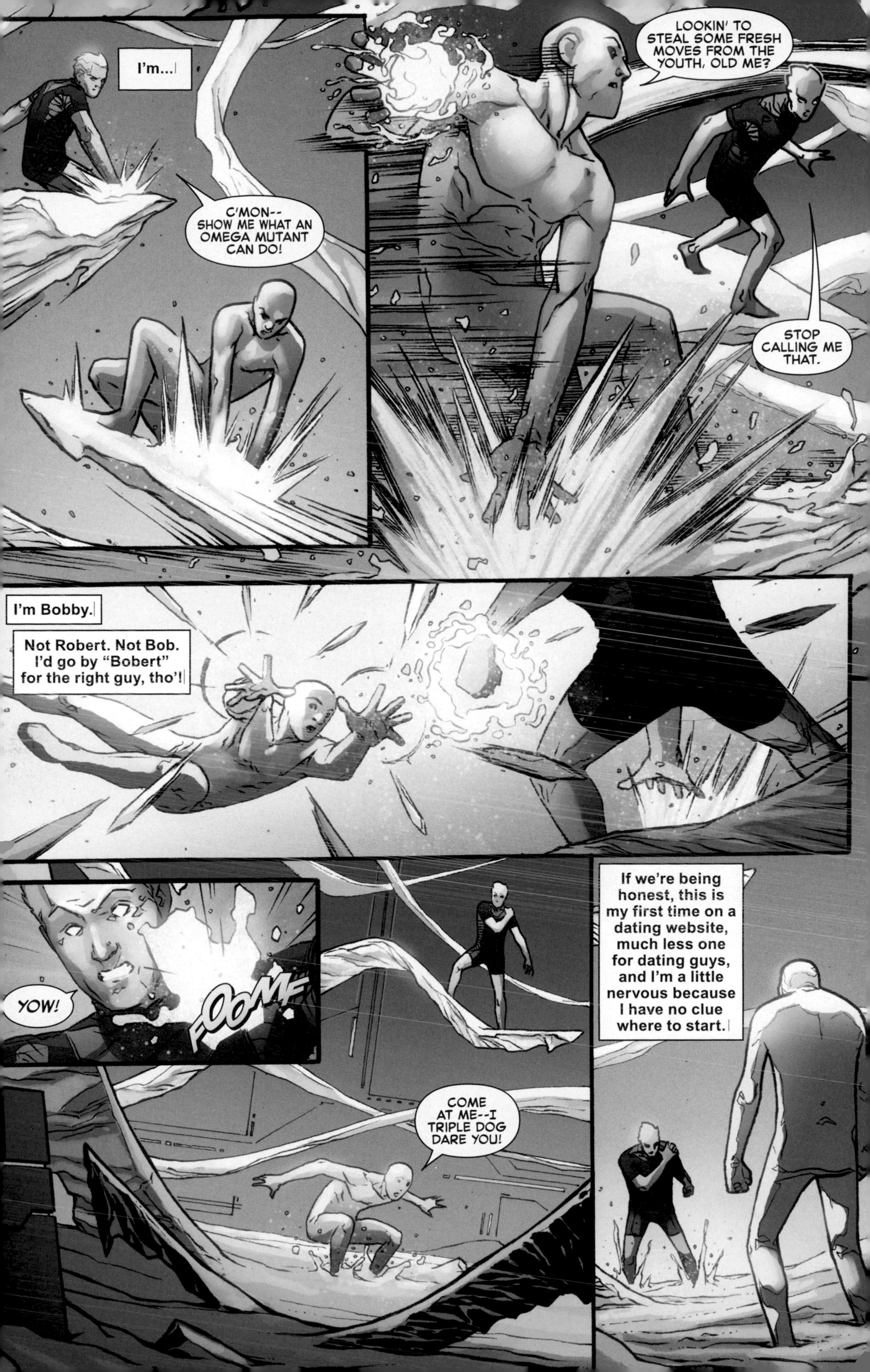
I'm...
C'MON--
SHOW ME WHAT AN OMEGA MUTANT CAN DO!
LOOKIN' TO STEAL SOME FRESH MOVES FROM THE YOUTH, OLD ME?
STOP CALLING ME THAT.
I'm Bobby.
Not Robert. Not Bob. I'd go by "Bobert" for the right guy, tho'!
YOW!
FOOMF
COME AT ME--I TRIPLE DOG DARE YOU!
If we're being honest, this is my first time on a dating website, much less one for dating guys, and I'm a little nervous because I have no clue where to start.

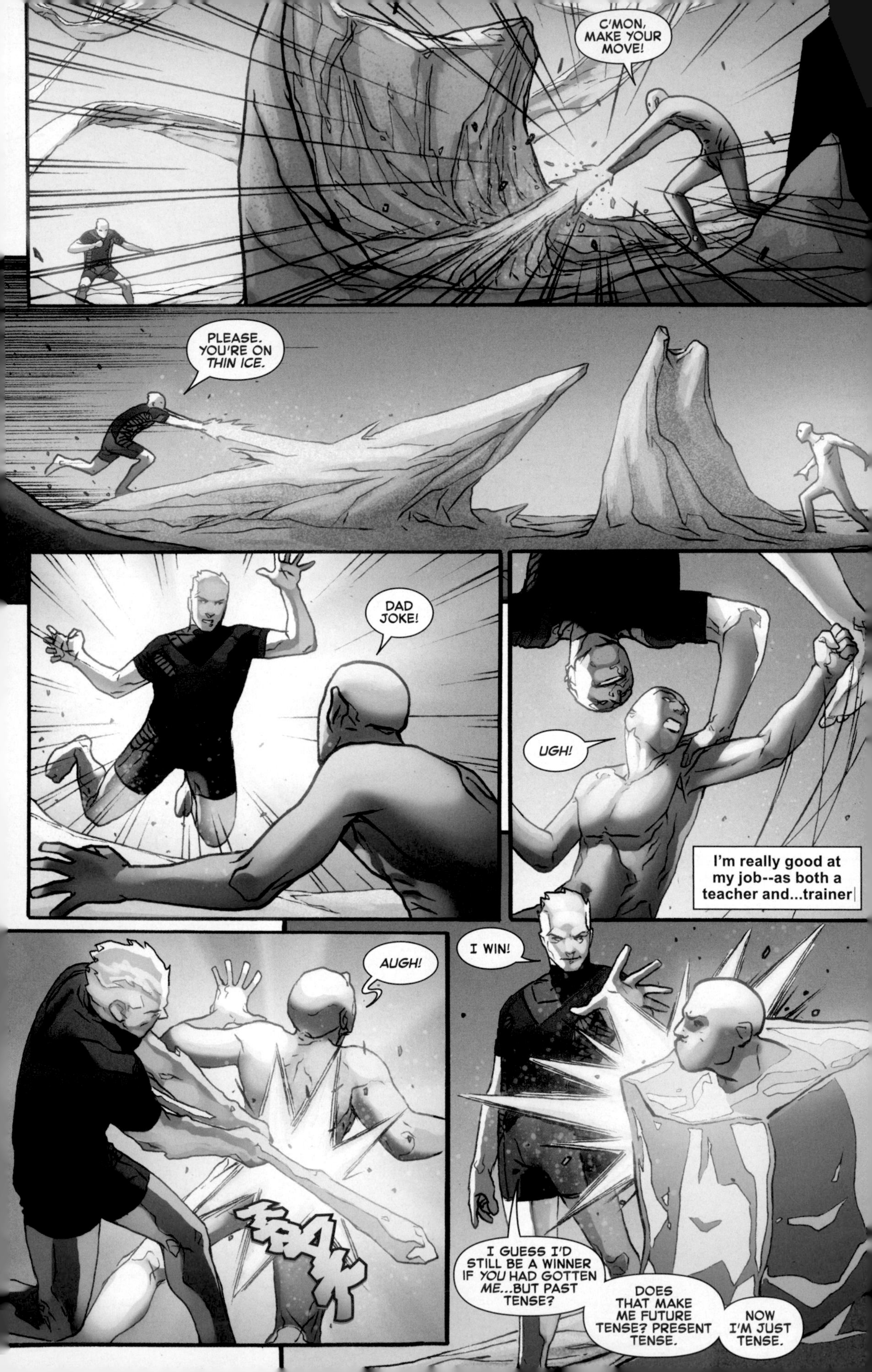
C'MON, MAKE YOUR MOVE!
PLEASE. YOU'RE ON THIN ICE.
DAD JOKE!
UGH!
I'm really good at my job--as both a teacher and...trainer
AUGH!
I WIN!
I GUESS I'D STILL BE A WINNER IF YOU HAD GOTTEN ME...BUT PAST TENSE?
DOES THAT MAKE ME FUTURE TENSE? PRESENT TENSE.
NOW I'M JUST TENSE.

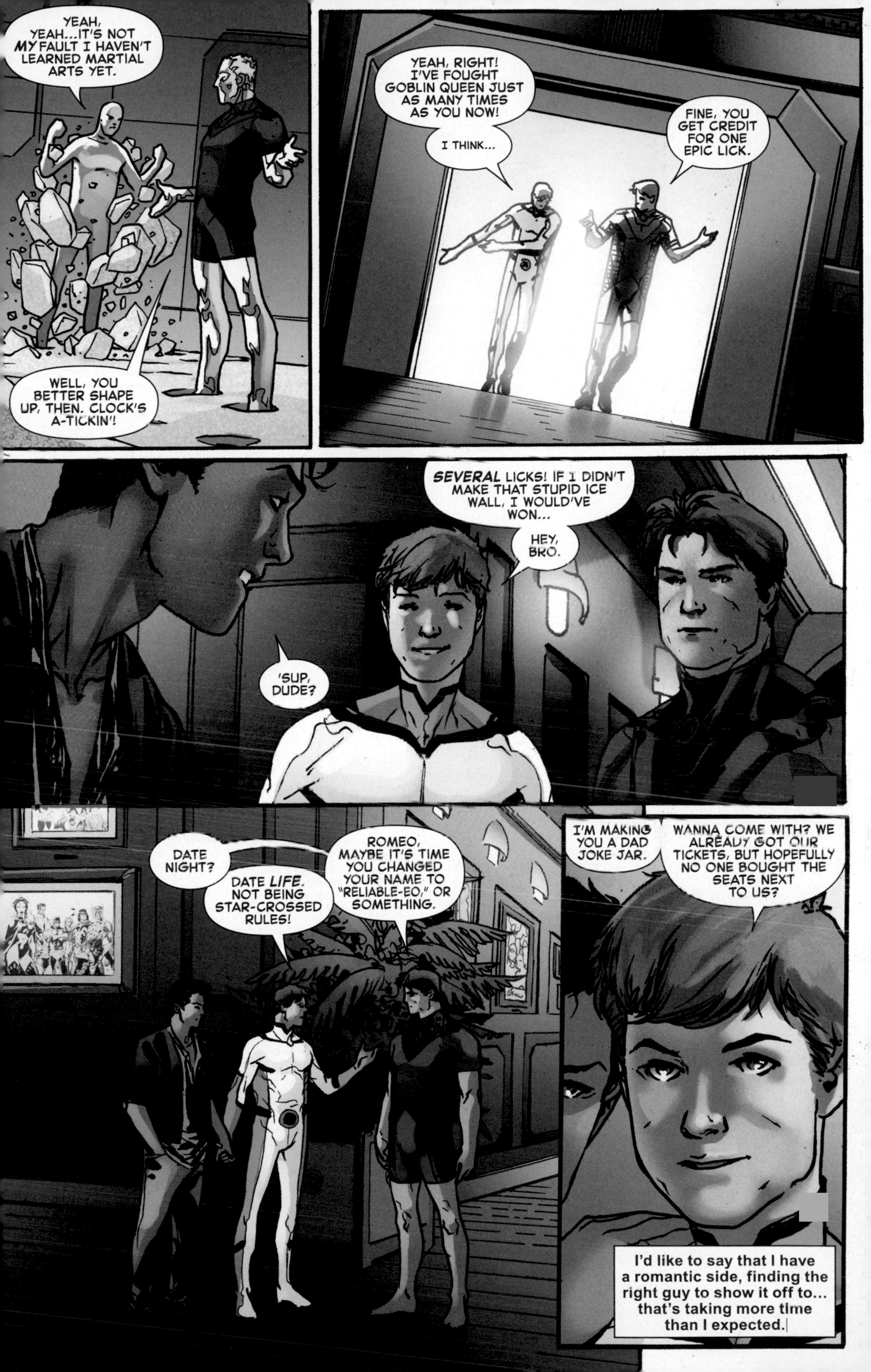
YEAH, YEAH...IT'S NOT MY FAULT I HAVEN'T LEARNED MARTIAL ARTS YET.
WELL, YOU BETTER SHAPE UP, THEN. CLOCK'S A-TICKIN'!
YEAH, RIGHT! I'VE FOUGHT GOBLIN QUEEN JUST AS MANY TIMES AS YOU NOW!
I THINK...
FINE, YOU GET CREDIT FOR ONE EPIC LICK.
SEVERAL LICKS! IF I DIDN'T MAKE THAT STUPID ICE WALL, I WOULD'VE WON...
HEY, BRO.
'SUP, DUDE?
DATE NIGHT?
DATE LIFE. NOT BEING STAR-CROSSED RULES!
ROMEO, MAYBE IT'S TIME YOU CHANGED YOUR NAME TO "RELIABLE-EO," OR SOMETHING.
I'M MAKING YOU A DAD JOKE JAR.
WANNA COME WITH? WE ALREADY GOT OUR TICKETS, BUT HOPEFULLY NO ONE BOUGHT THE SEATS NEXT TO US?
I'd like to say that I have a romantic side, finding the right guy to show it off to... that's taking more time than I expected.

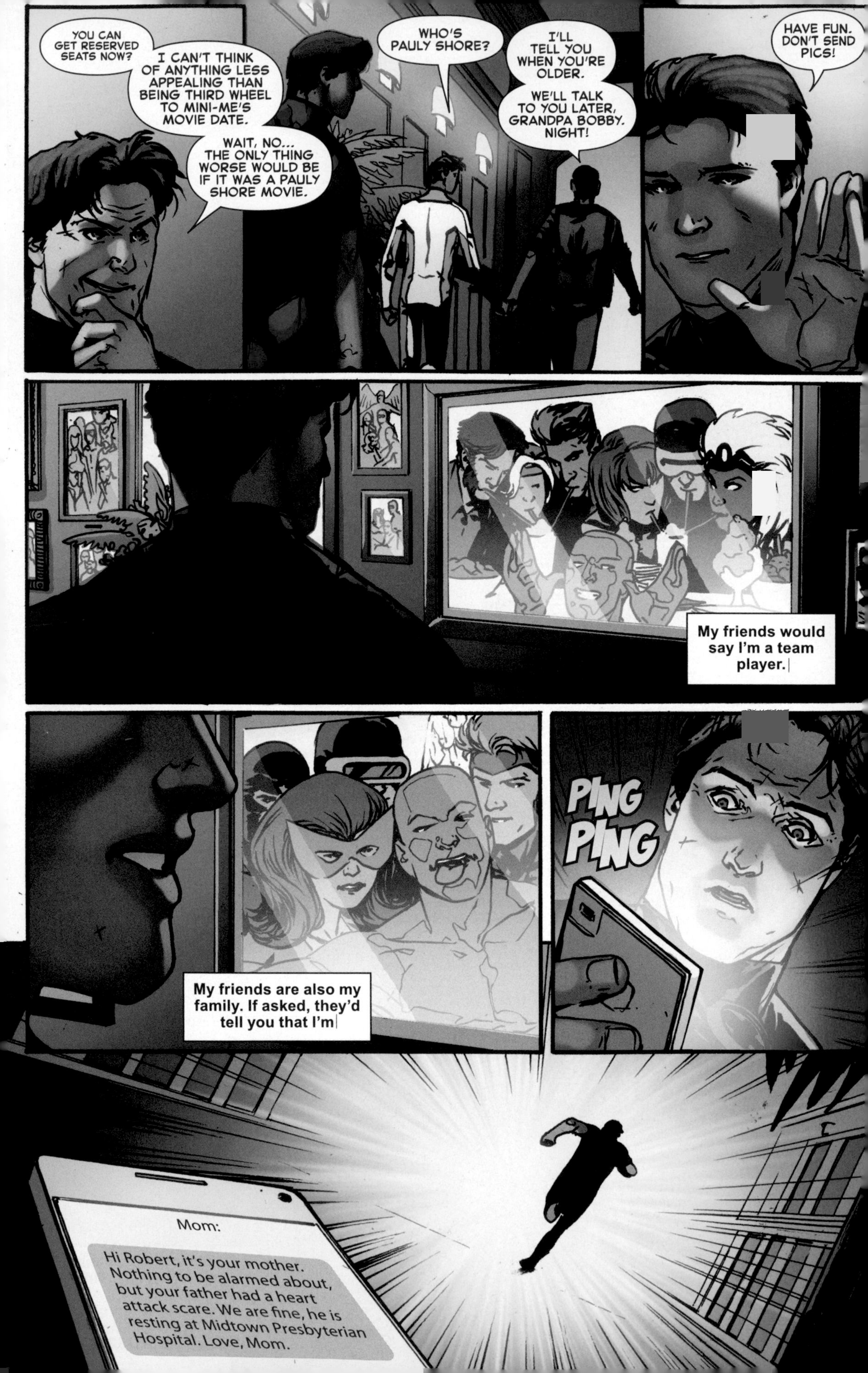

YOU CAN GET RESERVED SEATS NOW?
I CAN'T THINK OF ANYTHING LESS APPEALING THAN BEING THIRD WHEEL TO MINI-ME'S MOVIE DATE.
WAIT, NO... THE ONLY THING WORSE WOULD BE IF IT WAS A PAULY SHORE MOVIE.
WHO'S PAULY SHORE?
I'LL TELL YOU WHEN YOU'RE OLDER.
WE'LL TALK TO YOU LATER, GRANDPA BOBBY. NIGHT!
HAVE FUN. DON'T SEND PICS!
My friends would say I'm a team player.
My friends are also my family. If asked, they'd tell you that I'm
PING
PING
Mom:
Hi Robert, it's your mother. Nothing to be alarmed about, but your father had a heart attack scare. We are fine, he is resting at Midtown Presbyterian Hospital. Love, Mom.

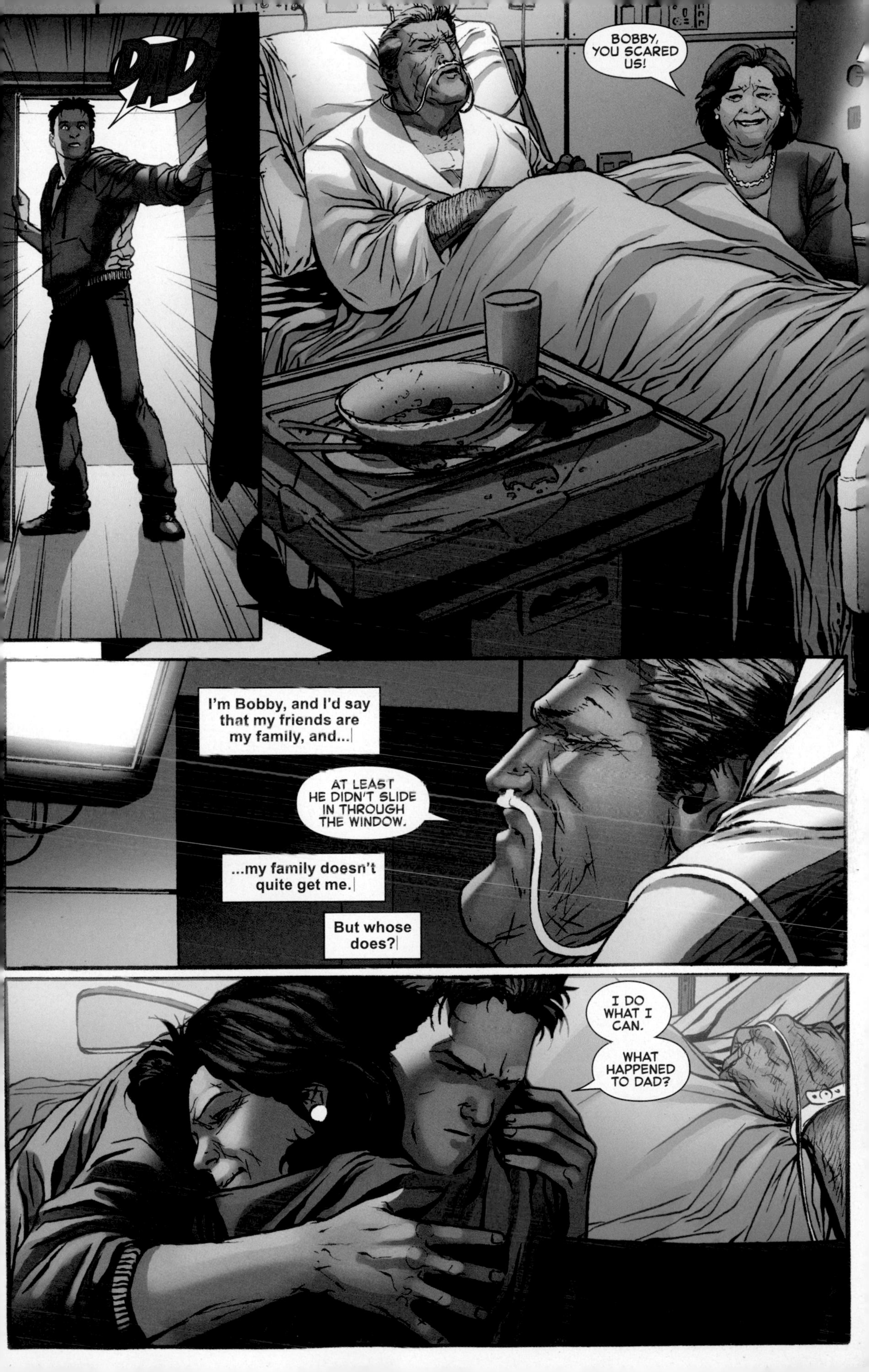
DAD!
BOBBY, YOU SCARED US!
I'm Bobby, and I'd say that my friends are my family, and...
AT LEAST HE DIDN'T SLIDE IN THROUGH THE WINDOW.
...my family doesn't quite get me.
But whose does?
I DO WHAT I CAN.
WHAT HAPPENED TO DAD?

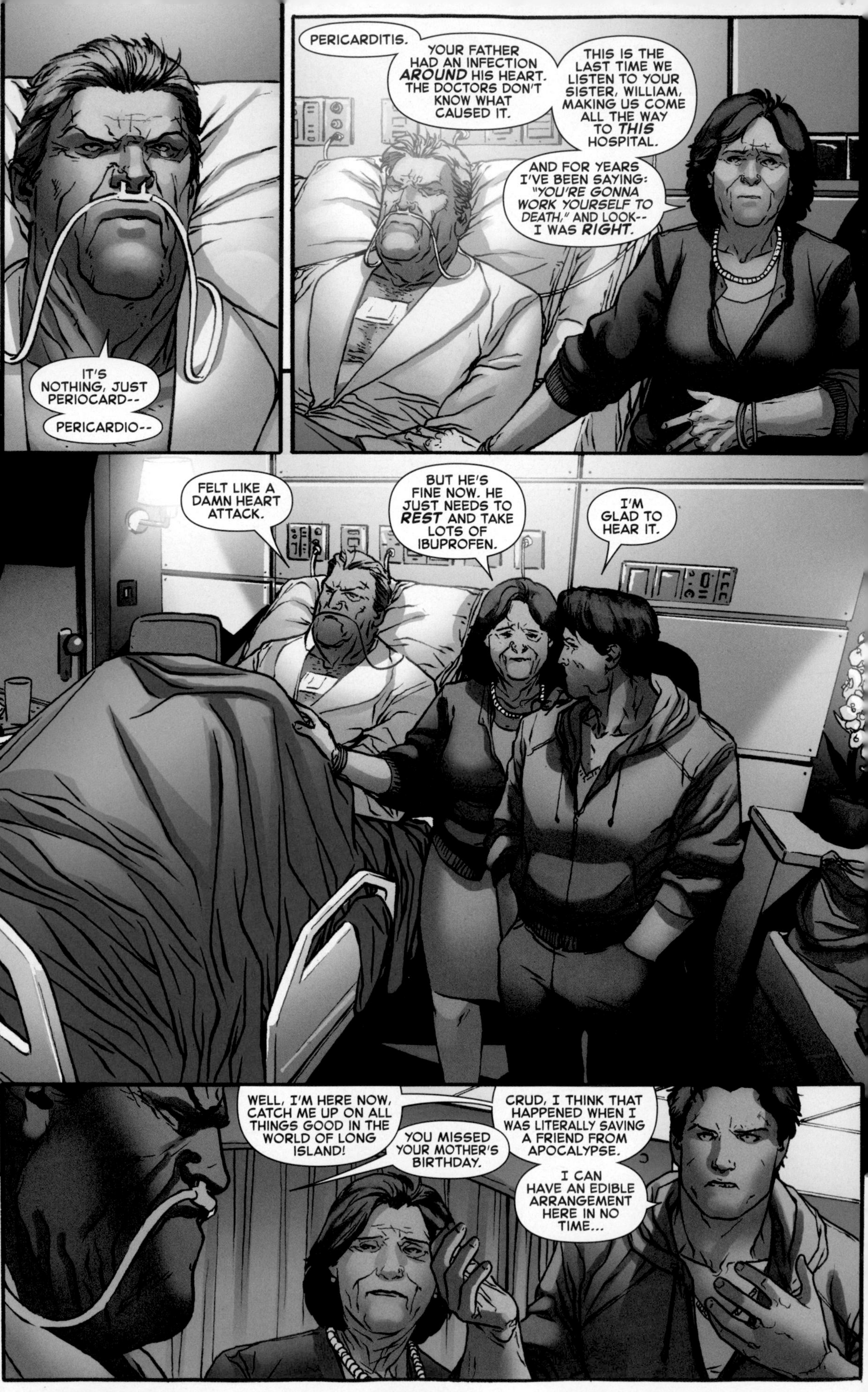
IT'S NOTHING, JUST PERIOCARD--
PERICARDIO--
PERICARDITIS.
YOUR FATHER HAD AN INFECTION AROUND HIS HEART. THE DOCTORS DON'T KNOW WHAT CAUSED IT.
THIS IS THE LAST TIME WE LISTEN TO YOUR SISTER, WILLIAM, MAKING US COME ALL THE WAY TO THIS HOSPITAL.
AND FOR YEARS I'VE BEEN SAYING: "YOU'RE GONNA WORK YOURSELF TO DEATH," AND LOOK-- I WAS RIGHT.
FELT LIKE A DAMN HEART ATTACK.
BUT HE'S FINE NOW. HE JUST NEEDS TO REST AND TAKE LOTS OF IBUPROFEN.
I'M GLAD TO HEAR IT.
WELL, I'M HERE NOW, CATCH ME UP ON ALL THINGS GOOD IN THE WORLD OF LONG ISLAND!
YOU MISSED YOUR MOTHER'S BIRTHDAY.
CRUD, I THINK THAT HAPPENED WHEN I WAS LITERALLY SAVING A FRIEND FROM APOCALYPSE.
I CAN HAVE AN EDIBLE ARRANGEMENT HERE IN NO TIME...

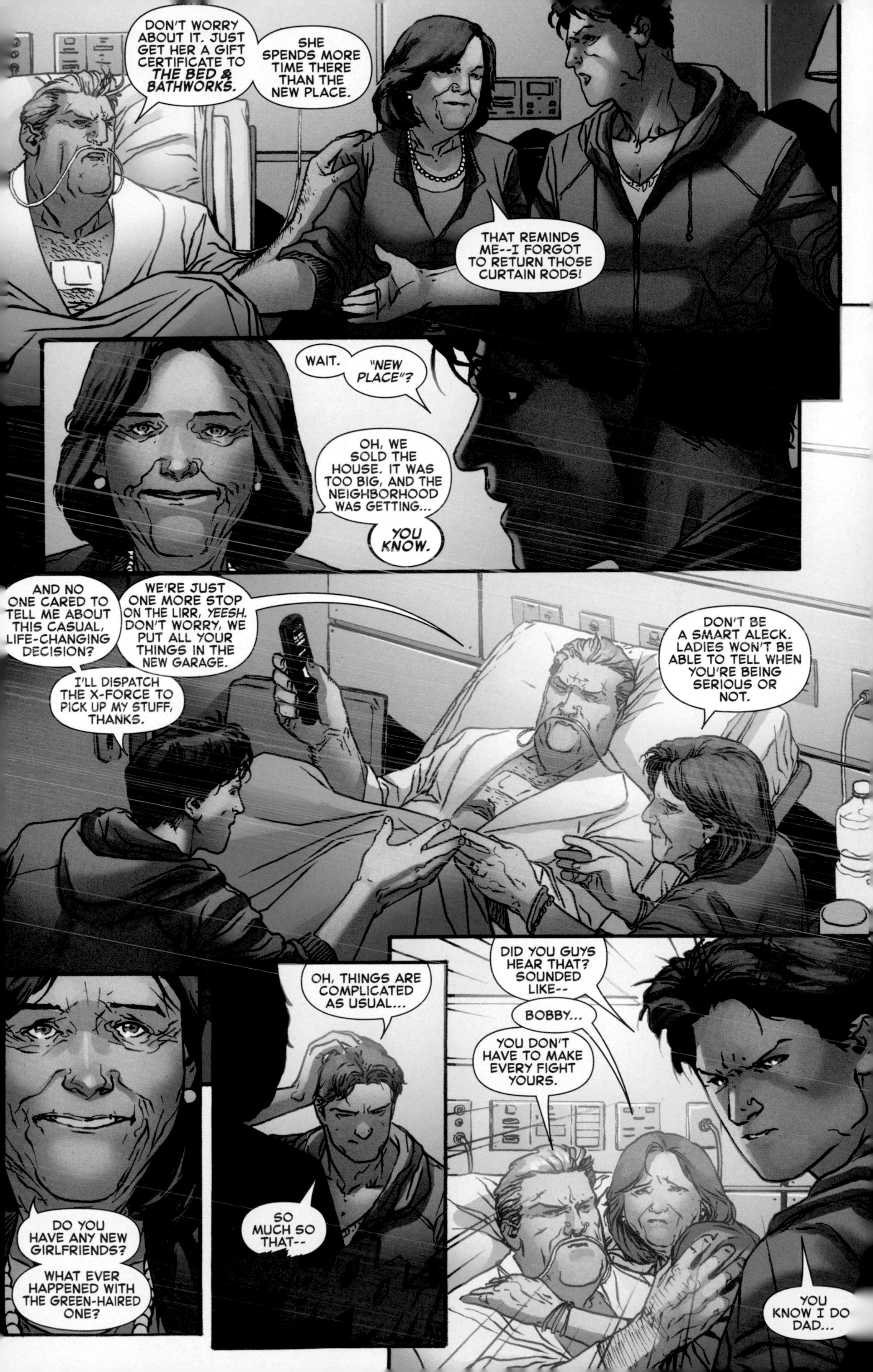
DON'T WORRY ABOUT IT. JUST GET HER A GIFT CERTIFICATE TO *THE BED & BATHWORKS.*
SHE SPENDS MORE TIME THERE THAN THE NEW PLACE.
THAT REMINDS ME--I FORGOT TO RETURN THOSE CURTAIN RODS!
WAIT. *"NEW PLACE"?*
OH, WE SOLD THE HOUSE. IT WAS TOO BIG, AND THE NEIGHBORHOOD WAS GETTING...
YOU KNOW.
AND NO ONE CARED TO TELL ME ABOUT THIS CASUAL, LIFE-CHANGING DECISION?
WE'RE JUST ONE MORE STOP ON THE LIRR, *YEESH.* DON'T WORRY, WE PUT ALL YOUR THINGS IN THE NEW GARAGE.
I'LL DISPATCH THE X-FORCE TO PICK UP MY STUFF, THANKS.
DON'T BE A SMART ALECK. LADIES WON'T BE ABLE TO TELL WHEN YOU'RE BEING SERIOUS OR NOT.
DO YOU HAVE ANY NEW GIRLFRIENDS?
WHAT EVER HAPPENED WITH THE GREEN-HAIRED ONE?
OH, THINGS ARE COMPLICATED AS USUAL...
SO MUCH SO THAT--
DID YOU GUYS HEAR THAT? SOUNDED LIKE--
BOBBY...
YOU DON'T HAVE TO MAKE EVERY FIGHT YOURS.
YOU KNOW I DO DAD...

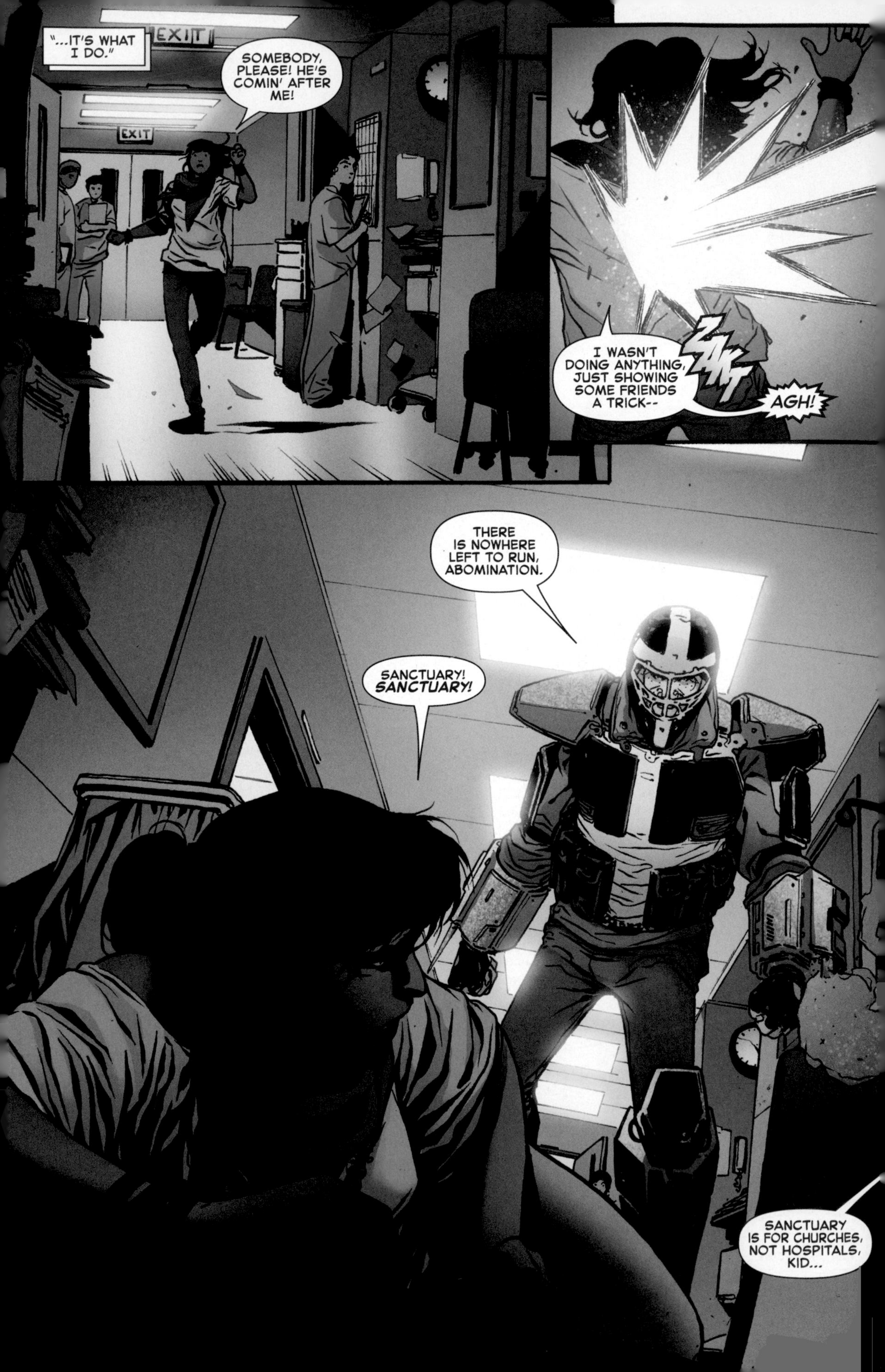
"...IT'S WHAT I DO."
EXIT
SOMEBODY, PLEASE! HE'S COMIN' AFTER ME!
EXIT
I WASN'T DOING ANYTHING, JUST SHOWING SOME FRIENDS A TRICK--
ZAKT
AGH!
THERE IS NOWHERE LEFT TO RUN, ABOMINATION.
SANCTUARY! *SANCTUARY!*
SANCTUARY IS FOR CHURCHES, NOT HOSPITALS, KID...

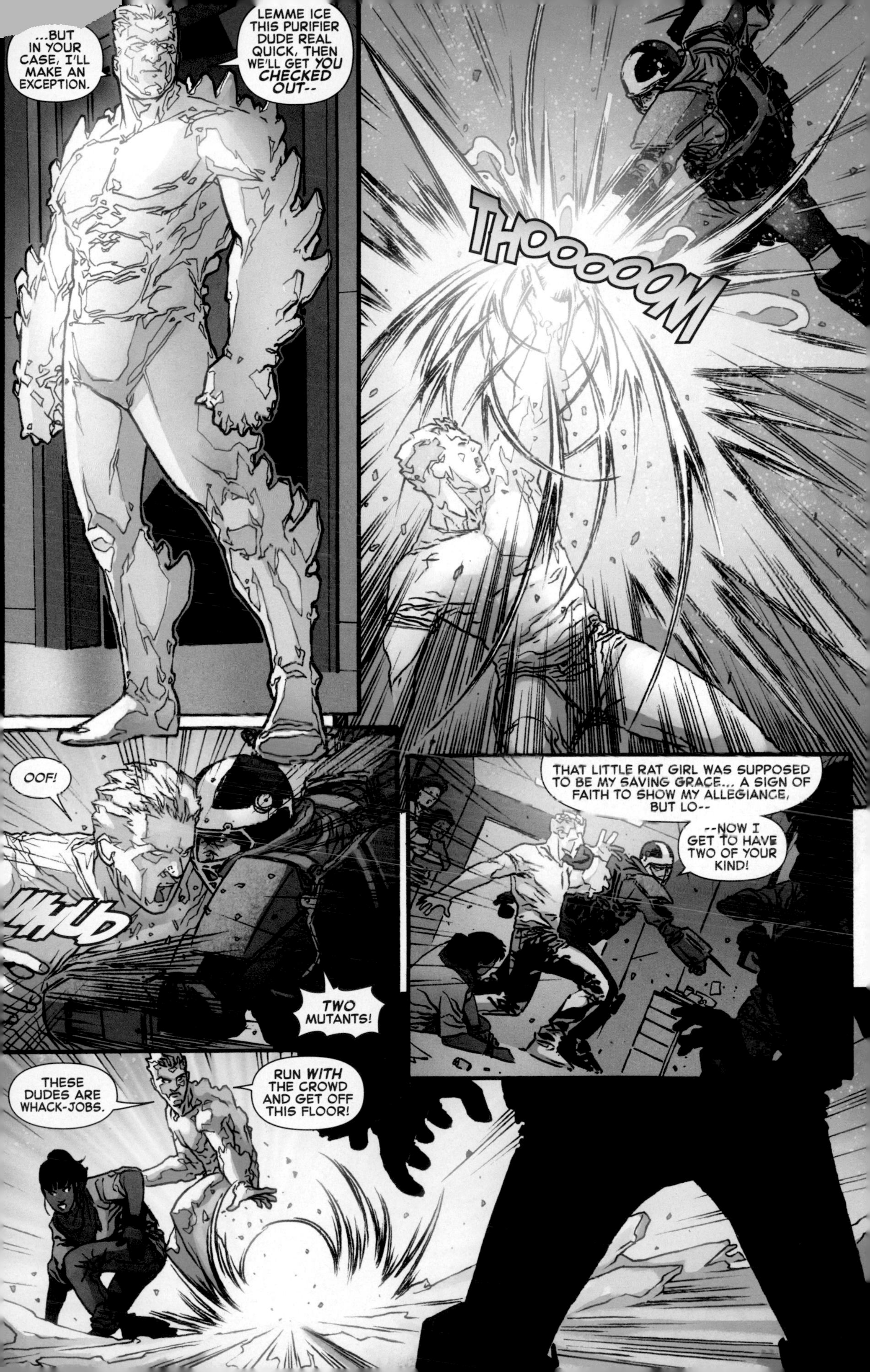
...BUT IN YOUR CASE, I'LL MAKE AN EXCEPTION.
LEMME ICE THIS PURIFIER DUDE REAL QUICK, THEN WE'LL GET YOU CHECKED OUT--
THOOOOOOM
OOF!
WHUD
TWO MUTANTS!
THAT LITTLE RAT GIRL WAS SUPPOSED TO BE MY SAVING GRACE... A SIGN OF FAITH TO SHOW MY ALLEGIANCE, BUT LO--
--NOW I GET TO HAVE TWO OF YOUR KIND!
THESE DUDES ARE WHACK-JOBS.
RUN WITH THE CROWD AND GET OFF THIS FLOOR!

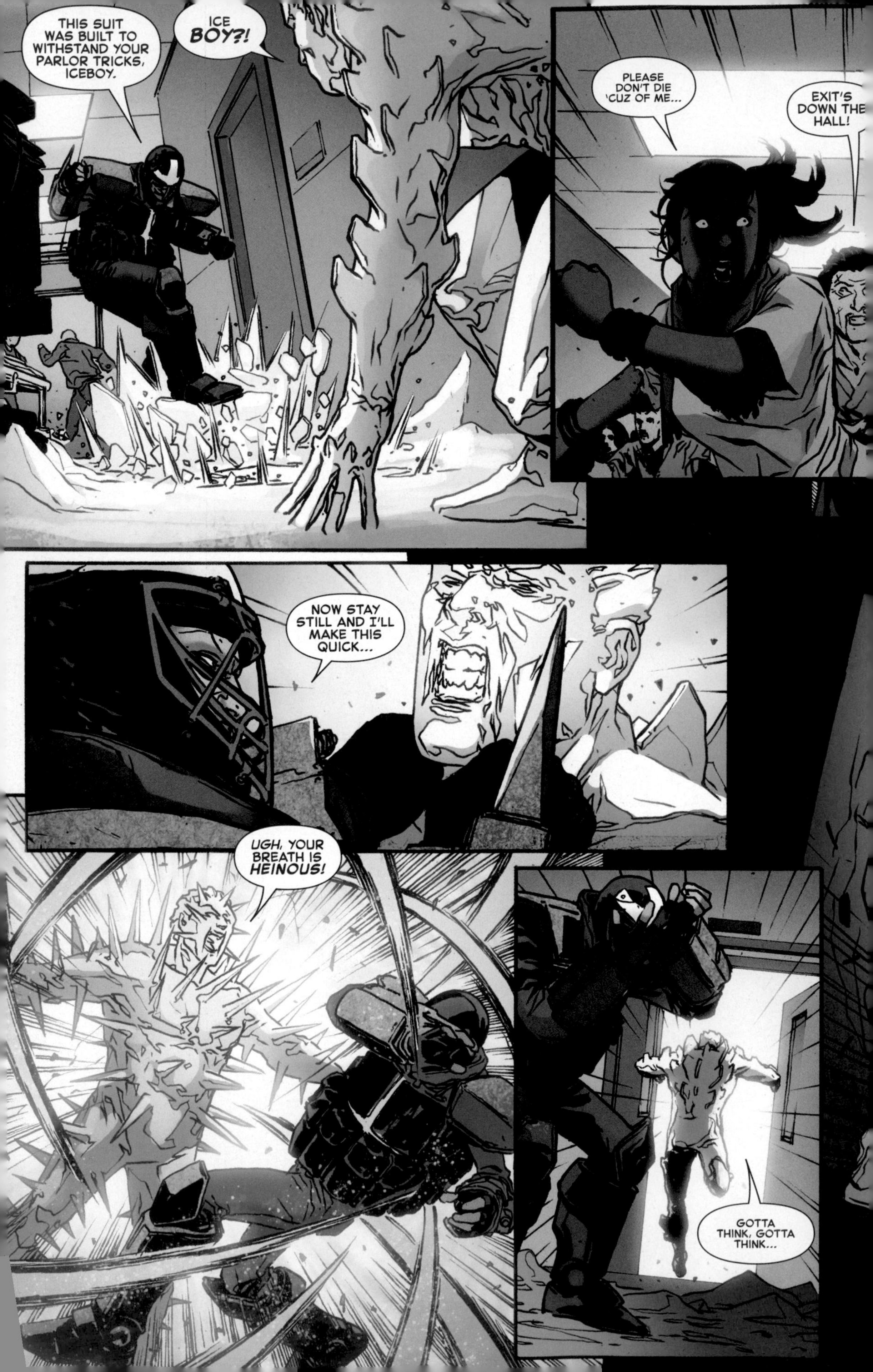
THIS SUIT WAS BUILT TO WITHSTAND YOUR PARLOR TRICKS, ICEBOY.
ICE BOY?!
PLEASE DON'T DIE 'CUZ OF ME...
EXIT'S DOWN THE HALL!
NOW STAY STILL AND I'LL MAKE THIS QUICK...
UGH, YOUR BREATH IS HEINOUS!
GOTTA THINK, GOTTA THINK...

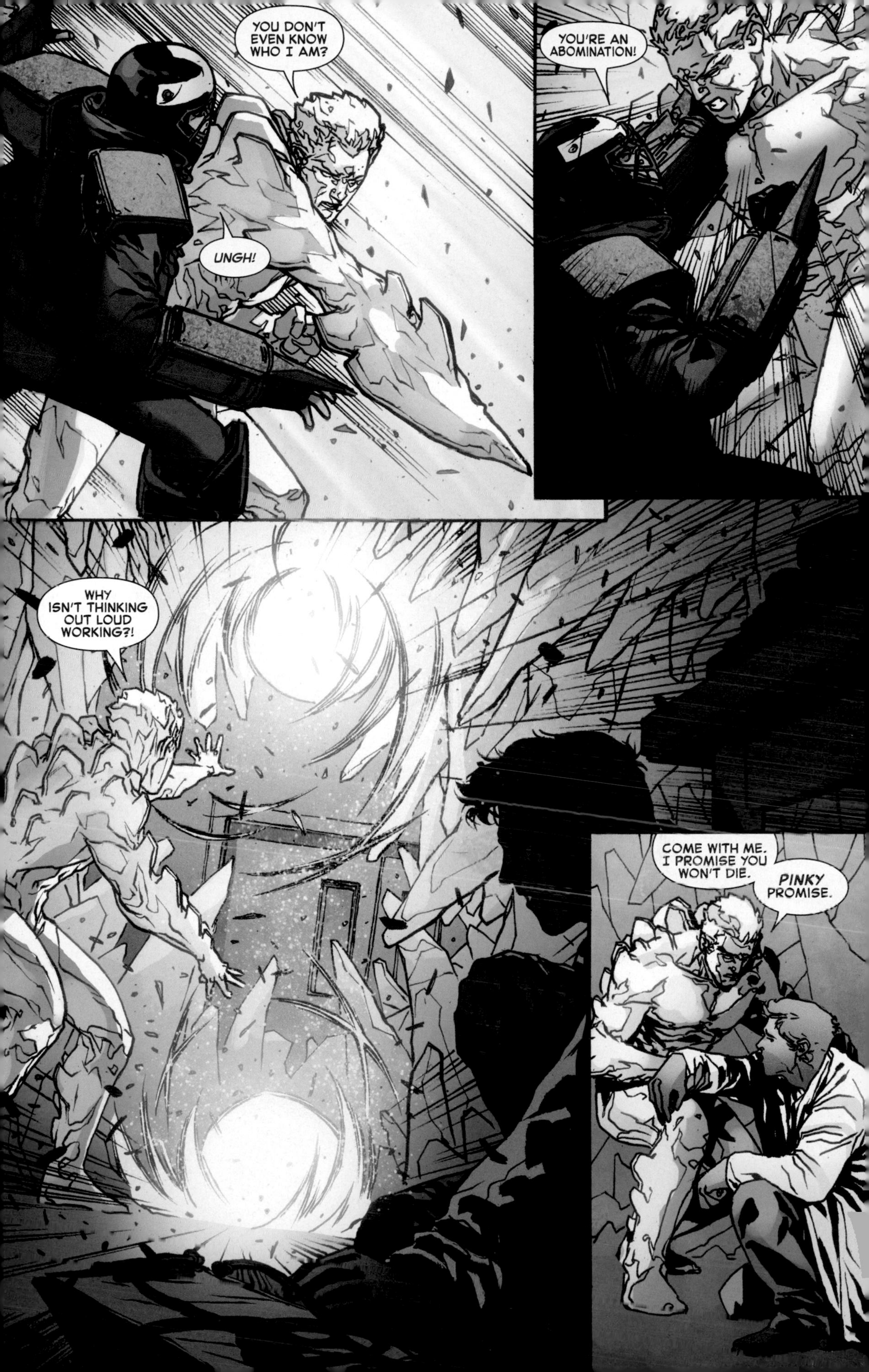
YOU DON'T EVEN KNOW WHO I AM?
UNGH!
YOU'RE AN ABOMINATION!
WHY ISN'T THINKING OUT LOUD WORKING?!
COME WITH ME. I PROMISE YOU WON'T DIE.
PINKY PROMISE.

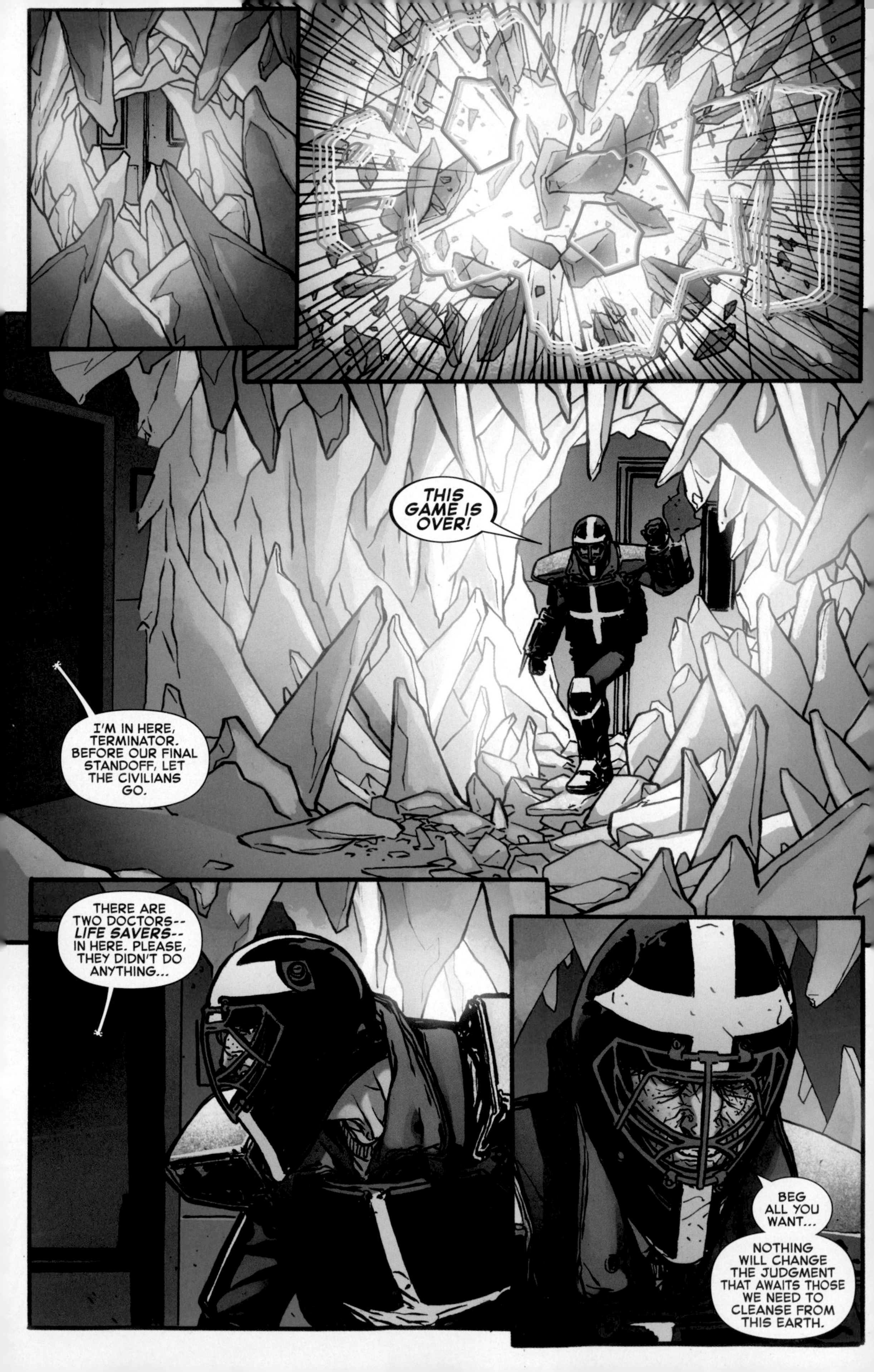
THIS GAME IS OVER!
I'M IN HERE, TERMINATOR. BEFORE OUR FINAL STANDOFF, LET THE CIVILIANS GO.
THERE ARE TWO DOCTORS-- *LIFE SAVERS*-- IN HERE. PLEASE, THEY DIDN'T DO ANYTHING...
BEG ALL YOU WANT...
NOTHING WILL CHANGE THE JUDGMENT THAT AWAITS THOSE WE NEED TO CLEANSE FROM THIS EARTH.

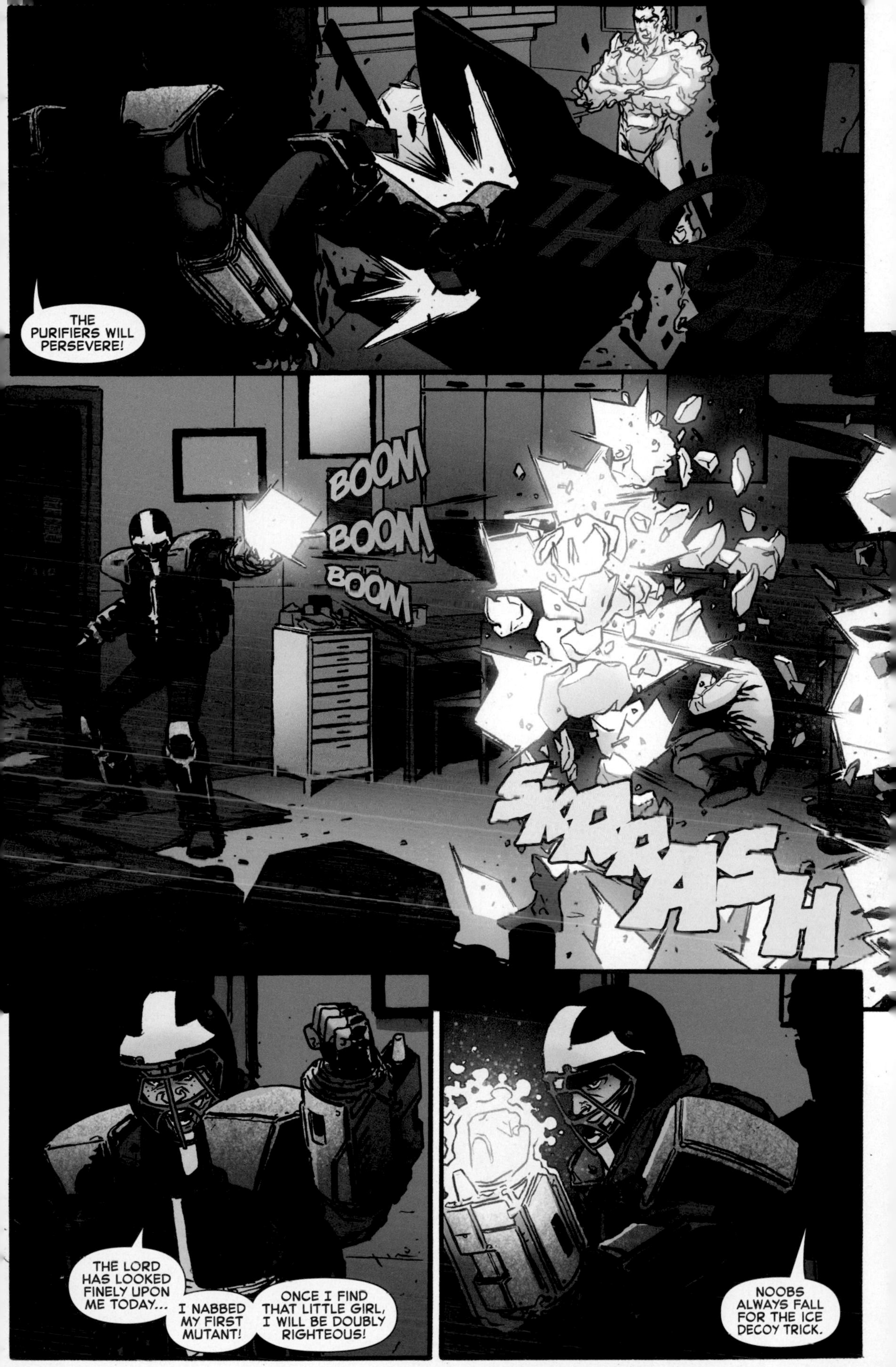
THE PURIFIERS WILL PERSEVERE!
BOOM
BOOM
BOOM
SKRRASH
THE LORD HAS LOOKED FINELY UPON ME TODAY...
I NABBED MY FIRST MUTANT!
ONCE I FIND THAT LITTLE GIRL, I WILL BE DOUBLY RIGHTEOUS!
NOOBS ALWAYS FALL FOR THE ICE DECOY TRICK.

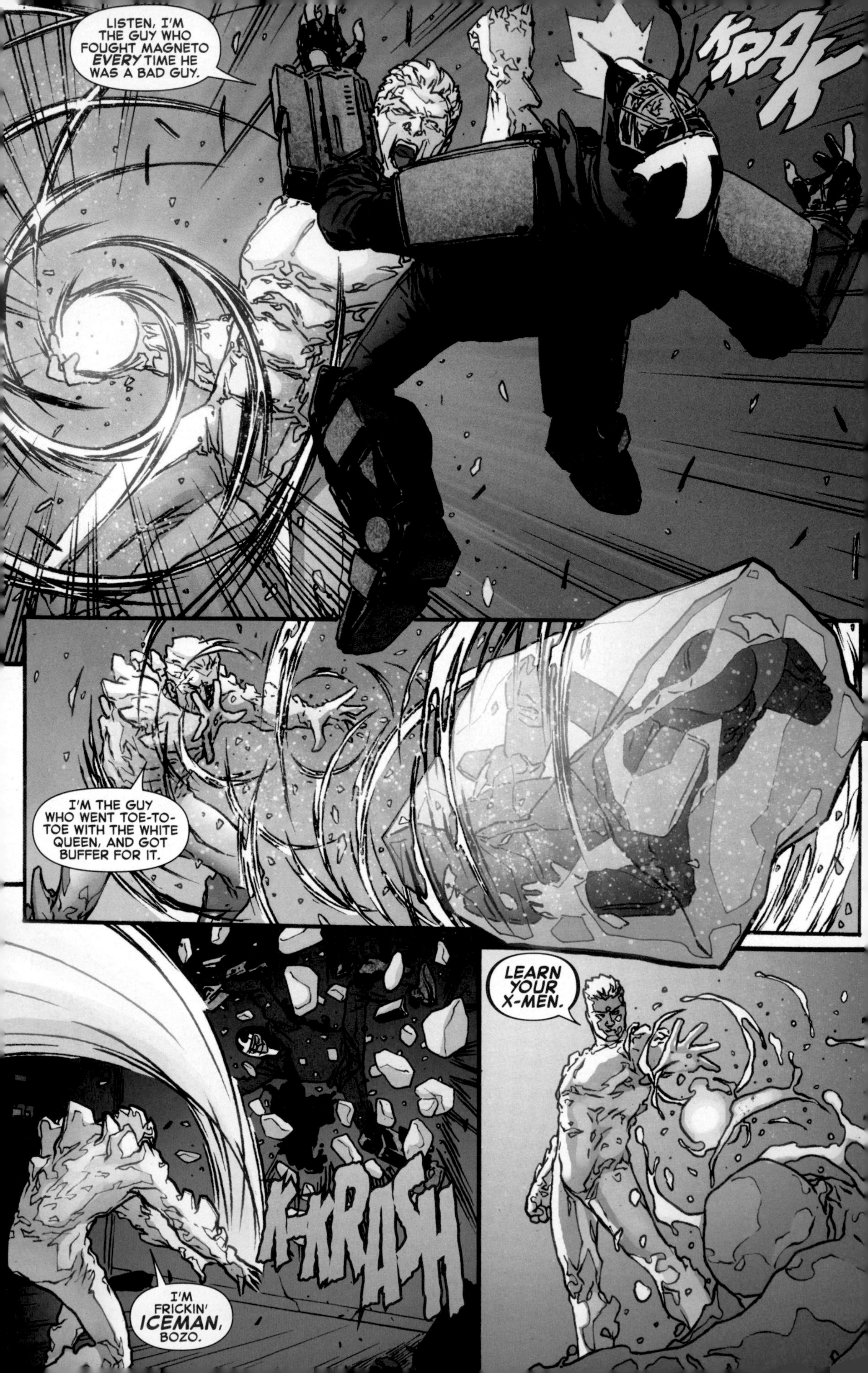
LISTEN, I'M THE GUY WHO FOUGHT MAGNETO *EVERY* TIME HE WAS A BAD GUY.
KRAK
I'M THE GUY WHO WENT TOE-TO-TOE WITH THE WHITE QUEEN, AND GOT BUFFER FOR IT.
K-KRASH
I'M FRICKIN' *ICEMAN*, BOZO.
LEARN YOUR X-MEN.

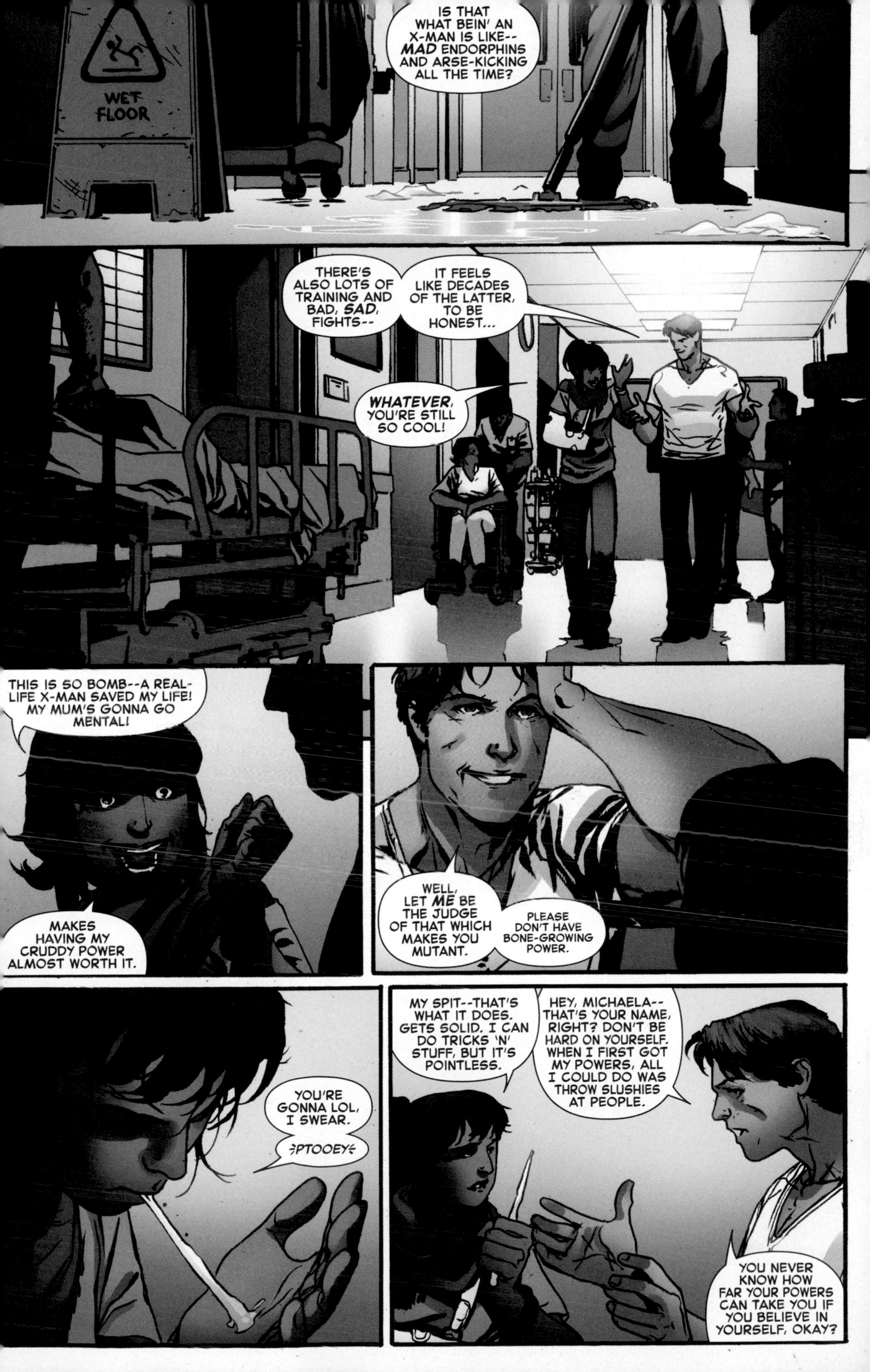
WET FLOOR
IS THAT WHAT BEIN' AN X-MAN IS LIKE-- MAD ENDORPHINS AND ARSE-KICKING ALL THE TIME?
THERE'S ALSO LOTS OF TRAINING AND BAD, SAD, FIGHTS--
IT FEELS LIKE DECADES OF THE LATTER, TO BE HONEST...
WHATEVER, YOU'RE STILL SO COOL!
THIS IS SO BOMB--A REAL-LIFE X-MAN SAVED MY LIFE! MY MUM'S GONNA GO MENTAL!
MAKES HAVING MY CRUDDY POWER ALMOST WORTH IT.
WELL, LET ME BE THE JUDGE OF THAT WHICH MAKES YOU MUTANT.
PLEASE DON'T HAVE BONE-GROWING POWER.
YOU'RE GONNA LOL, I SWEAR.
PTOOEY
MY SPIT--THAT'S WHAT IT DOES. GETS SOLID. I CAN DO TRICKS 'N' STUFF, BUT IT'S POINTLESS.
HEY, MICHAELA-- THAT'S YOUR NAME, RIGHT? DON'T BE HARD ON YOURSELF. WHEN I FIRST GOT MY POWERS, ALL I COULD DO WAS THROW SLUSHIES AT PEOPLE.
YOU NEVER KNOW HOW FAR YOUR POWERS CAN TAKE YOU IF YOU BELIEVE IN YOURSELF, OKAY?

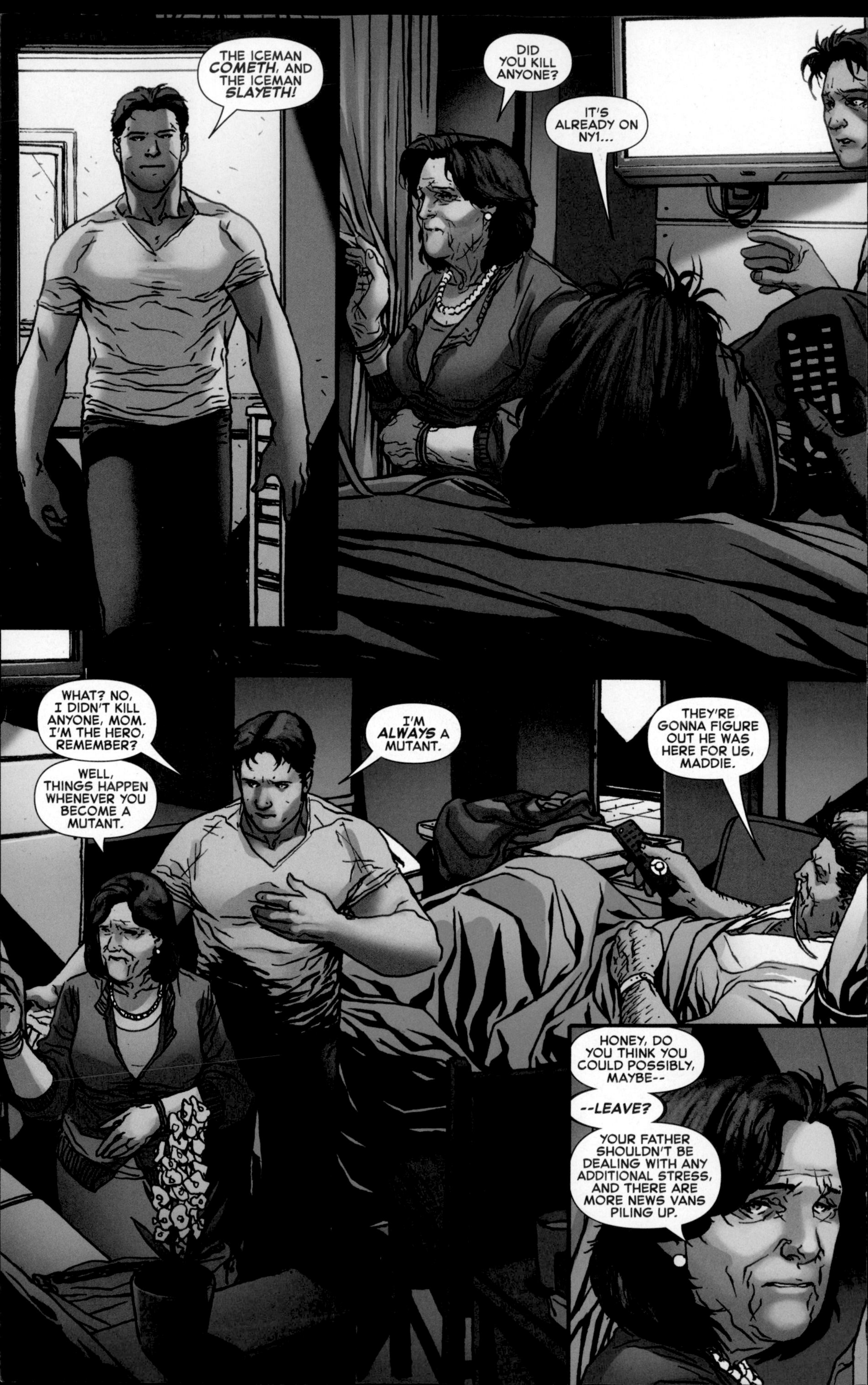
THE ICEMAN COMETH, AND THE ICEMAN SLAYETH!
DID YOU KILL ANYONE?
IT'S ALREADY ON NY1...
WHAT? NO, I DIDN'T KILL ANYONE, MOM. I'M THE HERO, REMEMBER?
WELL, THINGS HAPPEN WHENEVER YOU BECOME A MUTANT.
I'M ALWAYS A MUTANT.
THEY'RE GONNA FIGURE OUT HE WAS HERE FOR US, MADDIE.
HONEY, DO YOU THINK YOU COULD POSSIBLY, MAYBE--
--LEAVE?
YOUR FATHER SHOULDN'T BE DEALING WITH ANY ADDITIONAL STRESS, AND THERE ARE MORE NEWS VANS PILING UP.

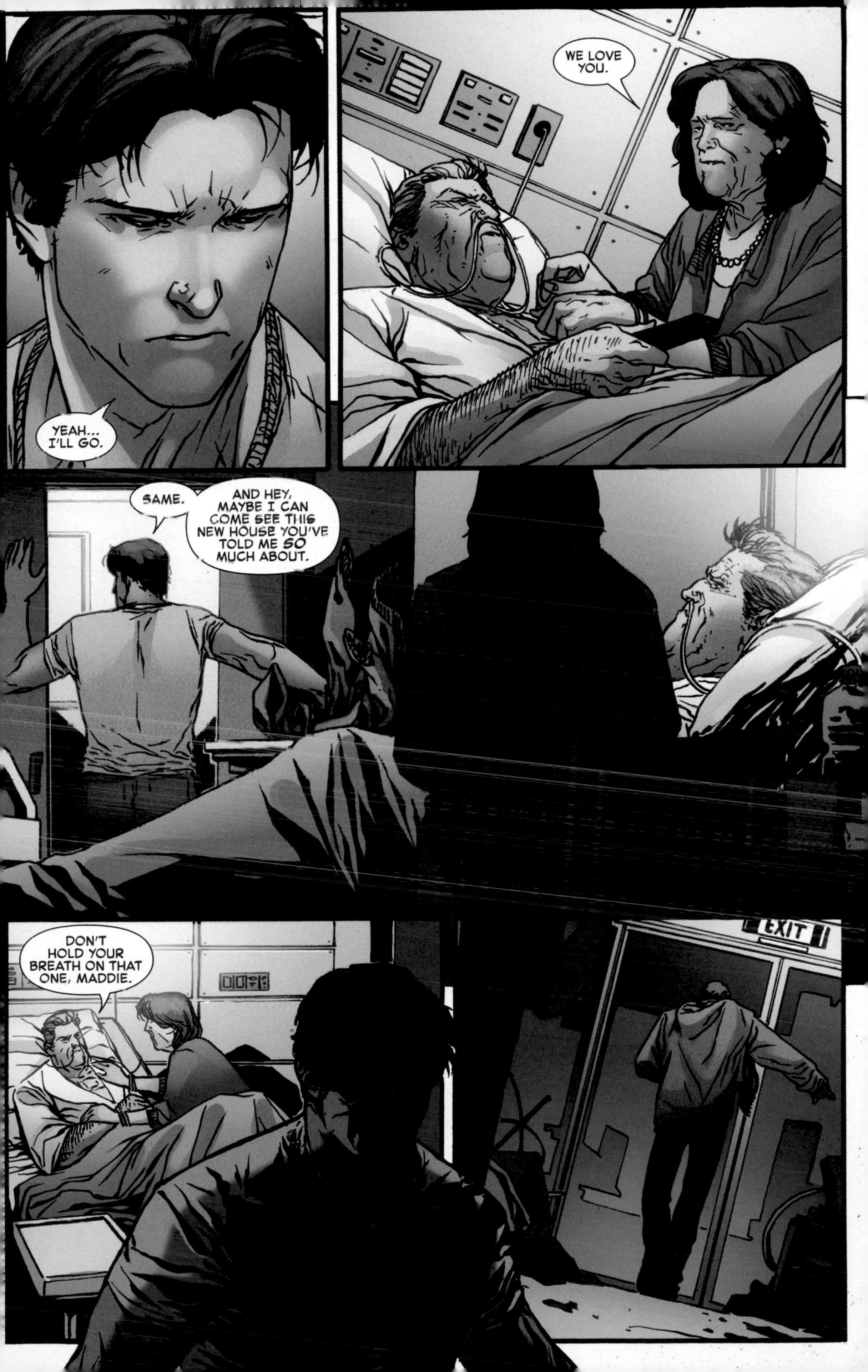
YEAH... I'LL GO.
WE LOVE YOU.
SAME.
AND HEY, MAYBE I CAN COME SEE THIS NEW HOUSE YOU'VE TOLD ME SO MUCH ABOUT.
DON'T HOLD YOUR BREATH ON THAT ONE, MADDIE.
EXIT

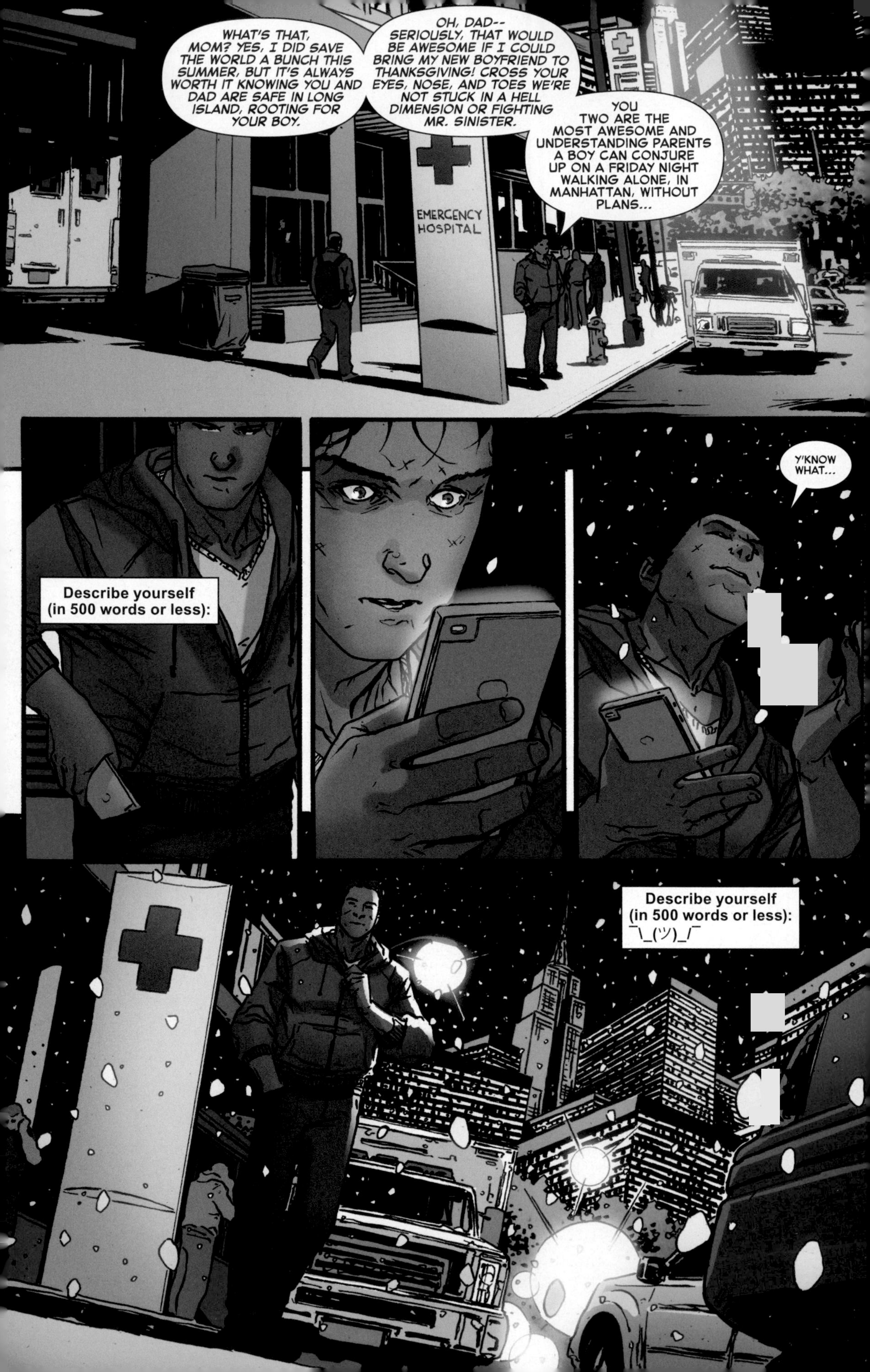
WHAT'S THAT, MOM? YES, I DID SAVE THE WORLD A BUNCH THIS SUMMER, BUT IT'S ALWAYS WORTH IT KNOWING YOU AND DAD ARE SAFE IN LONG ISLAND, ROOTING FOR YOUR BOY.
OH, DAD-- SERIOUSLY, THAT WOULD BE AWESOME IF I COULD BRING MY NEW BOYFRIEND TO THANKSGIVING! CROSS YOUR EYES, NOSE, AND TOES WE'RE NOT STUCK IN A HELL DIMENSION OR FIGHTING MR. SINISTER.
YOU TWO ARE THE MOST AWESOME AND UNDERSTANDING PARENTS A BOY CAN CONJURE UP ON A FRIDAY NIGHT WALKING ALONE, IN MANHATTAN, WITHOUT PLANS...
EMERGENCY HOSPITAL
Describe yourself (in 500 words or less):
Y'KNOW WHAT...
Describe yourself (in 500 words or less):
¯_(ツ)_/¯

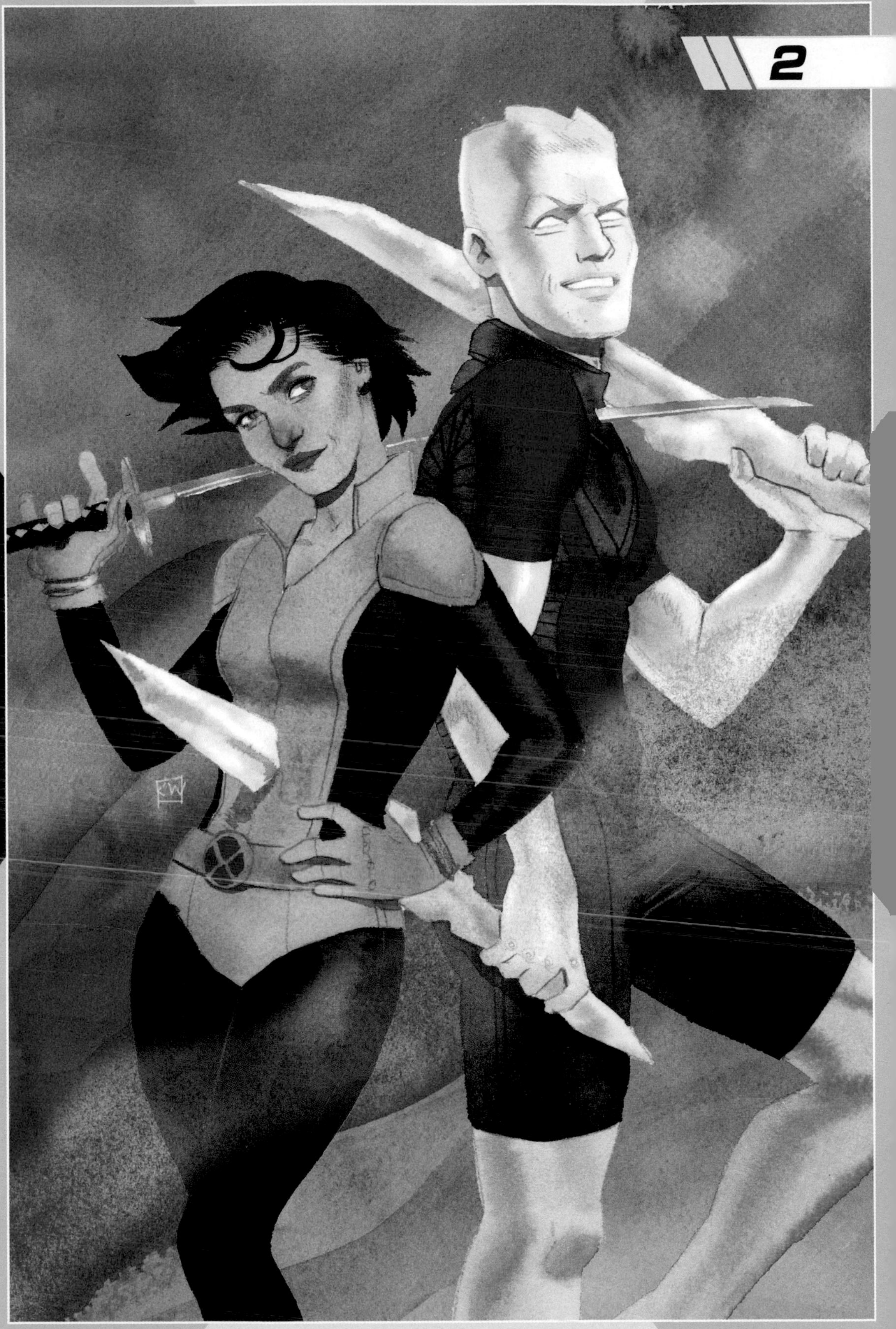
2
KW

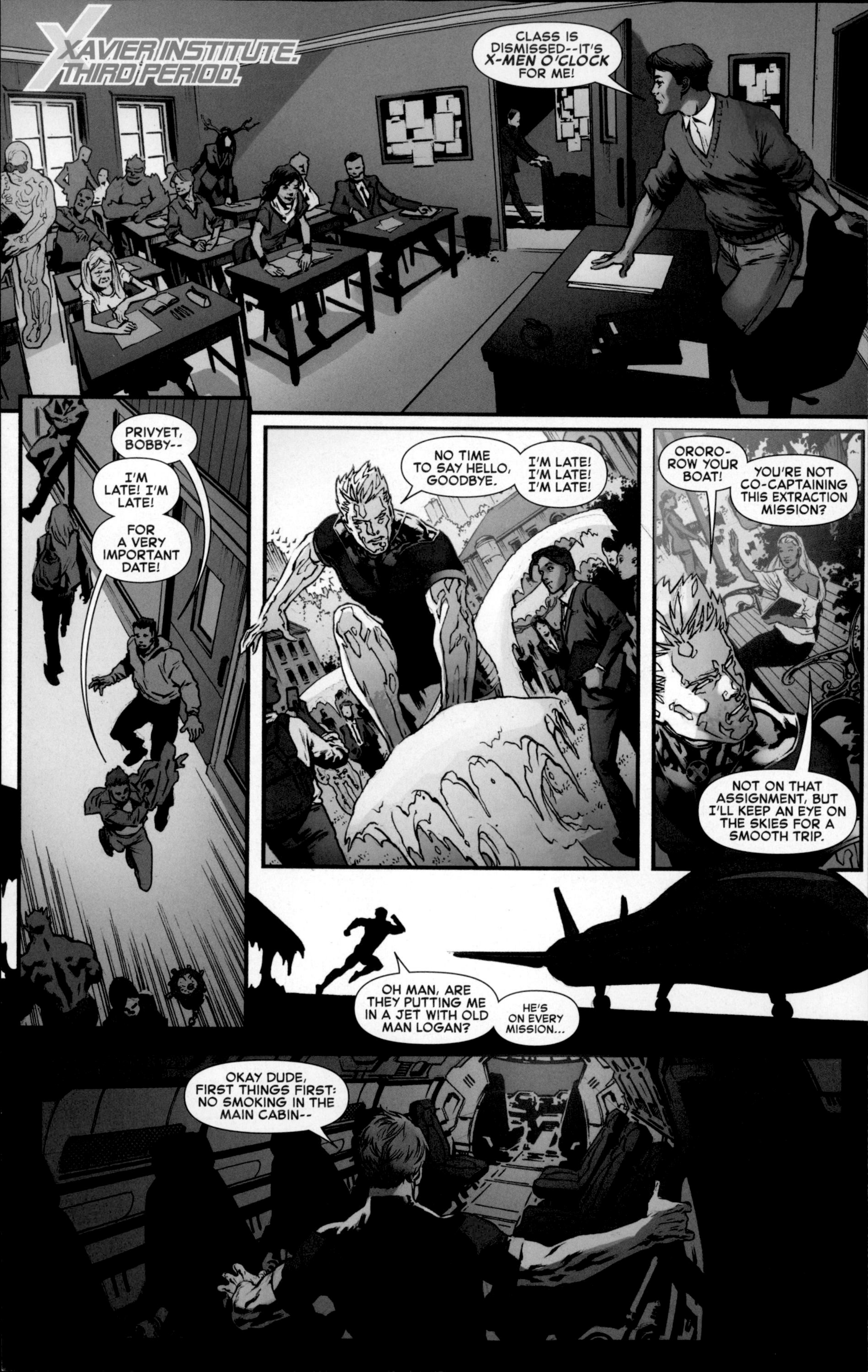
XAVIER INSTITUTE. THIRD PERIOD.
CLASS IS DISMISSED--IT'S X-MEN O'CLOCK FOR ME!
PRIVYET, BOBBY--
I'M LATE! I'M LATE!
FOR A VERY IMPORTANT DATE!
NO TIME TO SAY HELLO, GOODBYE.
I'M LATE! I'M LATE! I'M LATE!
ORORO-ROW YOUR BOAT!
YOU'RE NOT CO-CAPTAINING THIS EXTRACTION MISSION?
NOT ON THAT ASSIGNMENT, BUT I'LL KEEP AN EYE ON THE SKIES FOR A SMOOTH TRIP.
OH MAN, ARE THEY PUTTING ME IN A JET WITH OLD MAN LOGAN?
HE'S ON EVERY MISSION...
OKAY DUDE, FIRST THINGS FIRST: NO SMOKING IN THE MAIN CABIN--

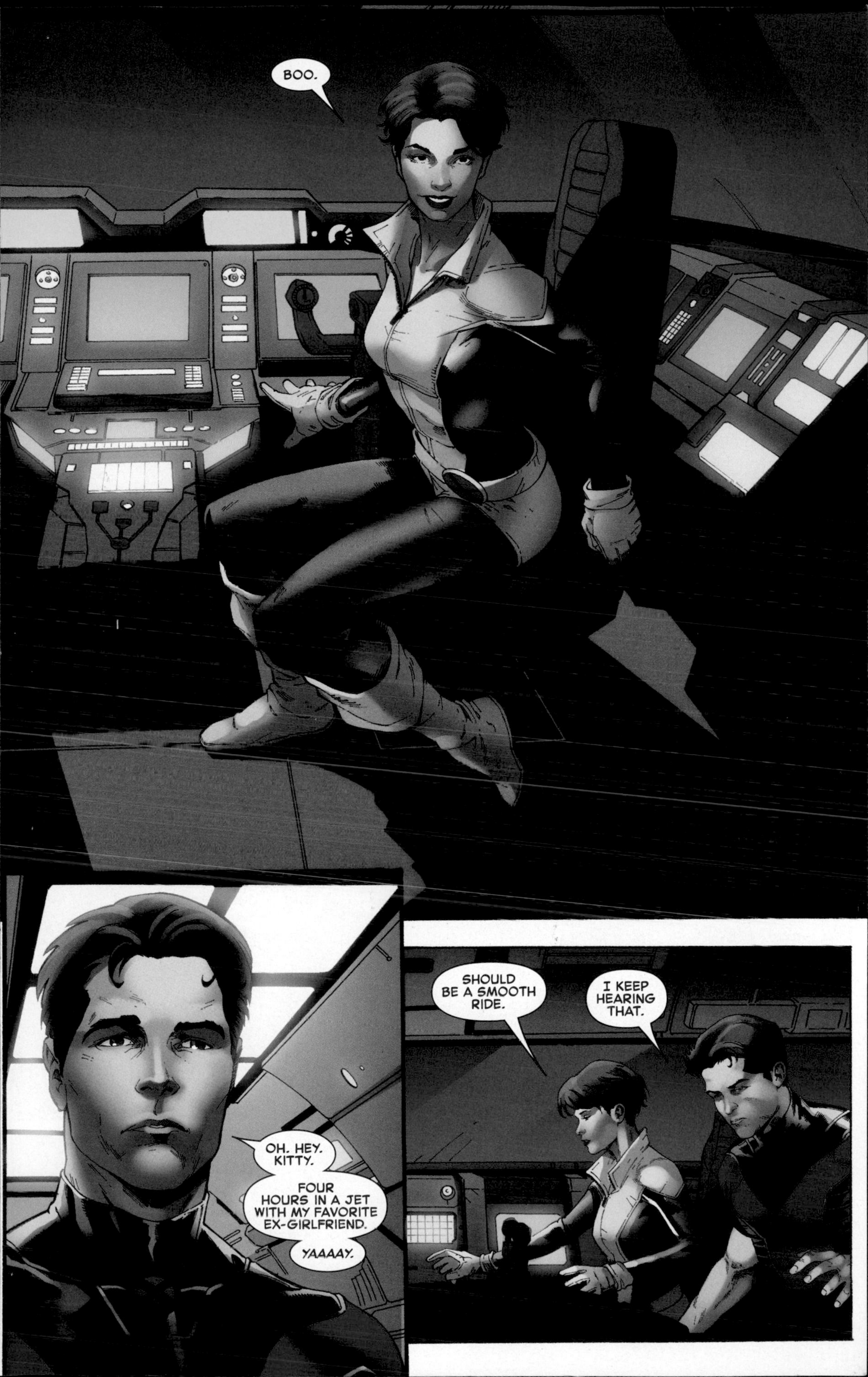
BOO.
OH. HEY. KITTY.
FOUR HOURS IN A JET WITH MY FAVORITE EX-GIRLFRIEND.
YAAAAY.
SHOULD BE A SMOOTH RIDE.
I KEEP HEARING THAT.

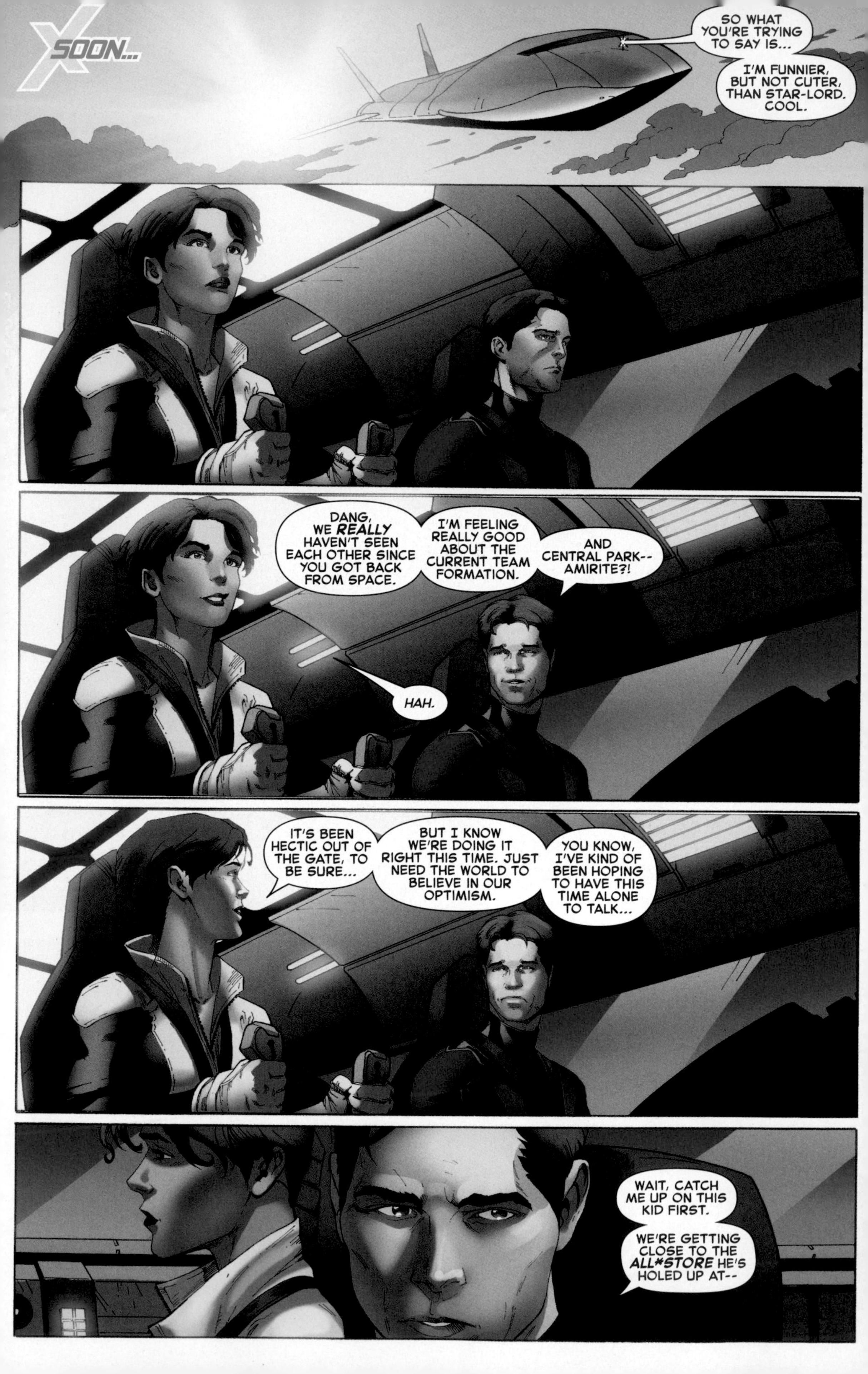
SOON...
SO WHAT YOU'RE TRYING TO SAY IS...
I'M FUNNIER, BUT NOT CUTER, THAN STAR-LORD. COOL.
DANG, WE REALLY HAVEN'T SEEN EACH OTHER SINCE YOU GOT BACK FROM SPACE.
I'M FEELING REALLY GOOD ABOUT THE CURRENT TEAM FORMATION.
AND CENTRAL PARK-- AMIRITE?!
HAH.
IT'S BEEN HECTIC OUT OF THE GATE, TO BE SURE...
BUT I KNOW WE'RE DOING IT RIGHT THIS TIME. JUST NEED THE WORLD TO BELIEVE IN OUR OPTIMISM.
YOU KNOW, I'VE KIND OF BEEN HOPING TO HAVE THIS TIME ALONE TO TALK...
WAIT, CATCH ME UP ON THIS KID FIRST.
WE'RE GETTING CLOSE TO THE ALL*STORE HE'S HOLED UP AT--

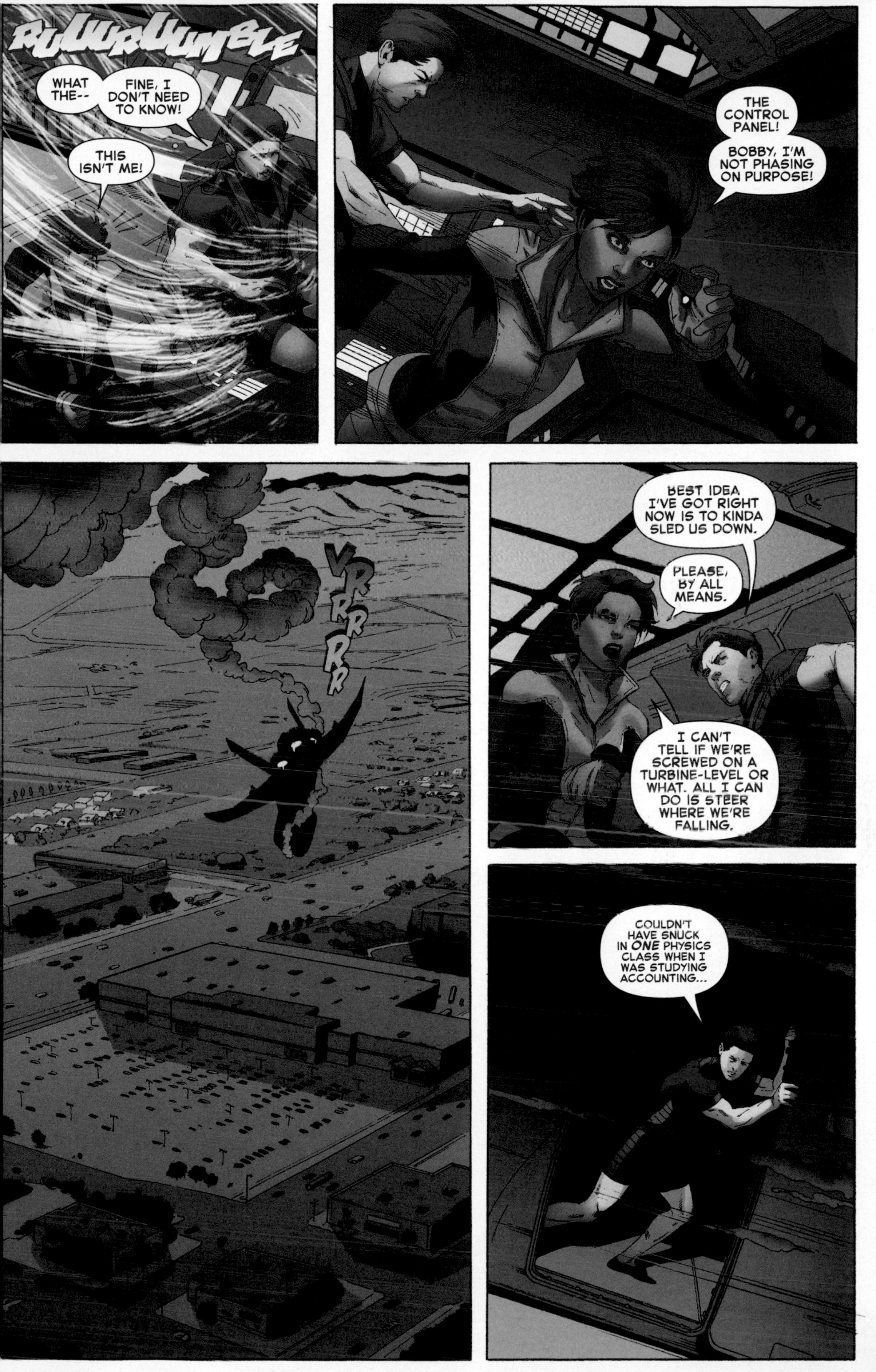
RUUURUUMBLE
WHAT THE--
FINE, I DON'T NEED TO KNOW!
THIS ISN'T ME!
THE CONTROL PANEL!
BOBBY, I'M NOT PHASING ON PURPOSE!
VRRRRR
BEST IDEA I'VE GOT RIGHT NOW IS TO KINDA SLED US DOWN.
PLEASE, BY ALL MEANS.
I CAN'T TELL IF WE'RE SCREWED ON A TURBINE-LEVEL OR WHAT. ALL I CAN DO IS STEER WHERE WE'RE FALLING.
COULDN'T HAVE SNUCK IN *ONE* PHYSICS CLASS WHEN I WAS STUDYING ACCOUNTING...

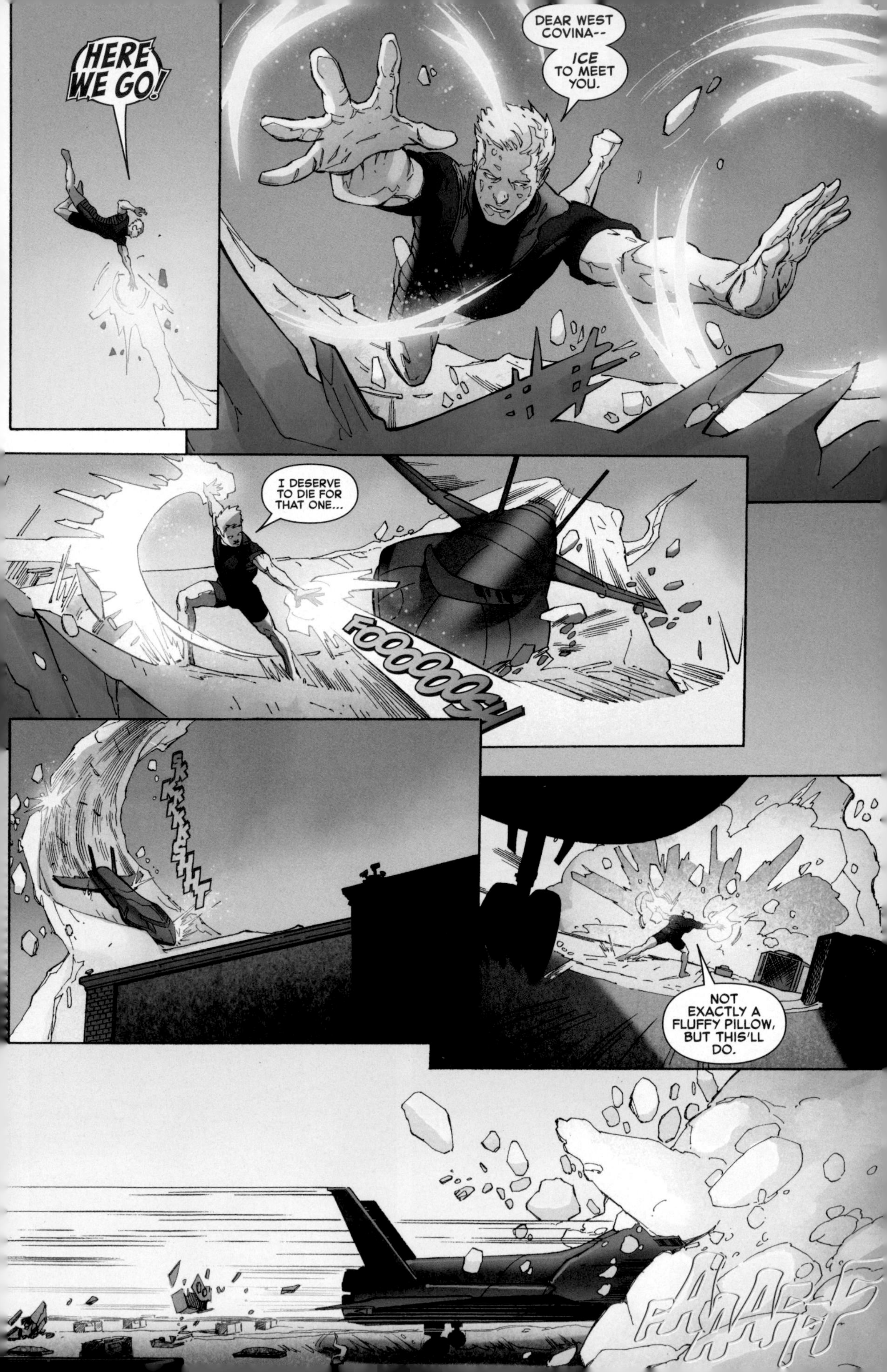
HERE WE GO!
DEAR WEST COVINA--
ICE TO MEET YOU.
I DESERVE TO DIE FOR THAT ONE...
FOOOOOOSH
SKRRKSHHT
NOT EXACTLY A FLUFFY PILLOW, BUT THIS'LL DO.
FWAAFF

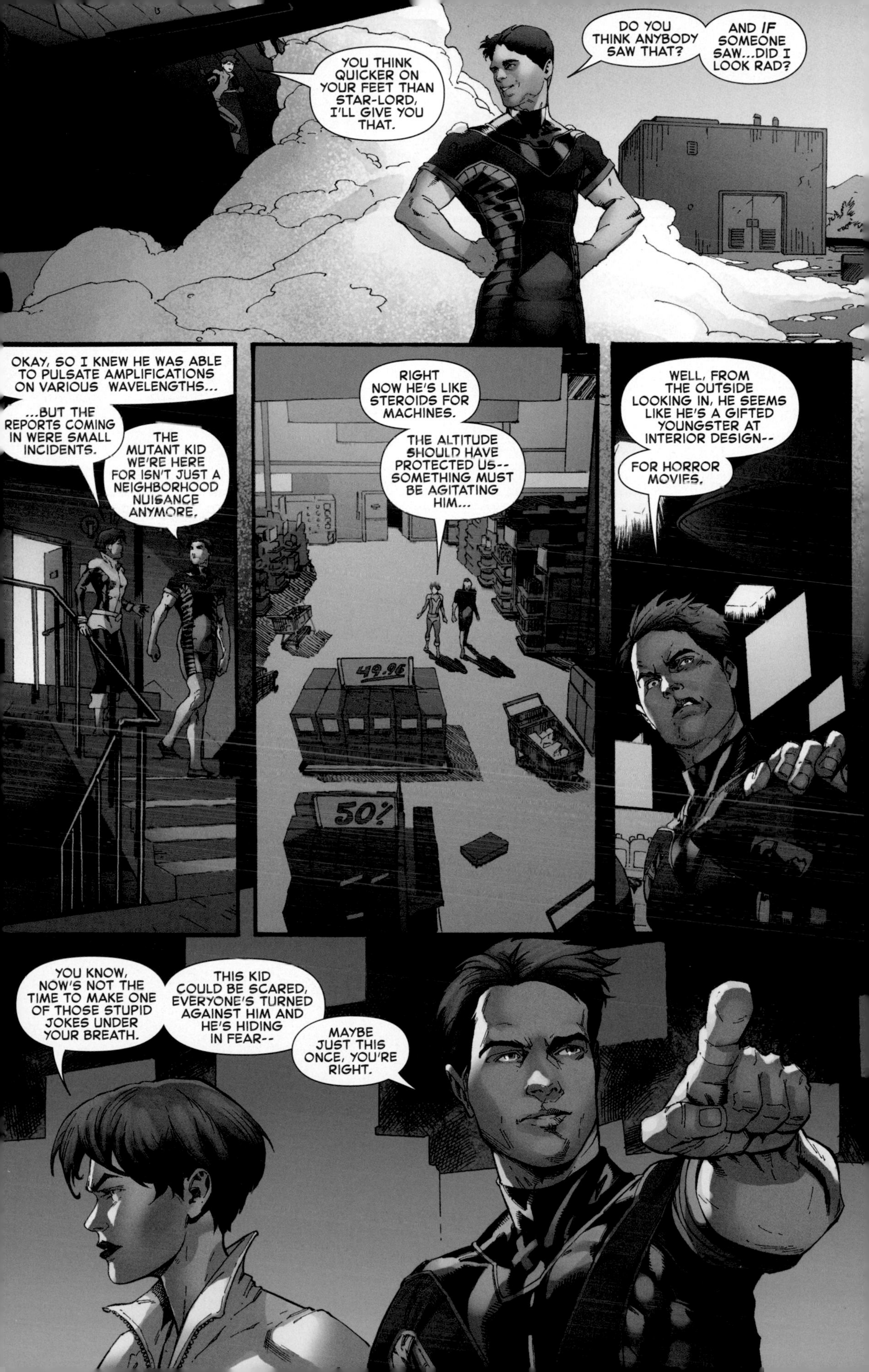
YOU THINK QUICKER ON YOUR FEET THAN STAR-LORD, I'LL GIVE YOU THAT.
DO YOU THINK ANYBODY SAW THAT?
AND IF SOMEONE SAW...DID I LOOK RAD?
OKAY, SO I KNEW HE WAS ABLE TO PULSATE AMPLIFICATIONS ON VARIOUS WAVELENGTHS...
...BUT THE REPORTS COMING IN WERE SMALL INCIDENTS.
THE MUTANT KID WE'RE HERE FOR ISN'T JUST A NEIGHBORHOOD NUISANCE ANYMORE.
RIGHT NOW HE'S LIKE STEROIDS FOR MACHINES.
THE ALTITUDE SHOULD HAVE PROTECTED US--SOMETHING MUST BE AGITATING HIM...
49.96
50%
WELL, FROM THE OUTSIDE LOOKING IN, HE SEEMS LIKE HE'S A GIFTED YOUNGSTER AT INTERIOR DESIGN--
FOR HORROR MOVIES.
YOU KNOW, NOW'S NOT THE TIME TO MAKE ONE OF THOSE STUPID JOKES UNDER YOUR BREATH.
THIS KID COULD BE SCARED, EVERYONE'S TURNED AGAINST HIM AND HE'S HIDING IN FEAR--
MAYBE JUST THIS ONCE, YOU'RE RIGHT.

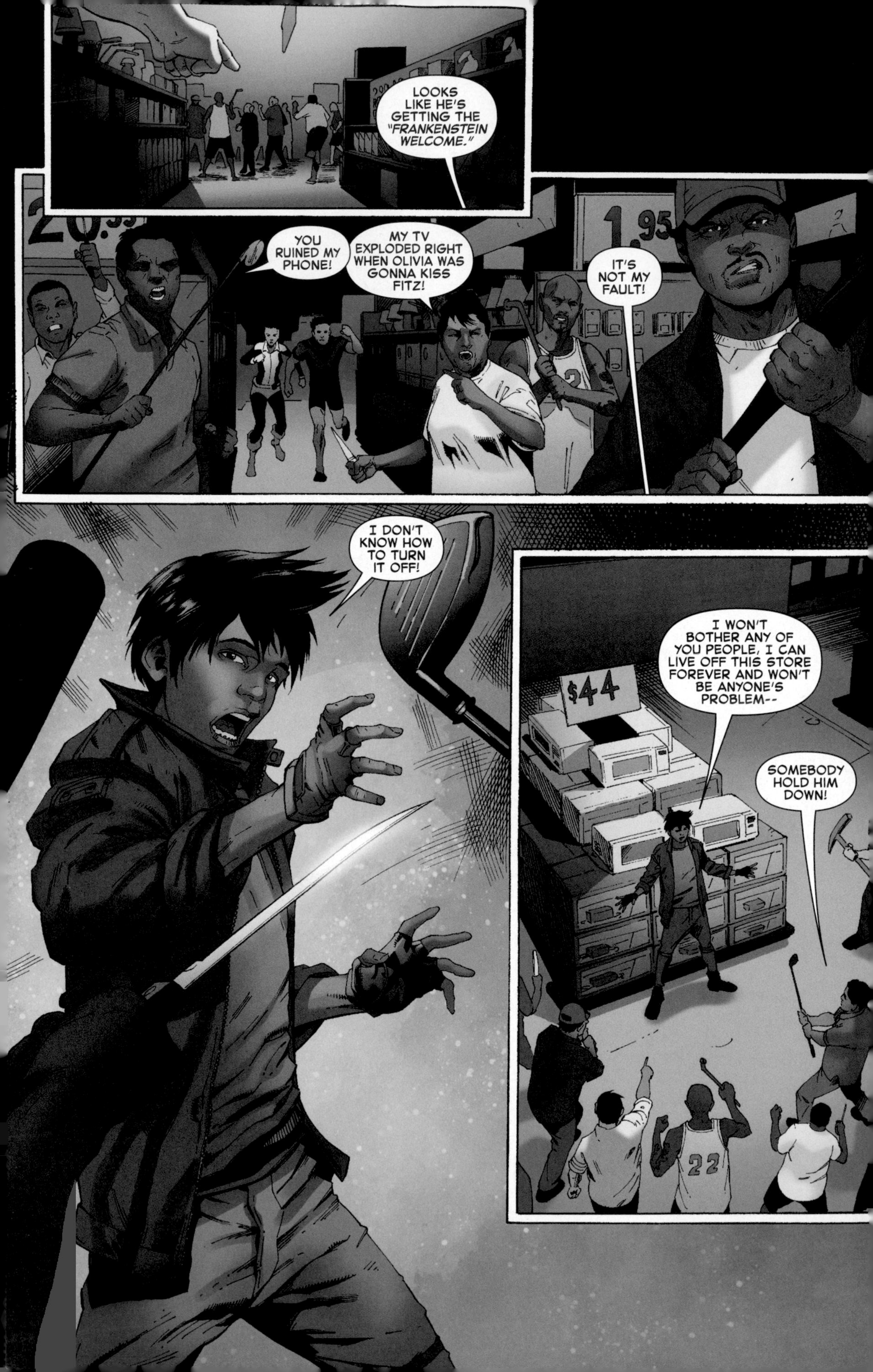
LOOKS LIKE HE'S GETTING THE "FRANKENSTEIN WELCOME."
YOU RUINED MY PHONE!
MY TV EXPLODED RIGHT WHEN OLIVIA WAS GONNA KISS FITZ!
IT'S NOT MY FAULT!
I DON'T KNOW HOW TO TURN IT OFF!
I WON'T BOTHER ANY OF YOU PEOPLE, I CAN LIVE OFF THIS STORE FOREVER AND WON'T BE ANYONE'S PROBLEM--
SOMEBODY HOLD HIM DOWN!
$44

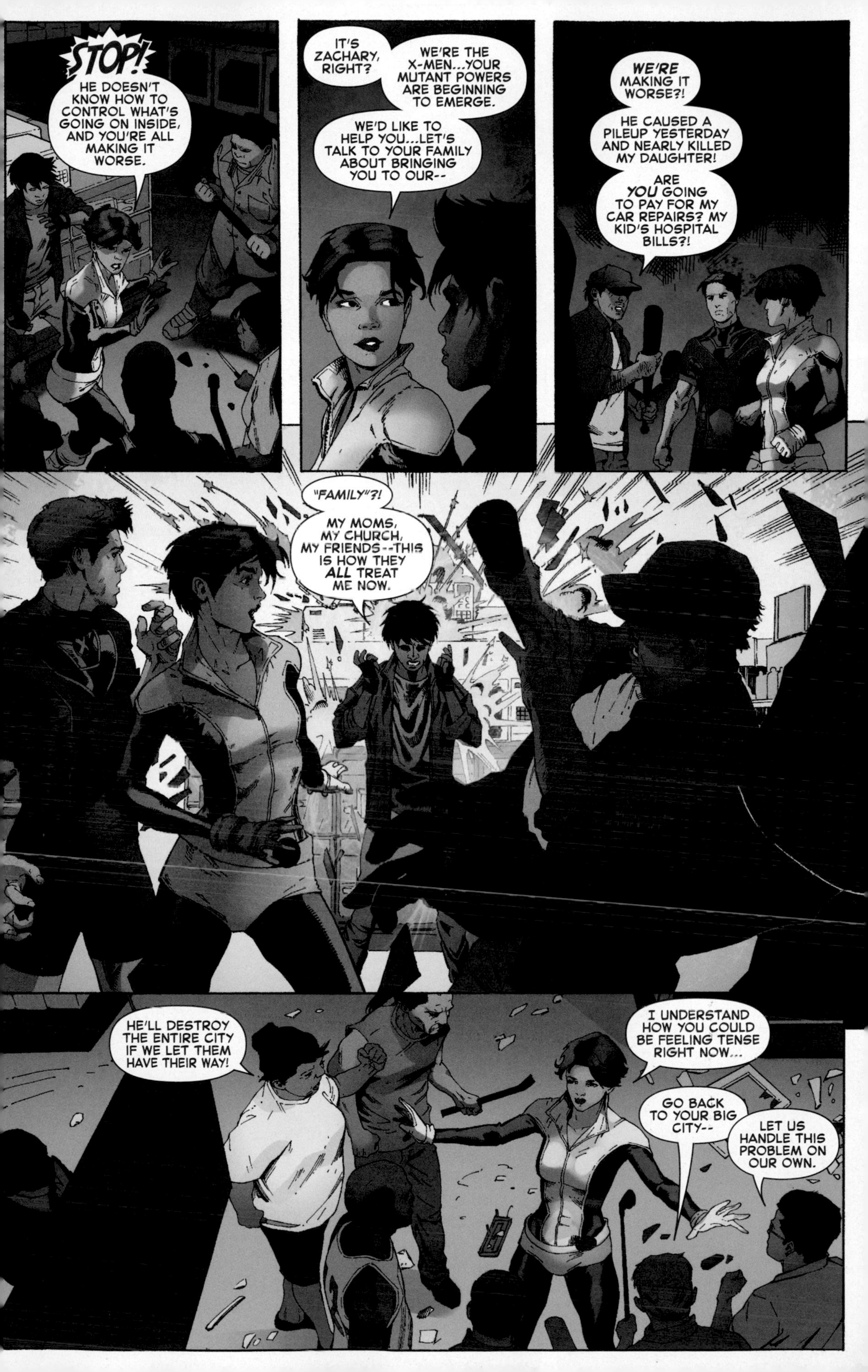
STOP!
HE DOESN'T KNOW HOW TO CONTROL WHAT'S GOING ON INSIDE, AND YOU'RE ALL MAKING IT WORSE.
IT'S ZACHARY, RIGHT?
WE'RE THE X-MEN...YOUR MUTANT POWERS ARE BEGINNING TO EMERGE.
WE'D LIKE TO HELP YOU...LET'S TALK TO YOUR FAMILY ABOUT BRINGING YOU TO OUR--
WE'RE MAKING IT WORSE?!
HE CAUSED A PILEUP YESTERDAY AND NEARLY KILLED MY DAUGHTER!
ARE YOU GOING TO PAY FOR MY CAR REPAIRS? MY KID'S HOSPITAL BILLS?!
"FAMILY"?!
MY MOMS, MY CHURCH, MY FRIENDS--THIS IS HOW THEY ALL TREAT ME NOW.
HE'LL DESTROY THE ENTIRE CITY IF WE LET THEM HAVE THEIR WAY!
I UNDERSTAND HOW YOU COULD BE FEELING TENSE RIGHT NOW...
GO BACK TO YOUR BIG CITY--
LET US HANDLE THIS PROBLEM ON OUR OWN.

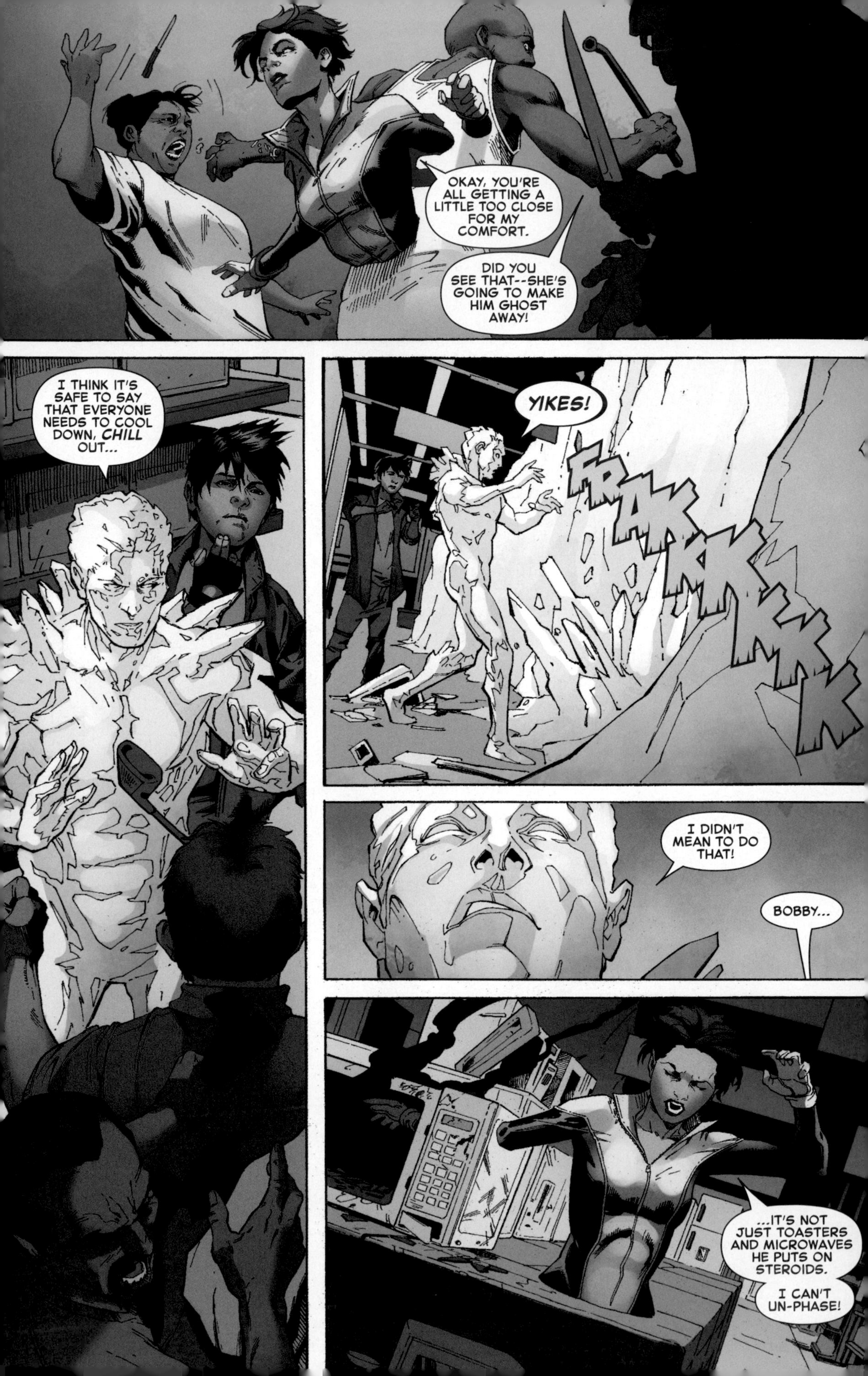

OKAY, YOU'RE ALL GETTING A LITTLE TOO CLOSE FOR MY COMFORT.
DID YOU SEE THAT--SHE'S GOING TO MAKE HIM GHOST AWAY!
I THINK IT'S SAFE TO SAY THAT EVERYONE NEEDS TO COOL DOWN, CHILL OUT...
YIKES!
FRAKKKKK
I DIDN'T MEAN TO DO THAT!
BOBBY...
...IT'S NOT JUST TOASTERS AND MICROWAVES HE PUTS ON STEROIDS.
I CAN'T UN-PHASE!

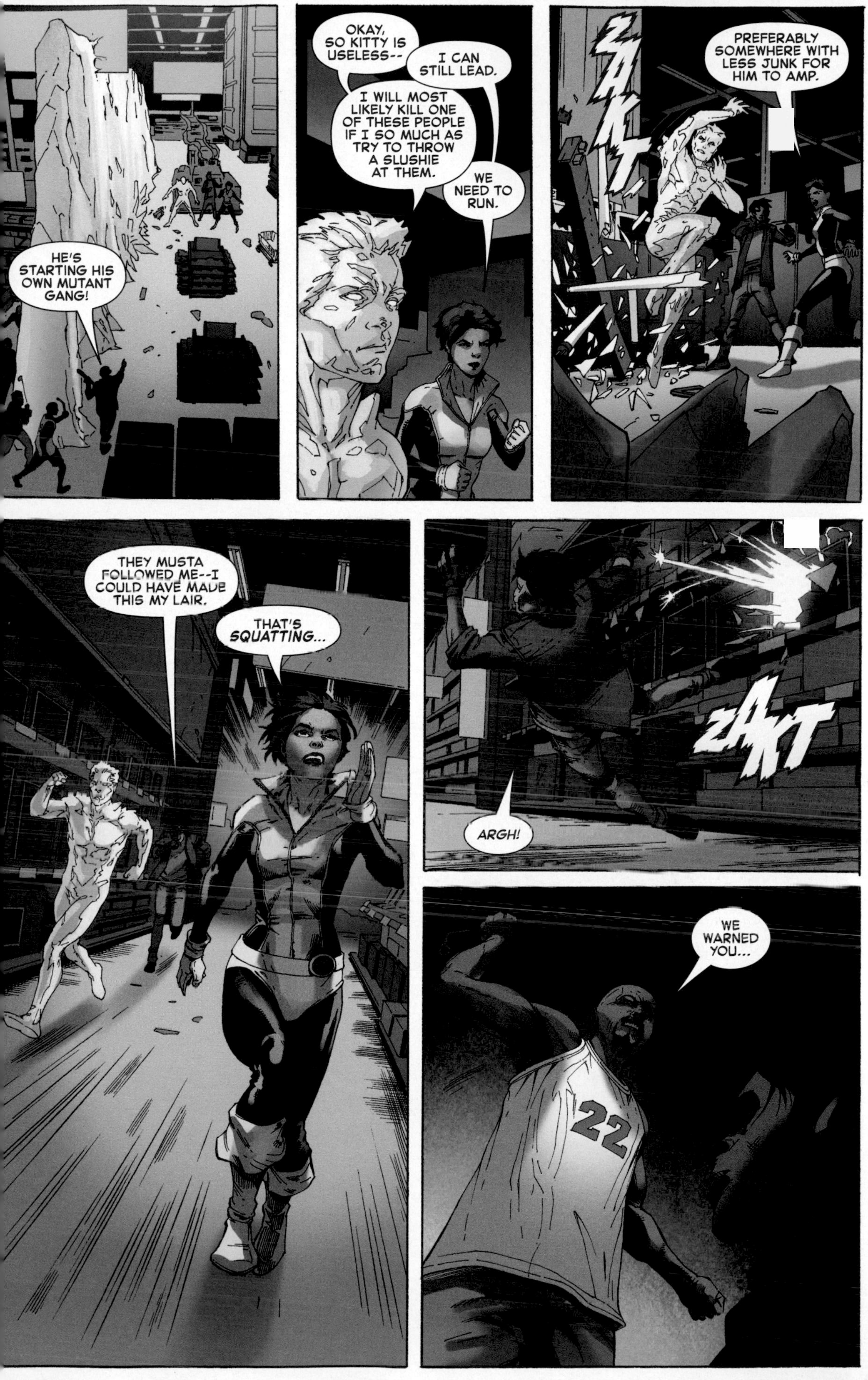
HE'S STARTING HIS OWN MUTANT GANG!
OKAY, SO KITTY IS USELESS--
I CAN STILL LEAD.
I WILL MOST LIKELY KILL ONE OF THESE PEOPLE IF I SO MUCH AS TRY TO THROW A SLUSHIE AT THEM.
WE NEED TO RUN.
ZAKT
PREFERABLY SOMEWHERE WITH LESS JUNK FOR HIM TO AMP.
THEY MUSTA FOLLOWED ME--I COULD HAVE MADE THIS MY LAIR.
THAT'S SQUATTING...
ZAKT
ARGH!
WE WARNED YOU...
22

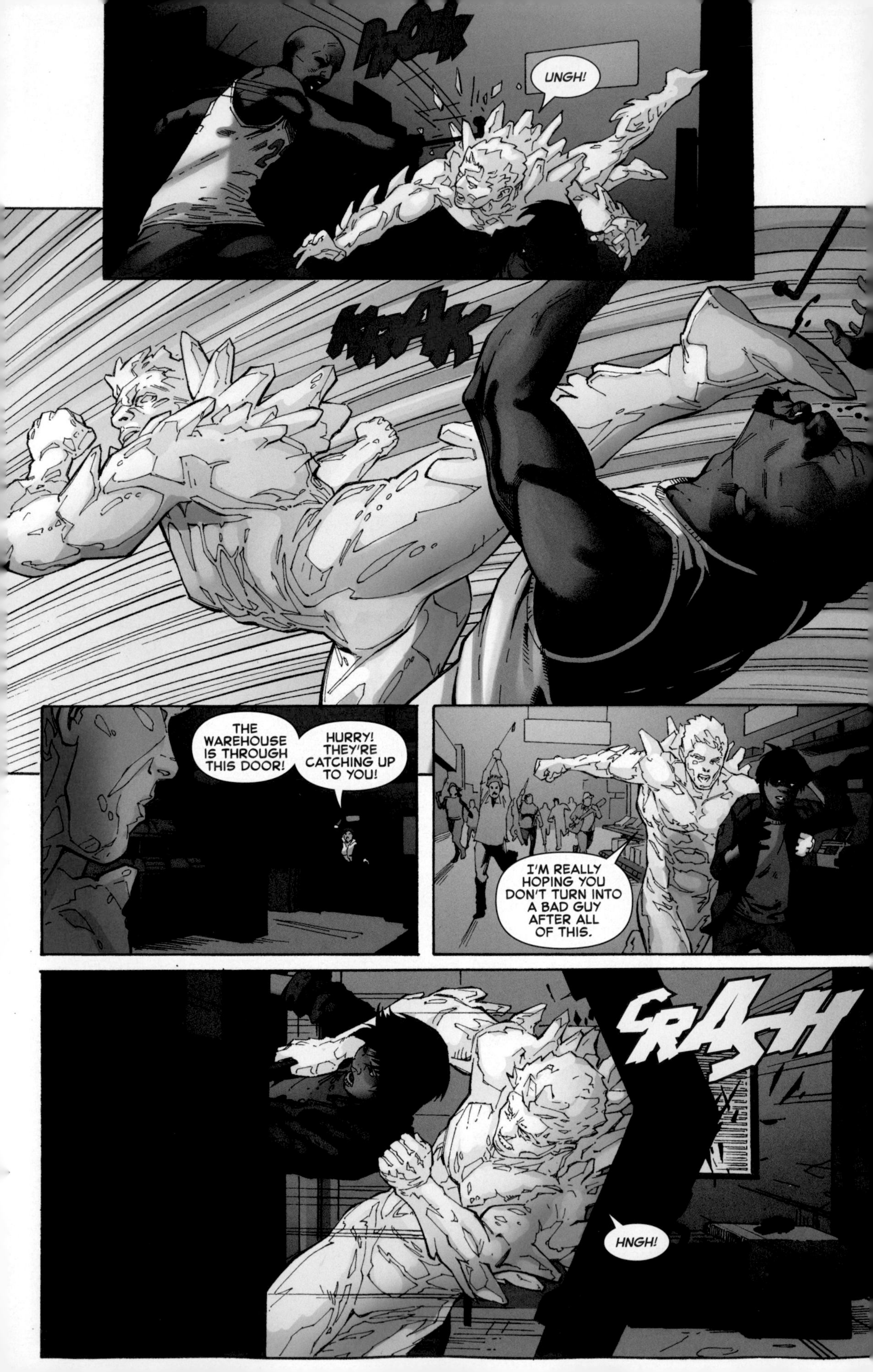
UNGH!
THE WAREHOUSE IS THROUGH THIS DOOR!
HURRY! THEY'RE CATCHING UP TO YOU!
I'M REALLY HOPING YOU DON'T TURN INTO A BAD GUY AFTER ALL OF THIS.
CRASH
HNGH!

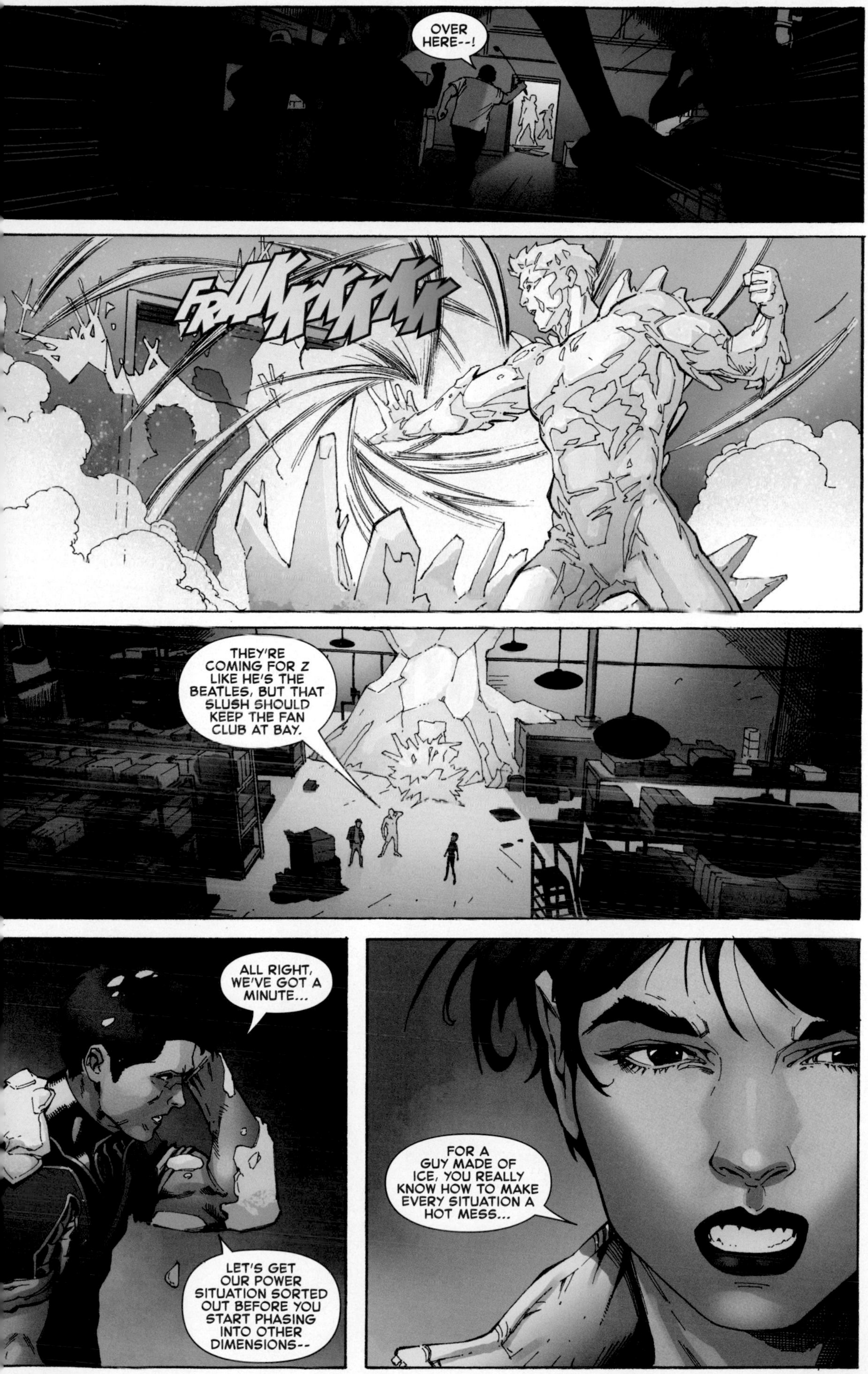
OVER HERE--!
FRAAKAKAKAK
THEY'RE COMING FOR Z LIKE HE'S THE BEATLES, BUT THAT SLUSH SHOULD KEEP THE FAN CLUB AT BAY.
ALL RIGHT, WE'VE GOT A MINUTE...
LET'S GET OUR POWER SITUATION SORTED OUT BEFORE YOU START PHASING INTO OTHER DIMENSIONS--
FOR A GUY MADE OF ICE, YOU REALLY KNOW HOW TO MAKE EVERY SITUATION A HOT MESS...

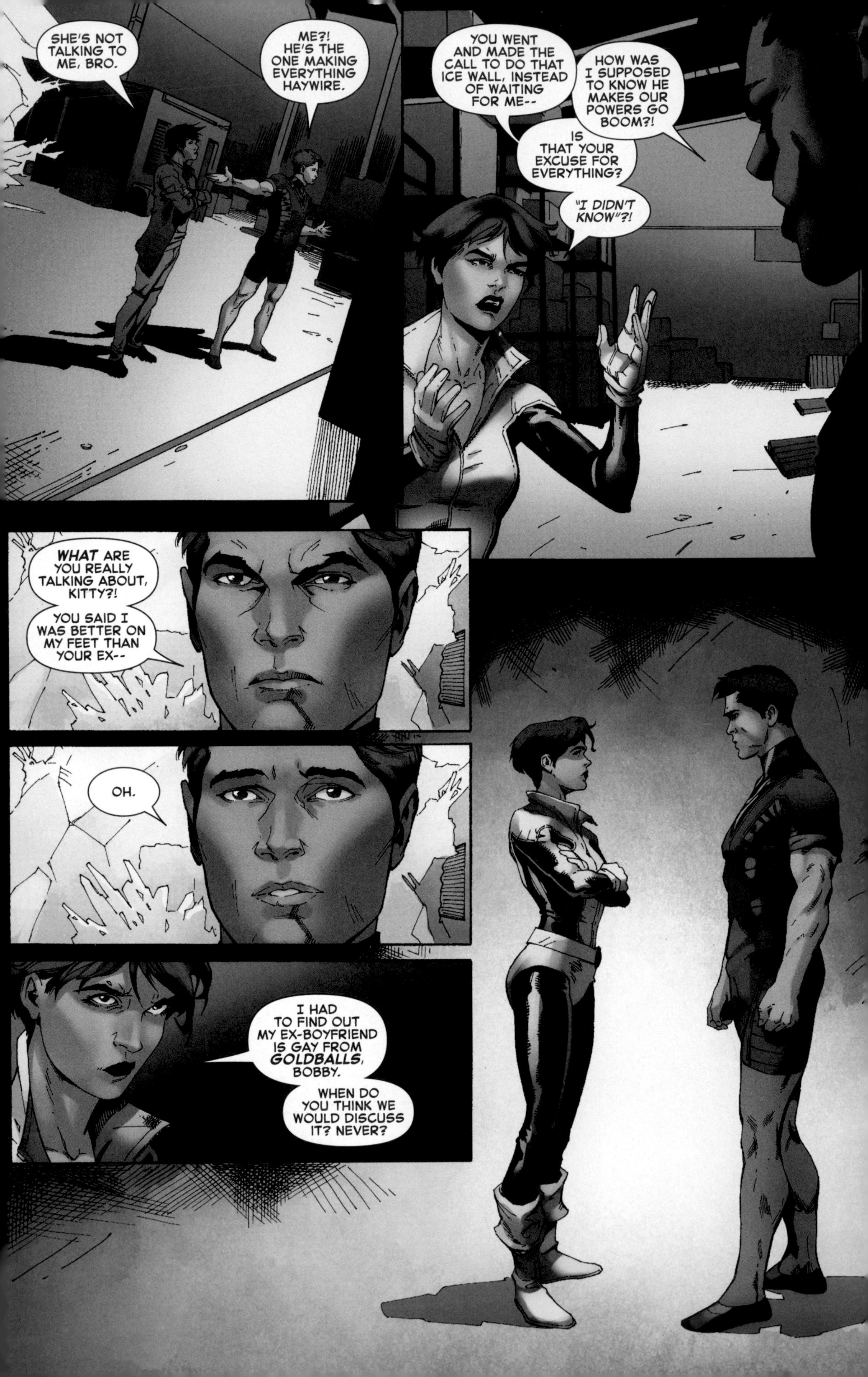
SHE'S NOT TALKING TO ME, BRO.
ME?! HE'S THE ONE MAKING EVERYTHING HAYWIRE.
YOU WENT AND MADE THE CALL TO DO THAT ICE WALL, INSTEAD OF WAITING FOR ME--
HOW WAS I SUPPOSED TO KNOW HE MAKES OUR POWERS GO BOOM?!
IS THAT YOUR EXCUSE FOR EVERYTHING?
"I DIDN'T KNOW"?!
WHAT ARE YOU REALLY TALKING ABOUT, KITTY?!
YOU SAID I WAS BETTER ON MY FEET THAN YOUR EX--
OH.
I HAD TO FIND OUT MY EX-BOYFRIEND IS GAY FROM GOLDBALLS, BOBBY.
WHEN DO YOU THINK WE WOULD DISCUSS IT? NEVER?

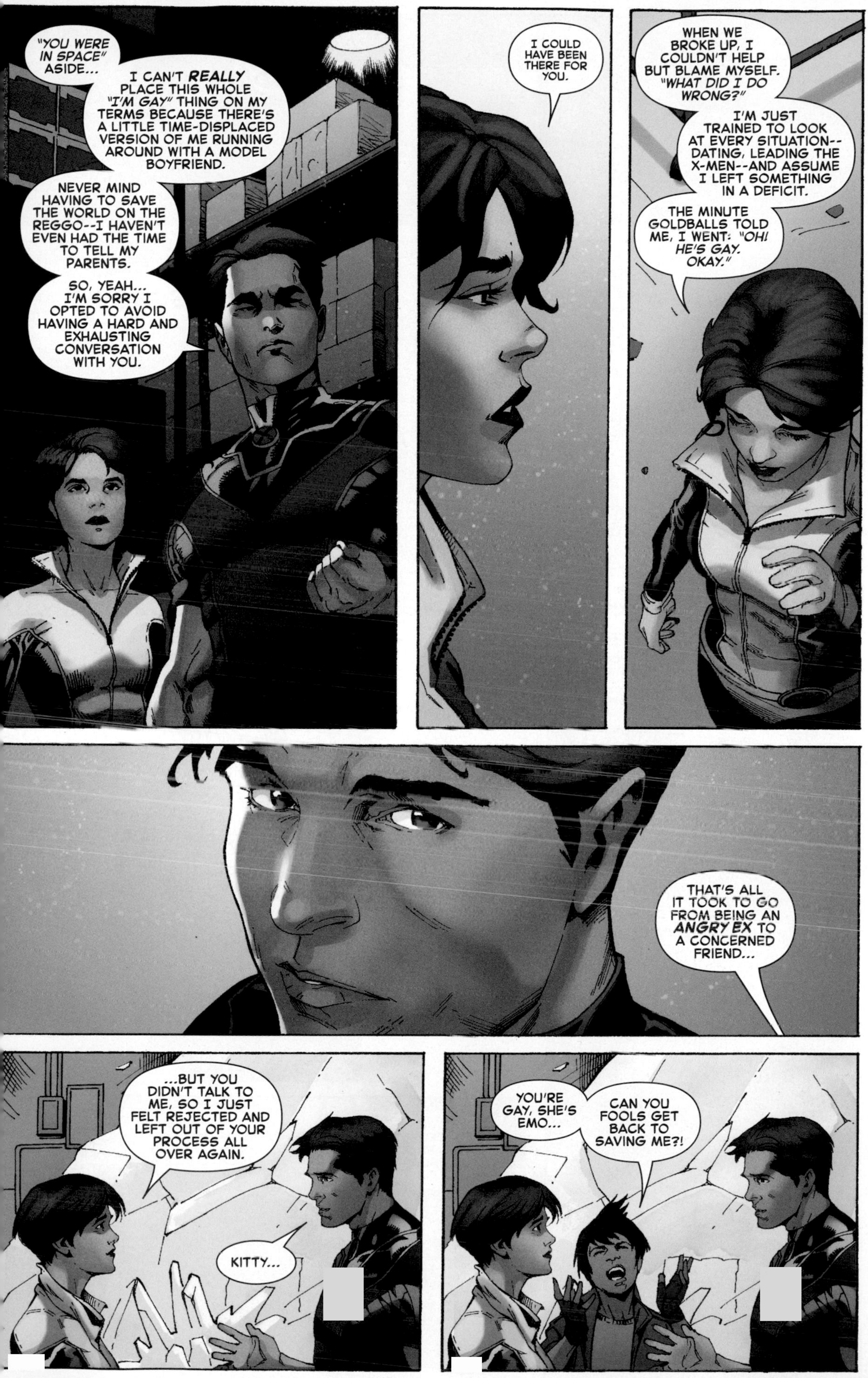
"YOU WERE IN SPACE" ASIDE...
I CAN'T REALLY PLACE THIS WHOLE "I'M GAY" THING ON MY TERMS BECAUSE THERE'S A LITTLE TIME-DISPLACED VERSION OF ME RUNNING AROUND WITH A MODEL BOYFRIEND.
NEVER MIND HAVING TO SAVE THE WORLD ON THE REGGO--I HAVEN'T EVEN HAD THE TIME TO TELL MY PARENTS.
SO, YEAH... I'M SORRY I OPTED TO AVOID HAVING A HARD AND EXHAUSTING CONVERSATION WITH YOU.
I COULD HAVE BEEN THERE FOR YOU.
WHEN WE BROKE UP, I COULDN'T HELP BUT BLAME MYSELF. "WHAT DID I DO WRONG?"
I'M JUST TRAINED TO LOOK AT EVERY SITUATION--DATING, LEADING THE X-MEN--AND ASSUME I LEFT SOMETHING IN A DEFICIT.
THE MINUTE GOLDBALLS TOLD ME, I WENT: "OH! HE'S GAY. OKAY."
THAT'S ALL IT TOOK TO GO FROM BEING AN ANGRY EX TO A CONCERNED FRIEND...
...BUT YOU DIDN'T TALK TO ME, SO I JUST FELT REJECTED AND LEFT OUT OF YOUR PROCESS ALL OVER AGAIN.
KITTY...
YOU'RE GAY, SHE'S EMO...
CAN YOU FOOLS GET BACK TO SAVING ME?!

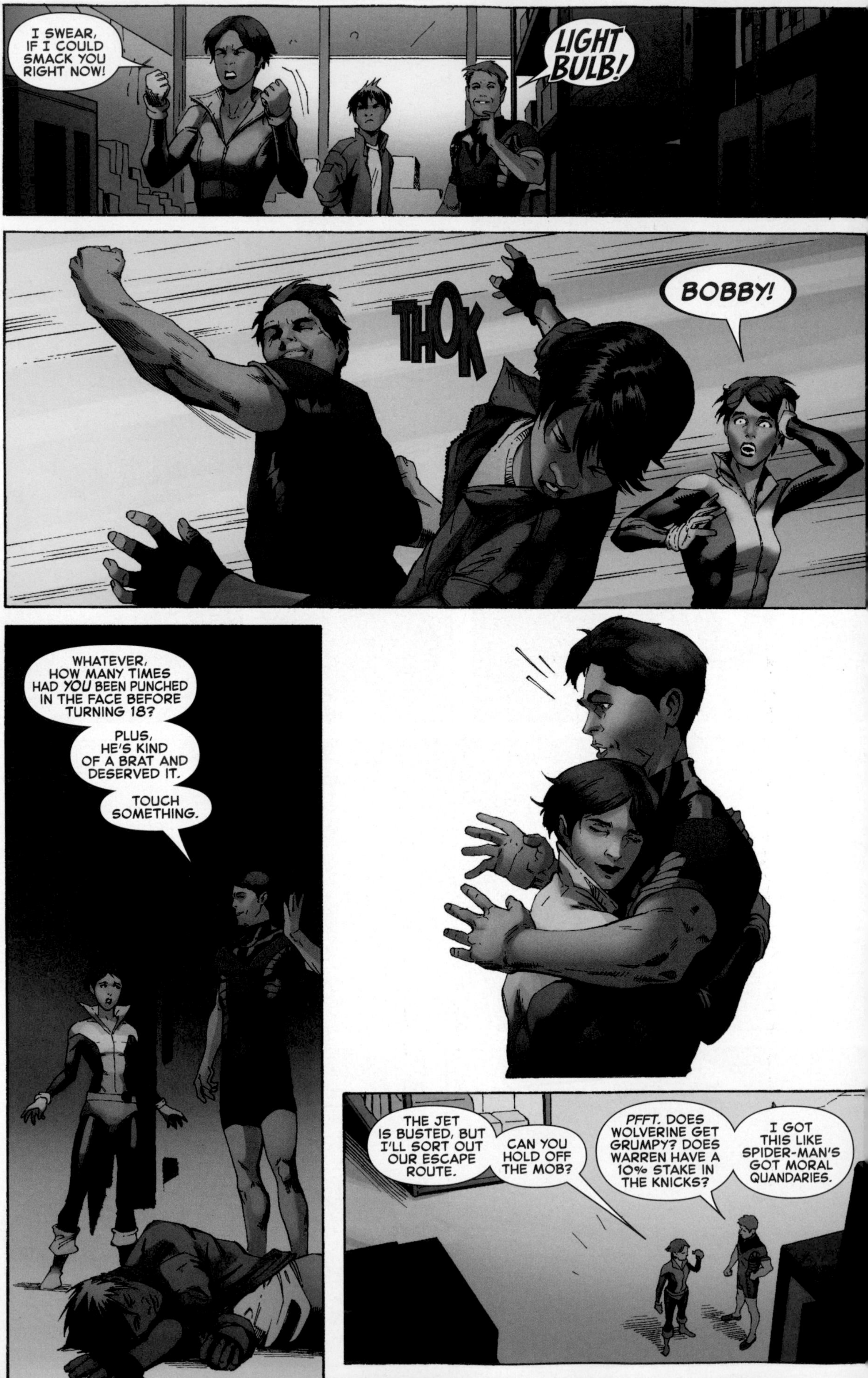

I SWEAR, IF I COULD SMACK YOU RIGHT NOW!
LIGHT BULB!
THOK
BOBBY!
WHATEVER, HOW MANY TIMES HAD *YOU* BEEN PUNCHED IN THE FACE BEFORE TURNING 18?
PLUS, HE'S KIND OF A BRAT AND DESERVED IT.
TOUCH SOMETHING.
THE JET IS BUSTED, BUT I'LL SORT OUT OUR ESCAPE ROUTE.
CAN YOU HOLD OFF THE MOB?
PFFT. DOES WOLVERINE GET GRUMPY? DOES WARREN HAVE A 10% STAKE IN THE KNICKS?
I GOT THIS LIKE SPIDER-MAN'S GOT MORAL QUANDARIES.

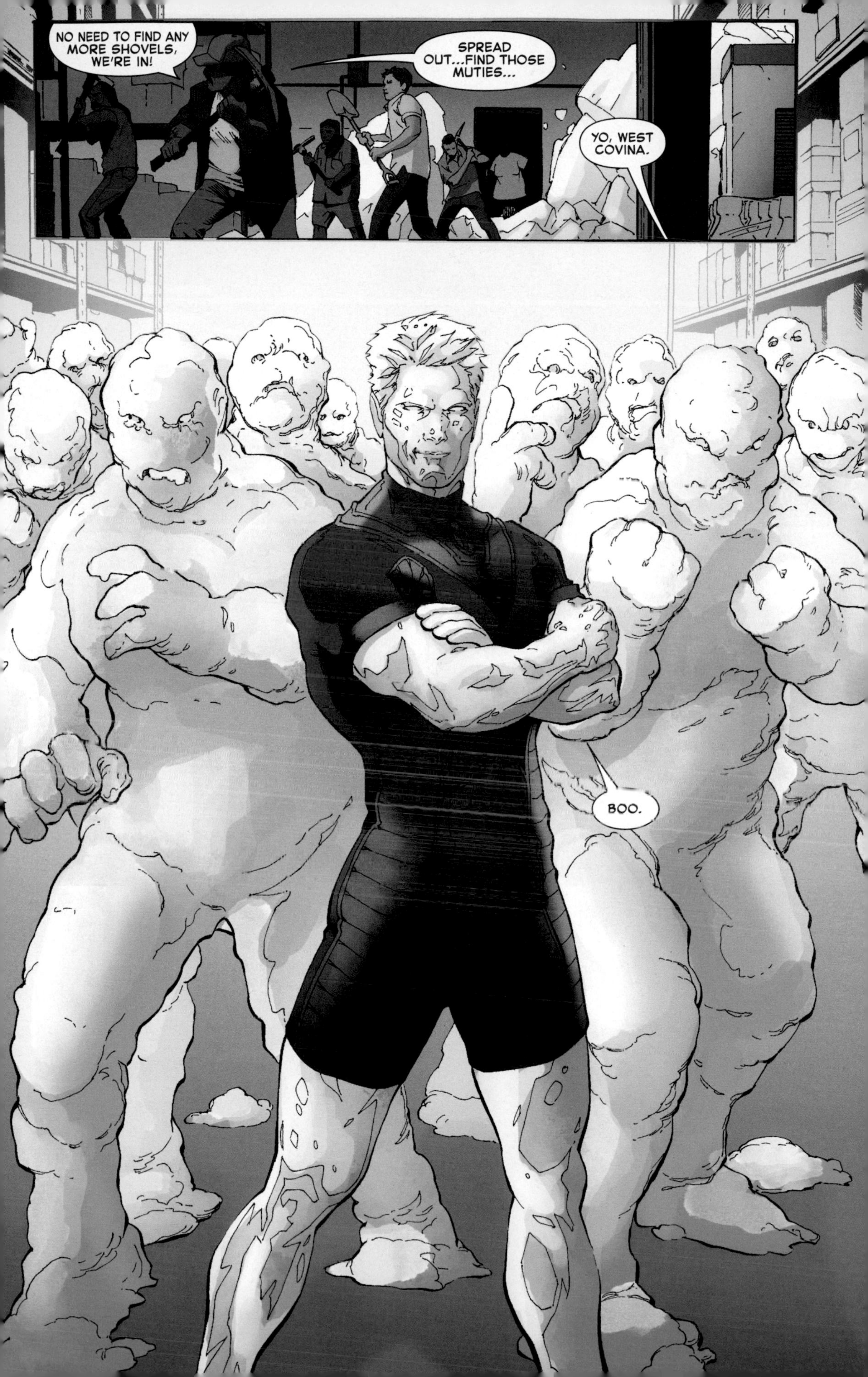
NO NEED TO FIND ANY MORE SHOVELS, WE'RE IN!
SPREAD OUT...FIND THOSE MUTIES...
YO, WEST COVINA.
BOO.

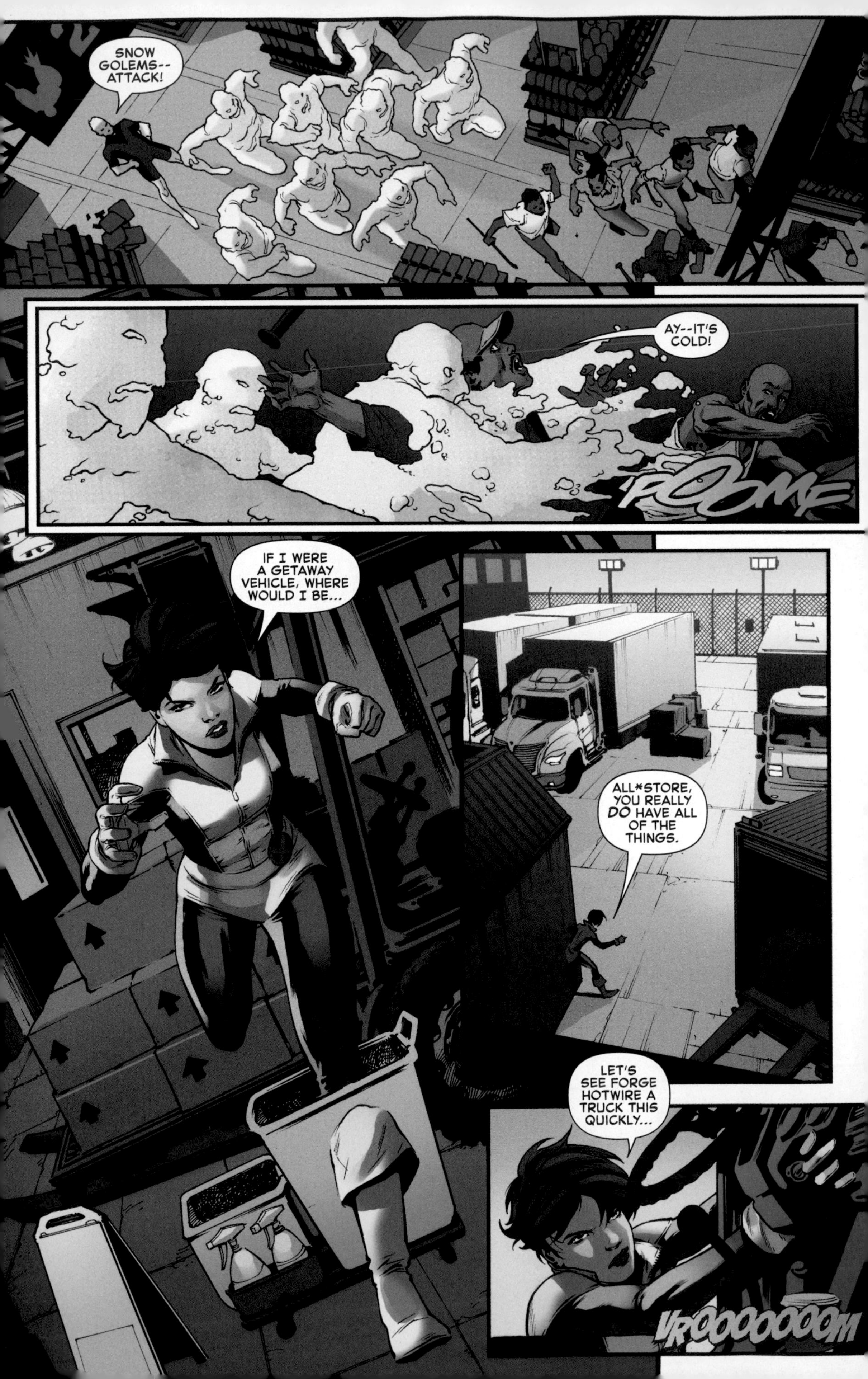
SNOW GOLEMS--ATTACK!
AY--IT'S COLD!
POOMF
IF I WERE A GETAWAY VEHICLE, WHERE WOULD I BE...
ALL*STORE, YOU REALLY DO HAVE ALL OF THE THINGS.
LET'S SEE FORGE HOTWIRE A TRUCK THIS QUICKLY...
VROOOOOOOOM

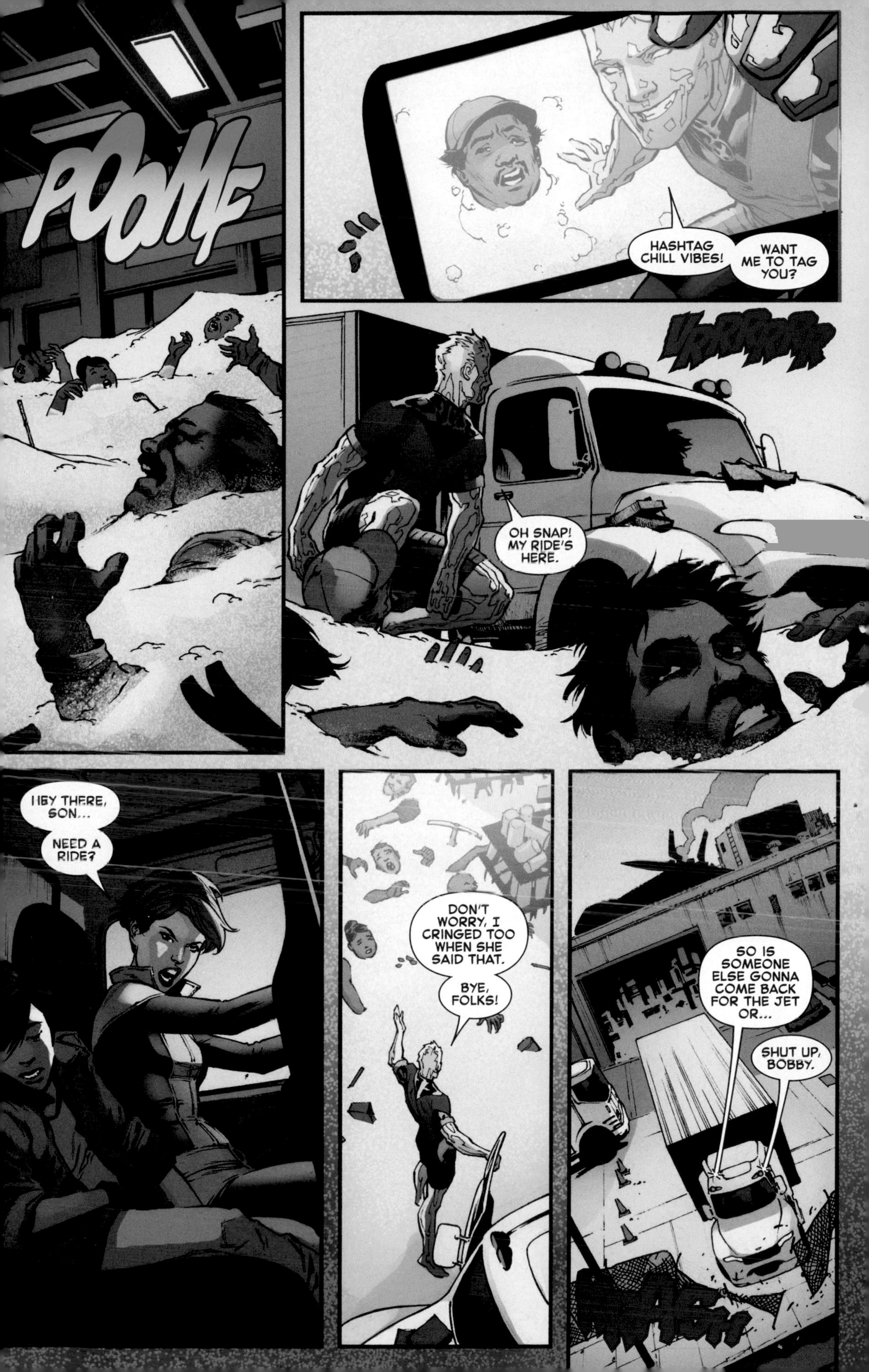
POOMF
HASHTAG CHILL VIBES!
WANT ME TO TAG YOU?
VRRRRRR
OH SNAP! MY RIDE'S HERE.
HEY THERE, SON...
NEED A RIDE?
DON'T WORRY, I CRINGED TOO WHEN SHE SAID THAT.
BYE, FOLKS!
SO IS SOMEONE ELSE GONNA COME BACK FOR THE JET OR...
SHUT UP, BOBBY.

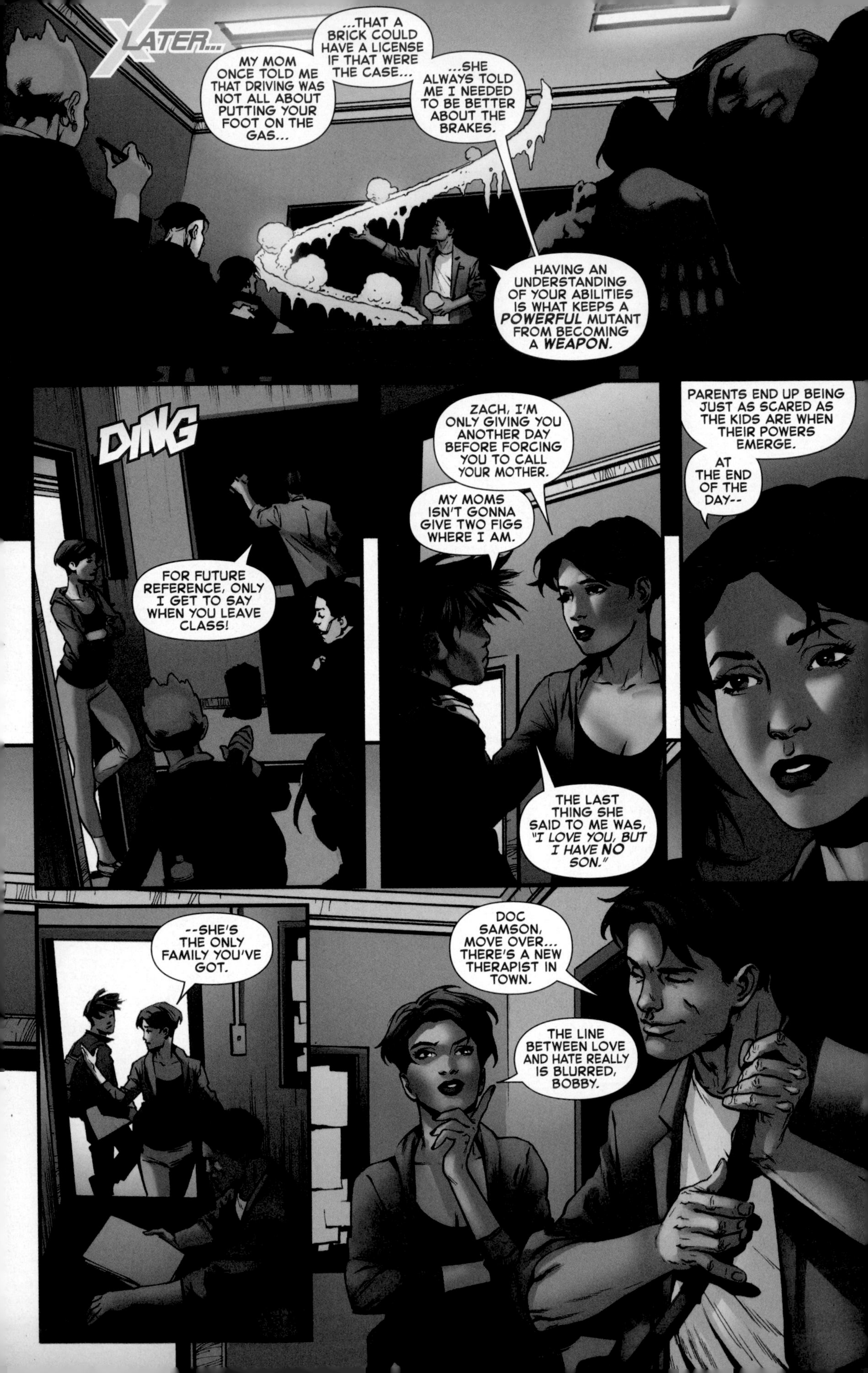
LATER...
MY MOM ONCE TOLD ME THAT DRIVING WAS NOT ALL ABOUT PUTTING YOUR FOOT ON THE GAS...
...THAT A BRICK COULD HAVE A LICENSE IF THAT WERE THE CASE...
...SHE ALWAYS TOLD ME I NEEDED TO BE BETTER ABOUT THE BRAKES.
HAVING AN UNDERSTANDING OF YOUR ABILITIES IS WHAT KEEPS A *POWERFUL* MUTANT FROM BECOMING A *WEAPON.*
DING
FOR FUTURE REFERENCE, ONLY I GET TO SAY WHEN YOU LEAVE CLASS!
ZACH, I'M ONLY GIVING YOU ANOTHER DAY BEFORE FORCING YOU TO CALL YOUR MOTHER.
MY MOMS ISN'T GONNA GIVE TWO FIGS WHERE I AM.
THE LAST THING SHE SAID TO ME WAS, *"I LOVE YOU, BUT I HAVE* ***NO*** *SON."*
PARENTS END UP BEING JUST AS SCARED AS THE KIDS ARE WHEN THEIR POWERS EMERGE.
AT THE END OF THE DAY--
--SHE'S THE ONLY FAMILY YOU'VE GOT.
DOC SAMSON, MOVE OVER... THERE'S A NEW THERAPIST IN TOWN.
THE LINE BETWEEN LOVE AND HATE REALLY IS BLURRED, BOBBY.

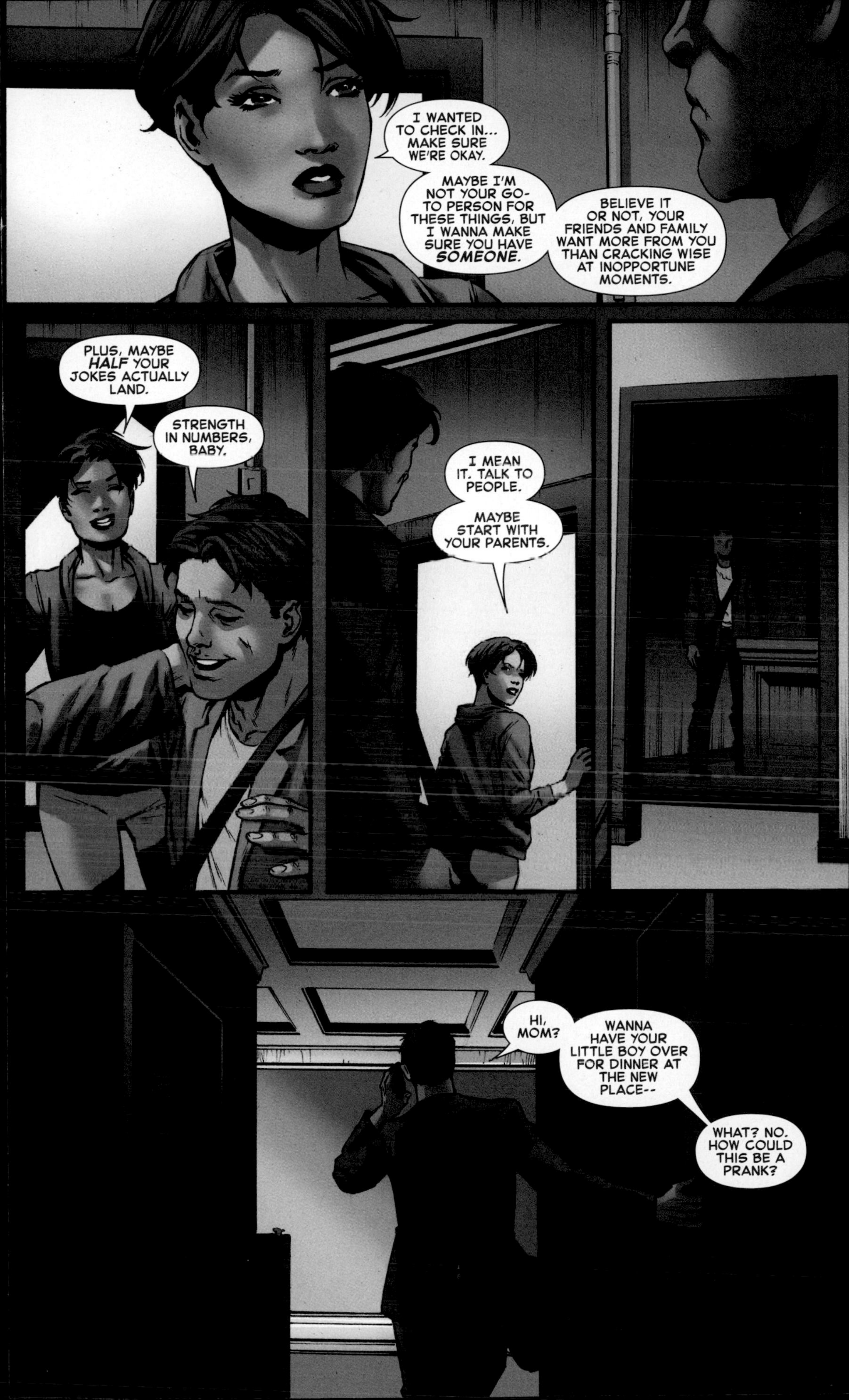
I WANTED TO CHECK IN... MAKE SURE WE'RE OKAY.
MAYBE I'M NOT YOUR GO-TO PERSON FOR THESE THINGS, BUT I WANNA MAKE SURE YOU HAVE SOMEONE.
BELIEVE IT OR NOT, YOUR FRIENDS AND FAMILY WANT MORE FROM YOU THAN CRACKING WISE AT INOPPORTUNE MOMENTS.
PLUS, MAYBE HALF YOUR JOKES ACTUALLY LAND.
STRENGTH IN NUMBERS, BABY.
I MEAN IT. TALK TO PEOPLE.
MAYBE START WITH YOUR PARENTS.
HI, MOM?
WANNA HAVE YOUR LITTLE BOY OVER FOR DINNER AT THE NEW PLACE--
WHAT? NO. HOW COULD THIS BE A PRANK?

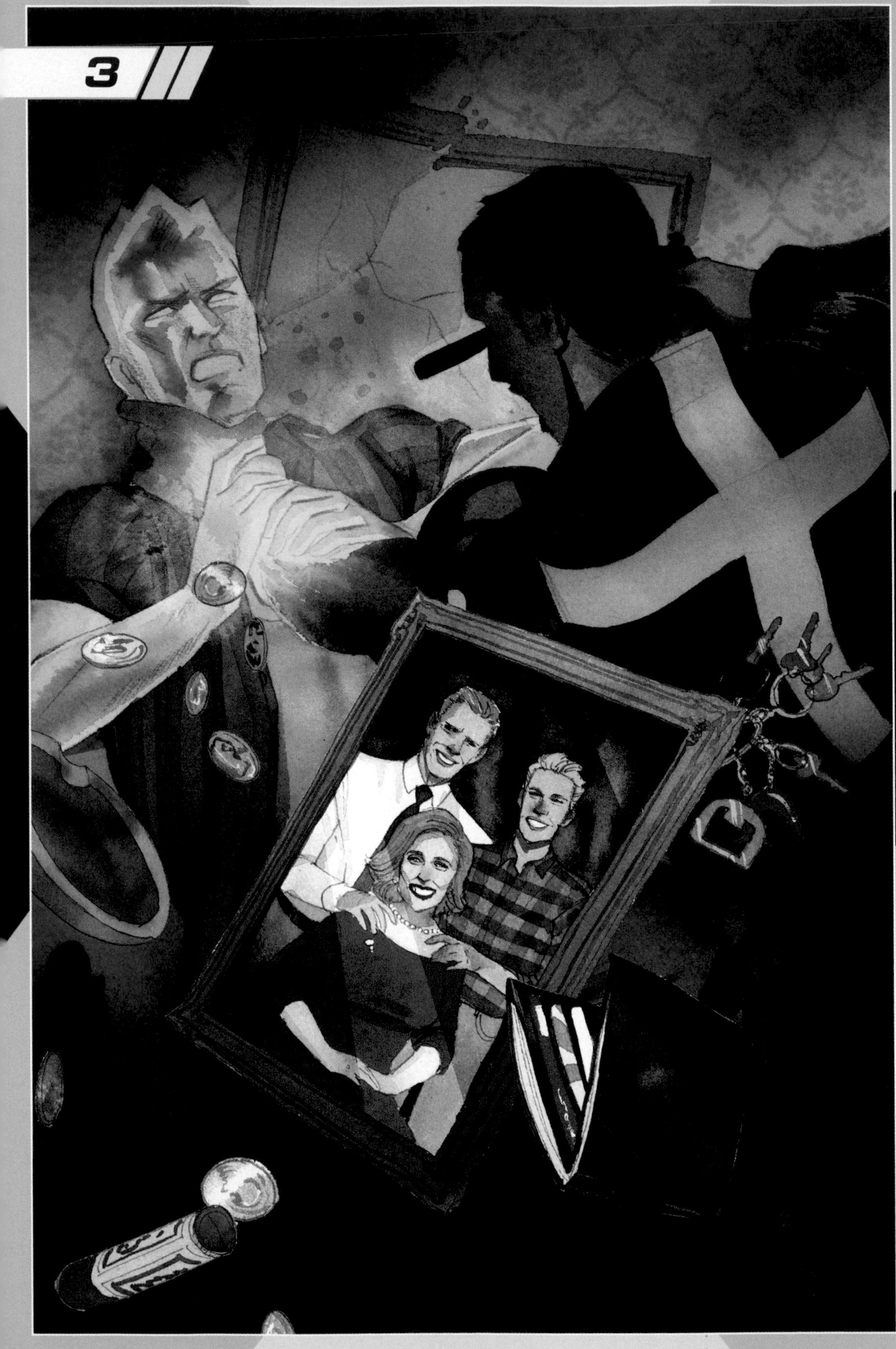
3

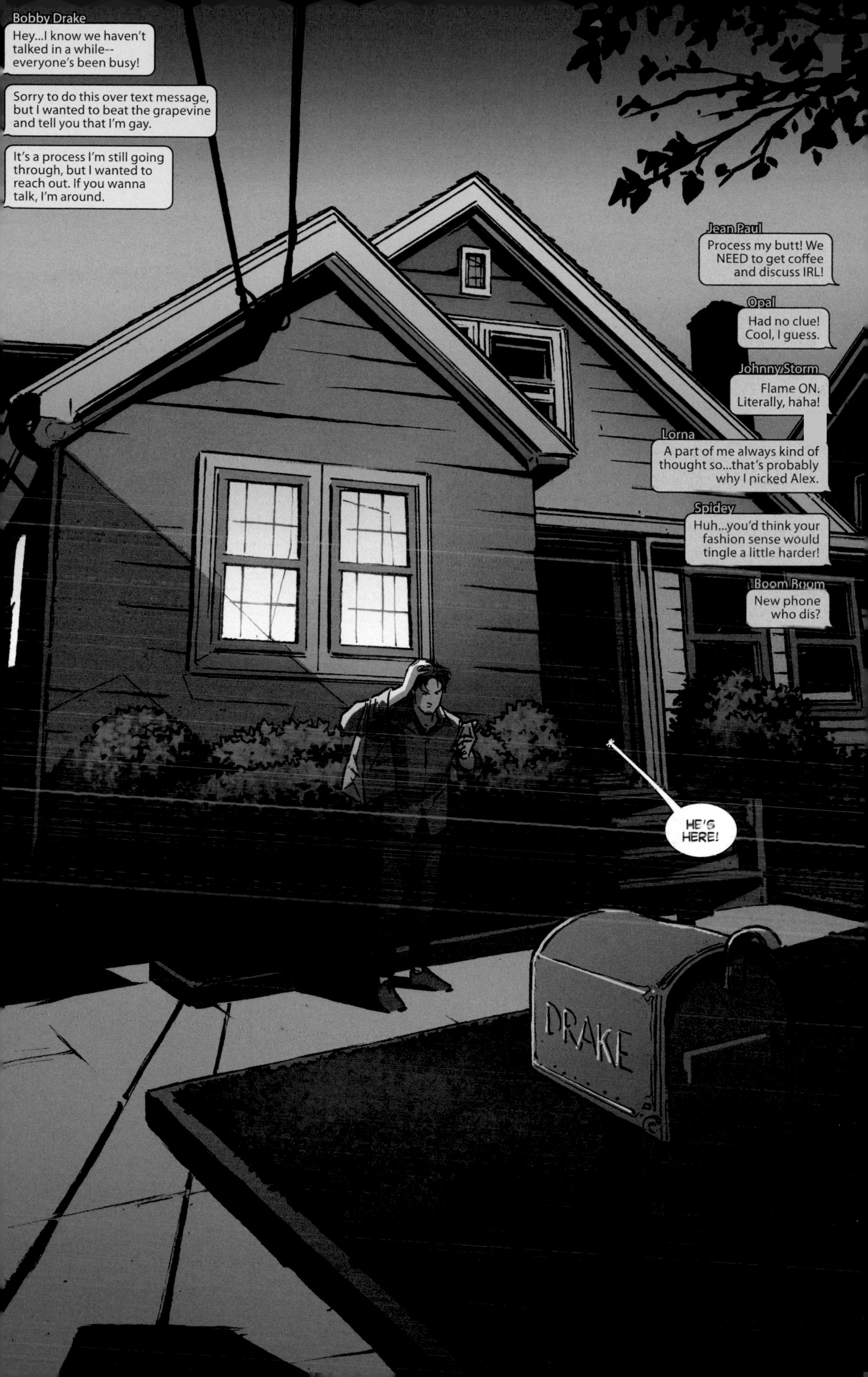
Bobby Drake
Hey...I know we haven't talked in a while-- everyone's been busy!
Sorry to do this over text message, but I wanted to beat the grapevine and tell you that I'm gay.
It's a process I'm still going through, but I wanted to reach out. If you wanna talk, I'm around.
Jean Paul
Process my butt! We NEED to get coffee and discuss IRL!
Opal
Had no clue! Cool, I guess.
Johnny Storm
Flame ON. Literally, haha!
Lorna
A part of me always kind of thought so...that's probably why I picked Alex.
Spidey
Huh...you'd think your fashion sense would tingle a little harder!
Boom Boom
New phone who dis?
HE'S HERE!
DRAKE

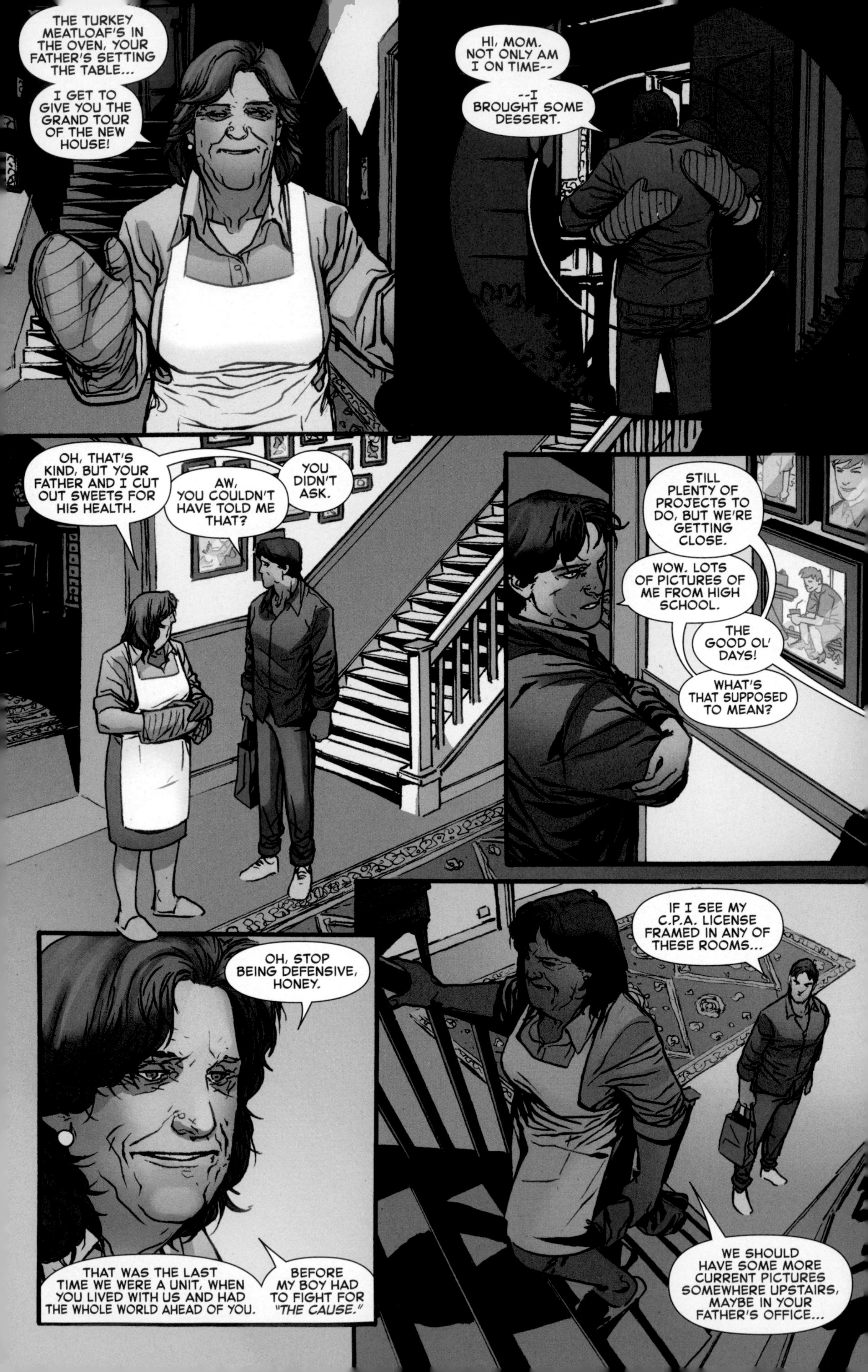
THE TURKEY MEATLOAF'S IN THE OVEN, YOUR FATHER'S SETTING THE TABLE...
I GET TO GIVE YOU THE GRAND TOUR OF THE NEW HOUSE!
HI, MOM. NOT ONLY AM I ON TIME--
--I BROUGHT SOME DESSERT.
OH, THAT'S KIND, BUT YOUR FATHER AND I CUT OUT SWEETS FOR HIS HEALTH.
AW, YOU COULDN'T HAVE TOLD ME THAT?
YOU DIDN'T ASK.
STILL PLENTY OF PROJECTS TO DO, BUT WE'RE GETTING CLOSE.
WOW. LOTS OF PICTURES OF ME FROM HIGH SCHOOL.
THE GOOD OL' DAYS!
WHAT'S THAT SUPPOSED TO MEAN?
OH, STOP BEING DEFENSIVE, HONEY.
THAT WAS THE LAST TIME WE WERE A UNIT, WHEN YOU LIVED WITH US AND HAD THE WHOLE WORLD AHEAD OF YOU.
BEFORE MY BOY HAD TO FIGHT FOR "THE CAUSE."
IF I SEE MY C.P.A. LICENSE FRAMED IN ANY OF THESE ROOMS...
WE SHOULD HAVE SOME MORE CURRENT PICTURES SOMEWHERE UPSTAIRS, MAYBE IN YOUR FATHER'S OFFICE...

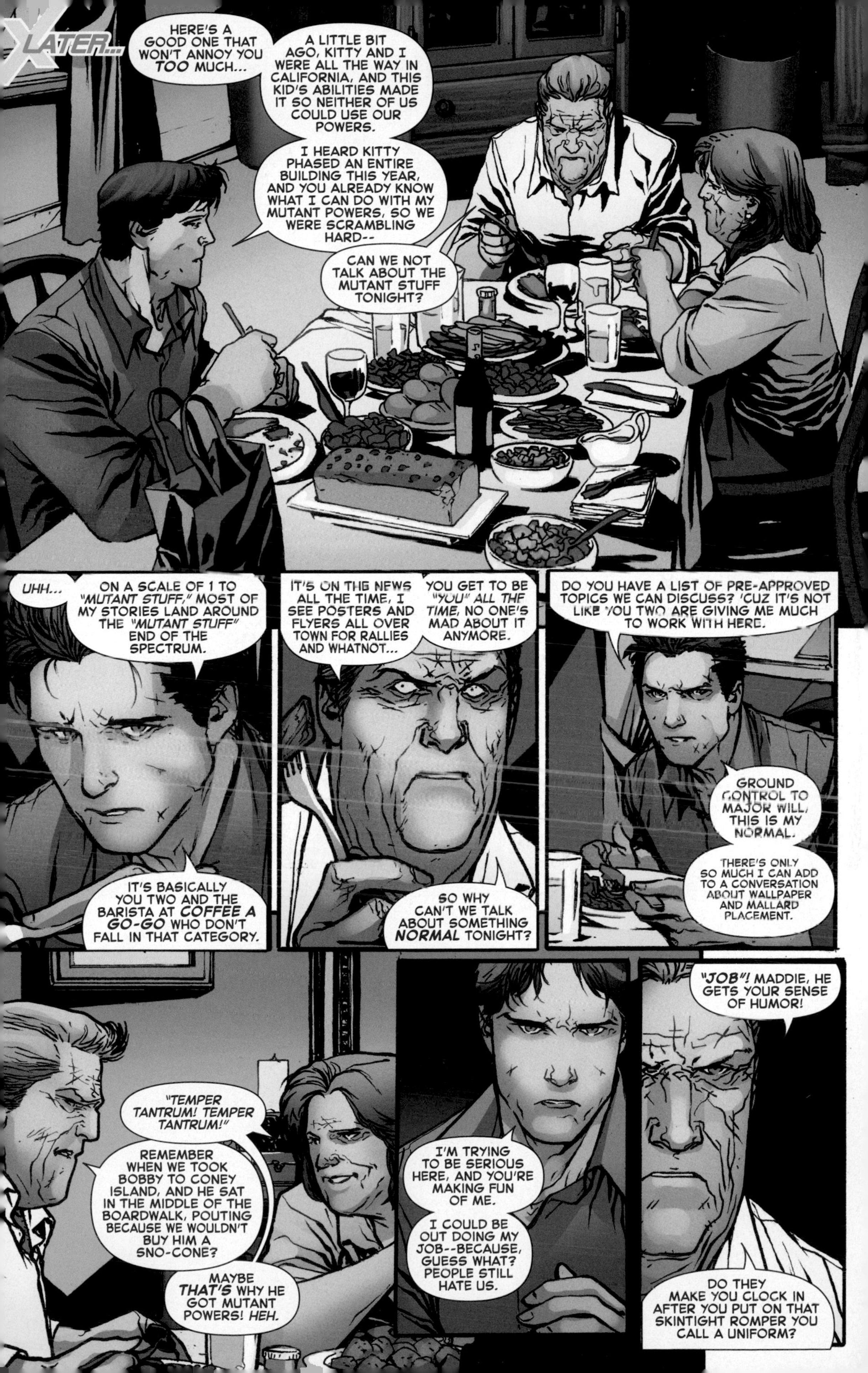
LATER...
HERE'S A GOOD ONE THAT WON'T ANNOY YOU TOO MUCH...
A LITTLE BIT AGO, KITTY AND I WERE ALL THE WAY IN CALIFORNIA, AND THIS KID'S ABILITIES MADE IT SO NEITHER OF US COULD USE OUR POWERS.
I HEARD KITTY PHASED AN ENTIRE BUILDING THIS YEAR, AND YOU ALREADY KNOW WHAT I CAN DO WITH MY MUTANT POWERS, SO WE WERE SCRAMBLING HARD--
CAN WE NOT TALK ABOUT THE MUTANT STUFF TONIGHT?
UHH...
ON A SCALE OF 1 TO "MUTANT STUFF," MOST OF MY STORIES LAND AROUND THE "MUTANT STUFF" END OF THE SPECTRUM.
IT'S BASICALLY YOU TWO AND THE BARISTA AT COFFEE A GO-GO WHO DON'T FALL IN THAT CATEGORY.
IT'S ON THE NEWS ALL THE TIME, I SEE POSTERS AND FLYERS ALL OVER TOWN FOR RALLIES AND WHATNOT...
YOU GET TO BE "YOU" ALL THE TIME, NO ONE'S MAD ABOUT IT ANYMORE.
SO WHY CAN'T WE TALK ABOUT SOMETHING NORMAL TONIGHT?
DO YOU HAVE A LIST OF PRE-APPROVED TOPICS WE CAN DISCUSS? 'CUZ IT'S NOT LIKE YOU TWO ARE GIVING ME MUCH TO WORK WITH HERE.
GROUND CONTROL TO MAJOR WILL, THIS IS MY NORMAL.
THERE'S ONLY SO MUCH I CAN ADD TO A CONVERSATION ABOUT WALLPAPER AND MALLARD PLACEMENT.
"TEMPER TANTRUM! TEMPER TANTRUM!"
REMEMBER WHEN WE TOOK BOBBY TO CONEY ISLAND, AND HE SAT IN THE MIDDLE OF THE BOARDWALK, POUTING BECAUSE WE WOULDN'T BUY HIM A SNO-CONE?
MAYBE THAT'S WHY HE GOT MUTANT POWERS! HEH.
I'M TRYING TO BE SERIOUS HERE, AND YOU'RE MAKING FUN OF ME.
I COULD BE OUT DOING MY JOB--BECAUSE, GUESS WHAT? PEOPLE STILL HATE US.
"JOB"! MADDIE, HE GETS YOUR SENSE OF HUMOR!
DO THEY MAKE YOU CLOCK IN AFTER YOU PUT ON THAT SKINTIGHT ROMPER YOU CALL A UNIFORM?

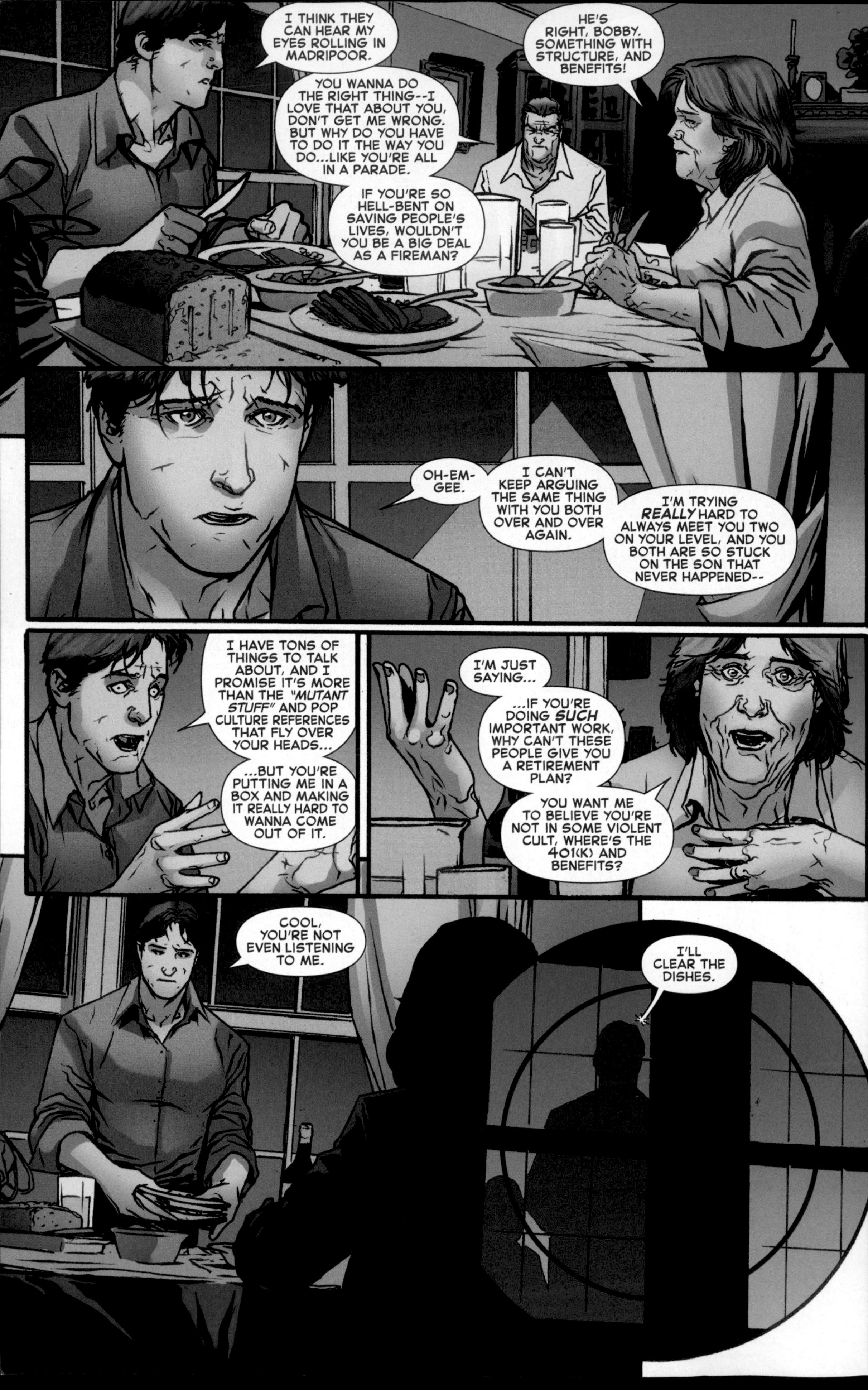
I THINK THEY CAN HEAR MY EYES ROLLING IN MADRIPOOR.
HE'S RIGHT, BOBBY. SOMETHING WITH STRUCTURE, AND BENEFITS!
YOU WANNA DO THE RIGHT THING--I LOVE THAT ABOUT YOU, DON'T GET ME WRONG. BUT WHY DO YOU HAVE TO DO IT THE WAY YOU DO...LIKE YOU'RE ALL IN A PARADE.
IF YOU'RE SO HELL-BENT ON SAVING PEOPLE'S LIVES, WOULDN'T YOU BE A BIG DEAL AS A FIREMAN?
OH-EM-GEE.
I CAN'T KEEP ARGUING THE SAME THING WITH YOU BOTH OVER AND OVER AGAIN.
I'M TRYING *REALLY* HARD TO ALWAYS MEET YOU TWO ON YOUR LEVEL, AND YOU BOTH ARE SO STUCK ON THE SON THAT NEVER HAPPENED--
I HAVE TONS OF THINGS TO TALK ABOUT, AND I PROMISE IT'S MORE THAN THE *"MUTANT STUFF"* AND POP CULTURE REFERENCES THAT FLY OVER YOUR HEADS...
...BUT YOU'RE PUTTING ME IN A BOX AND MAKING IT REALLY HARD TO WANNA COME OUT OF IT.
I'M JUST SAYING...
...IF YOU'RE DOING *SUCH* IMPORTANT WORK, WHY CAN'T THESE PEOPLE GIVE YOU A RETIREMENT PLAN?
YOU WANT ME TO BELIEVE YOU'RE NOT IN SOME VIOLENT CULT, WHERE'S THE 401(K) AND BENEFITS?
COOL, YOU'RE NOT EVEN LISTENING TO ME.
I'LL CLEAR THE DISHES.

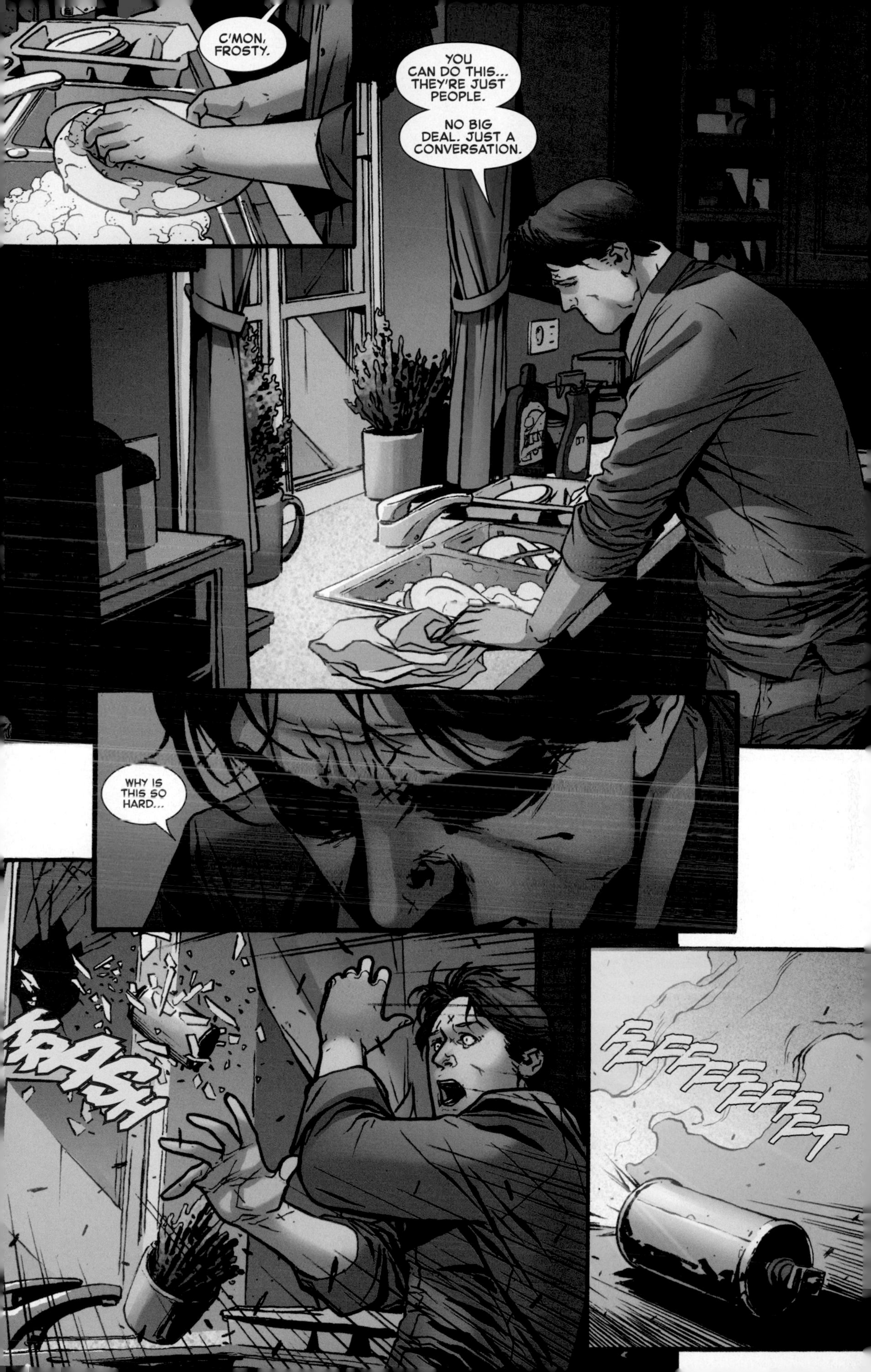
C'MON, FROSTY.
YOU CAN DO THIS... THEY'RE JUST PEOPLE.
NO BIG DEAL. JUST A CONVERSATION.
WHY IS THIS SO HARD...
KRASH
FSSSSSSSSSSSSSSSSSSSSSSSSSSST

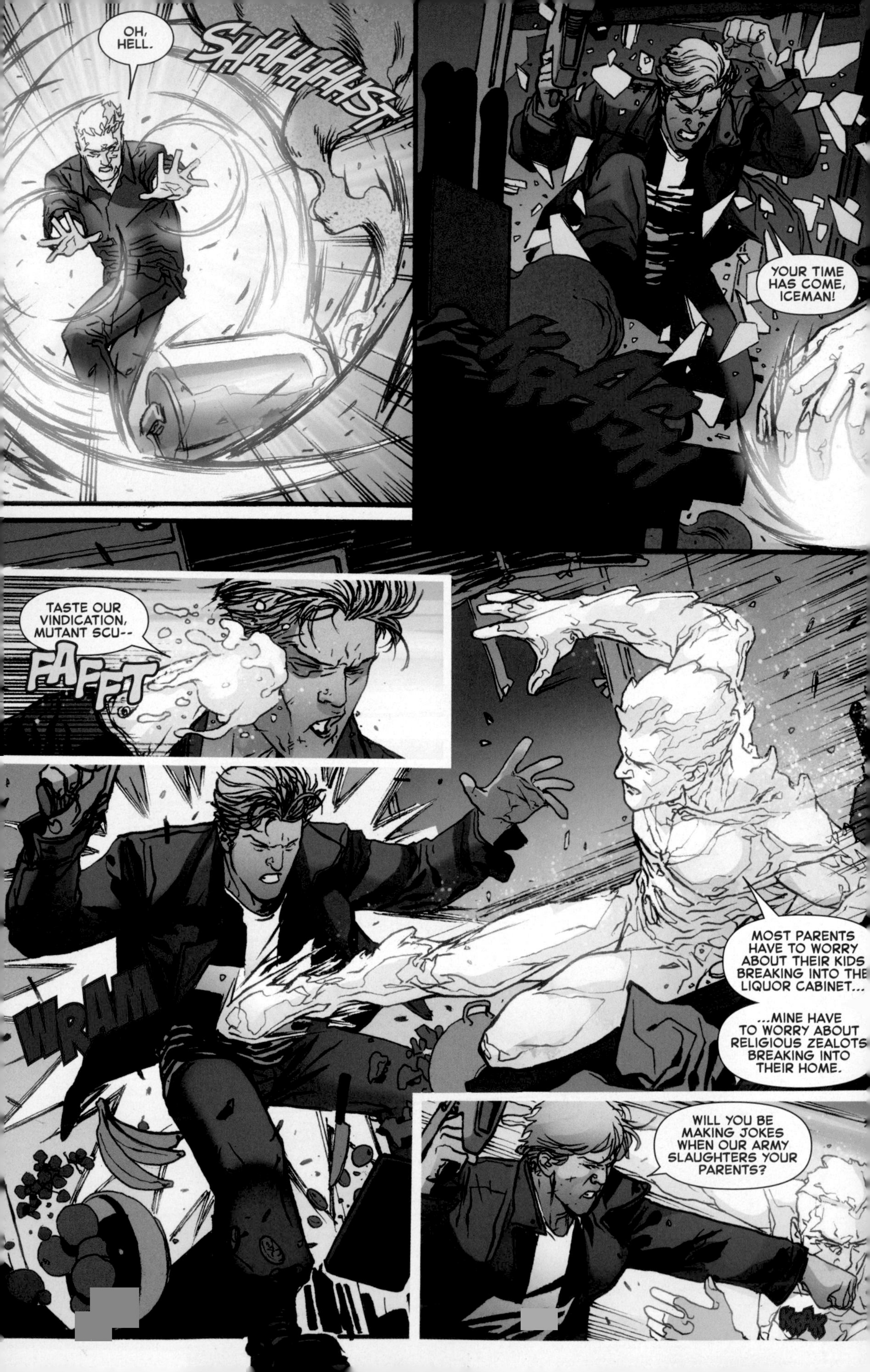
OH, HELL.
SHHHHHST
YOUR TIME HAS COME, ICEMAN!
TASTE OUR VINDICATION, MUTANT SCU--
FAFFT
WRAM
MOST PARENTS HAVE TO WORRY ABOUT THEIR KIDS BREAKING INTO THE LIQUOR CABINET...
...MINE HAVE TO WORRY ABOUT RELIGIOUS ZEALOTS BREAKING INTO THEIR HOME.
WILL YOU BE MAKING JOKES WHEN OUR ARMY SLAUGHTERS YOUR PARENTS?

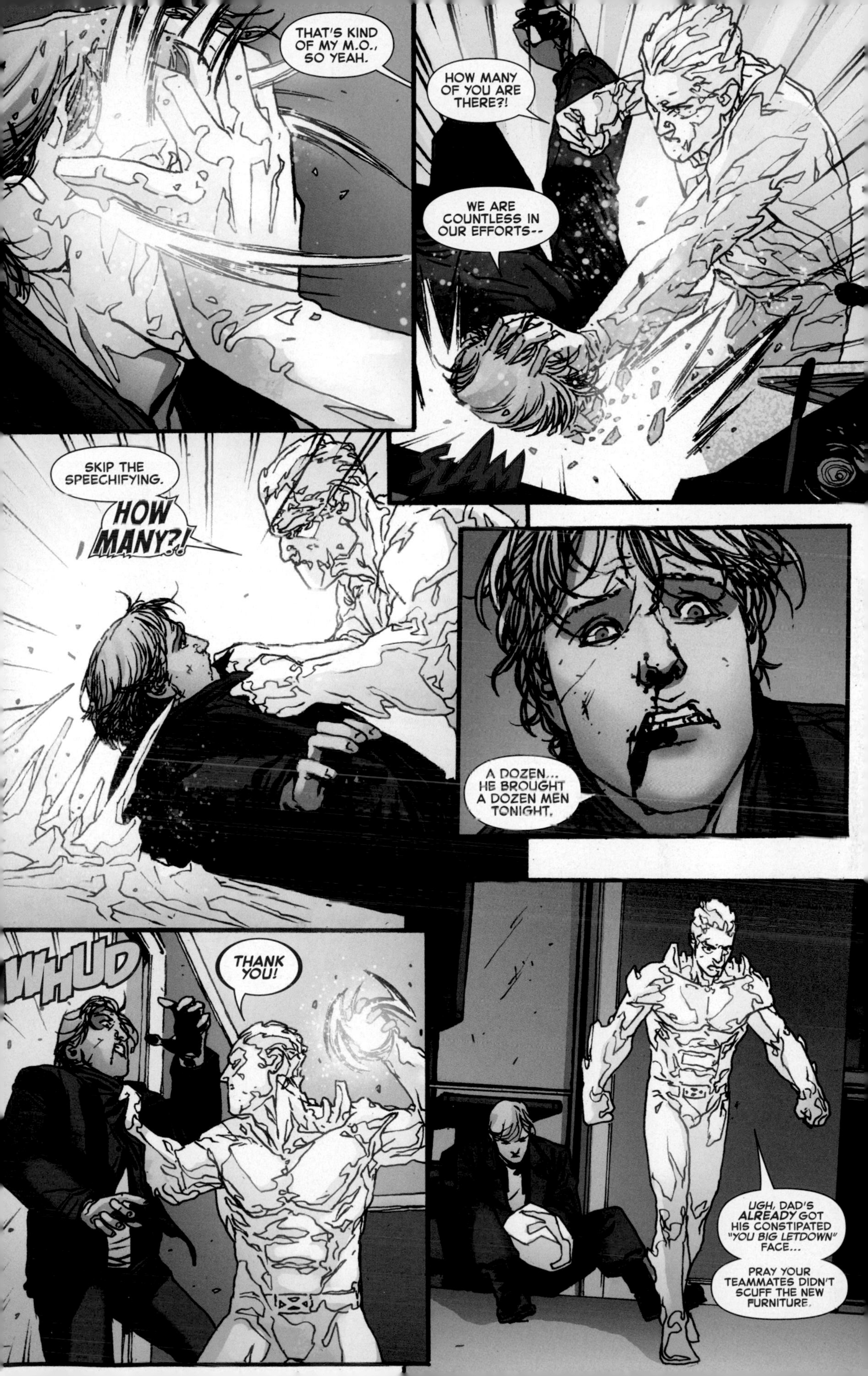
THAT'S KIND OF MY M.O., SO YEAH.
HOW MANY OF YOU ARE THERE?!
WE ARE COUNTLESS IN OUR EFFORTS--
SLAM
SKIP THE SPEECHIFYING.
HOW MANY?!
A DOZEN... HE BROUGHT A DOZEN MEN TONIGHT.
WHUD
THANK YOU!
UGH, DAD'S ALREADY GOT HIS CONSTIPATED "YOU BIG LETDOWN" FACE...
PRAY YOUR TEAMMATES DIDN'T SCUFF THE NEW FURNITURE.

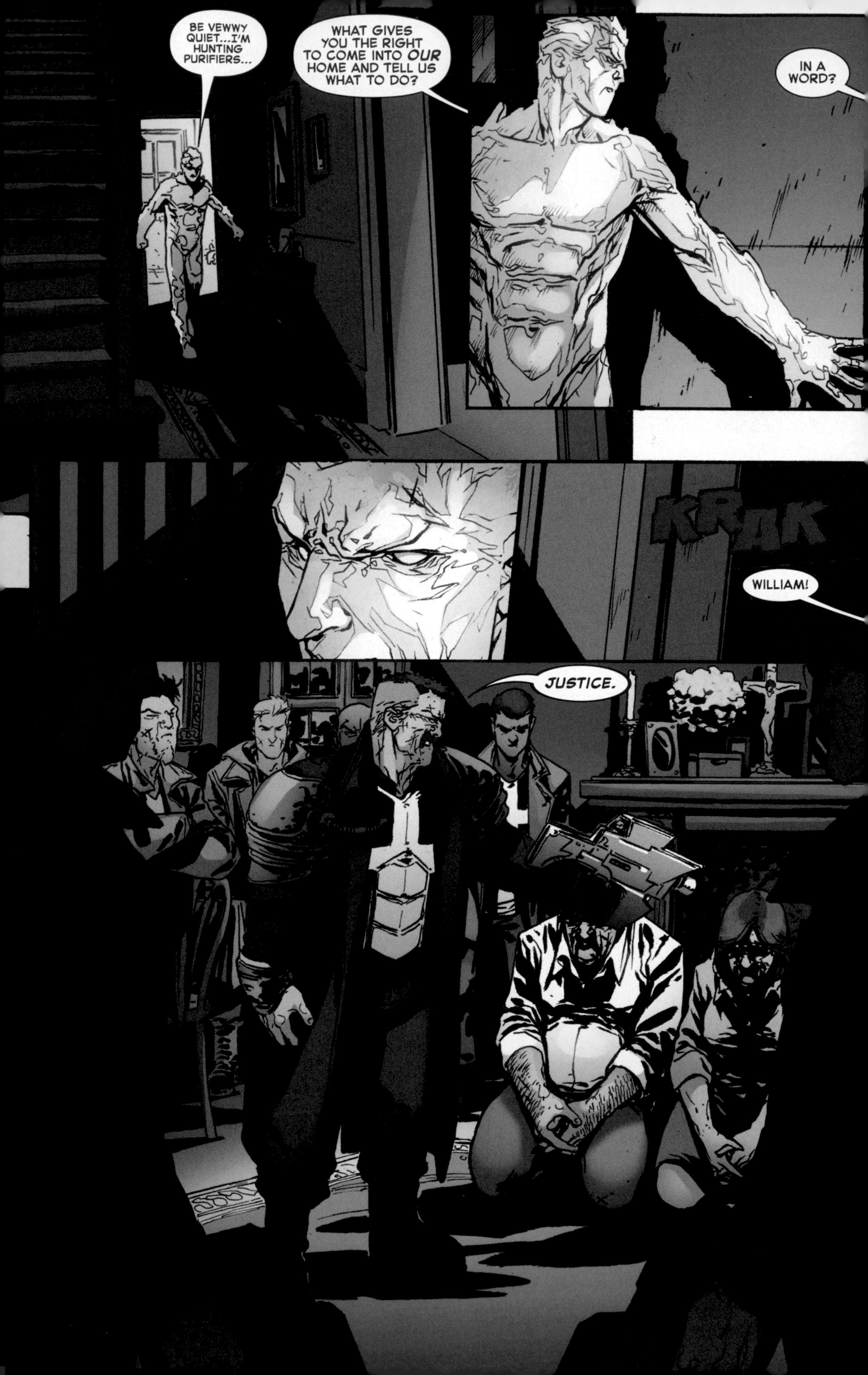
BE VEWWY QUIET...I'M HUNTING PURIFIERS...
WHAT GIVES YOU THE RIGHT TO COME INTO OUR HOME AND TELL US WHAT TO DO?
IN A WORD?
KRAK
WILLIAM!
JUSTICE.

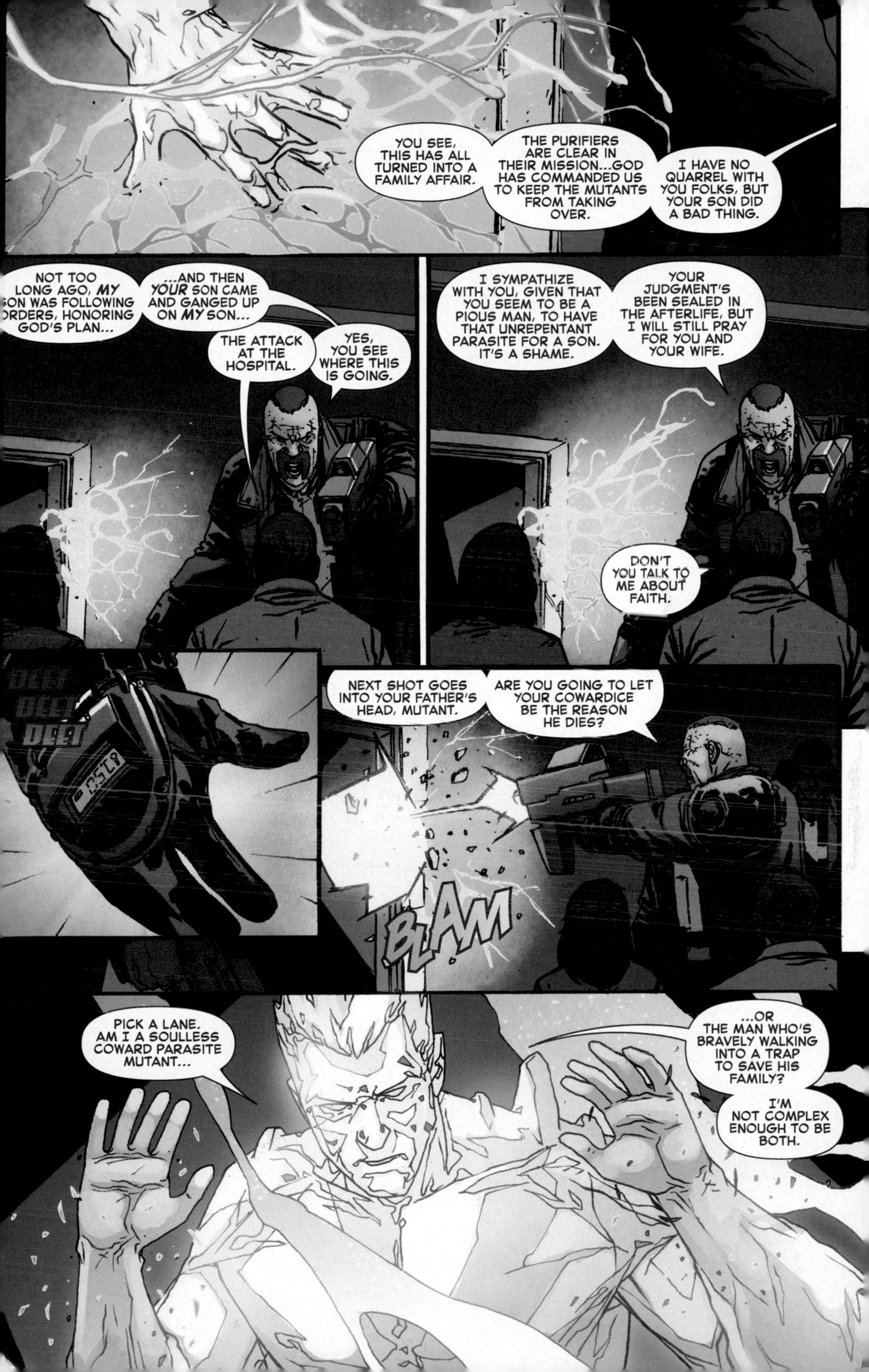
YOU SEE, THIS HAS ALL TURNED INTO A FAMILY AFFAIR.
THE PURIFIERS ARE CLEAR IN THEIR MISSION...GOD HAS COMMANDED US TO KEEP THE MUTANTS FROM TAKING OVER.
I HAVE NO QUARREL WITH YOU FOLKS, BUT YOUR SON DID A BAD THING.
NOT TOO LONG AGO, MY SON WAS FOLLOWING ORDERS, HONORING GOD'S PLAN...
...AND THEN YOUR SON CAME AND GANGED UP ON MY SON...
THE ATTACK AT THE HOSPITAL.
YES, YOU SEE WHERE THIS IS GOING.
I SYMPATHIZE WITH YOU, GIVEN THAT YOU SEEM TO BE A PIOUS MAN, TO HAVE THAT UNREPENTANT PARASITE FOR A SON. IT'S A SHAME.
YOUR JUDGMENT'S BEEN SEALED IN THE AFTERLIFE, BUT I WILL STILL PRAY FOR YOU AND YOUR WIFE.
DON'T YOU TALK TO ME ABOUT FAITH.
DEET
DEET
DEET
NEXT SHOT GOES INTO YOUR FATHER'S HEAD, MUTANT.
ARE YOU GOING TO LET YOUR COWARDICE BE THE REASON HE DIES?
BLAM
PICK A LANE. AM I A SOULLESS COWARD PARASITE MUTANT...
...OR THE MAN WHO'S BRAVELY WALKING INTO A TRAP TO SAVE HIS FAMILY?
I'M NOT COMPLEX ENOUGH TO BE BOTH.

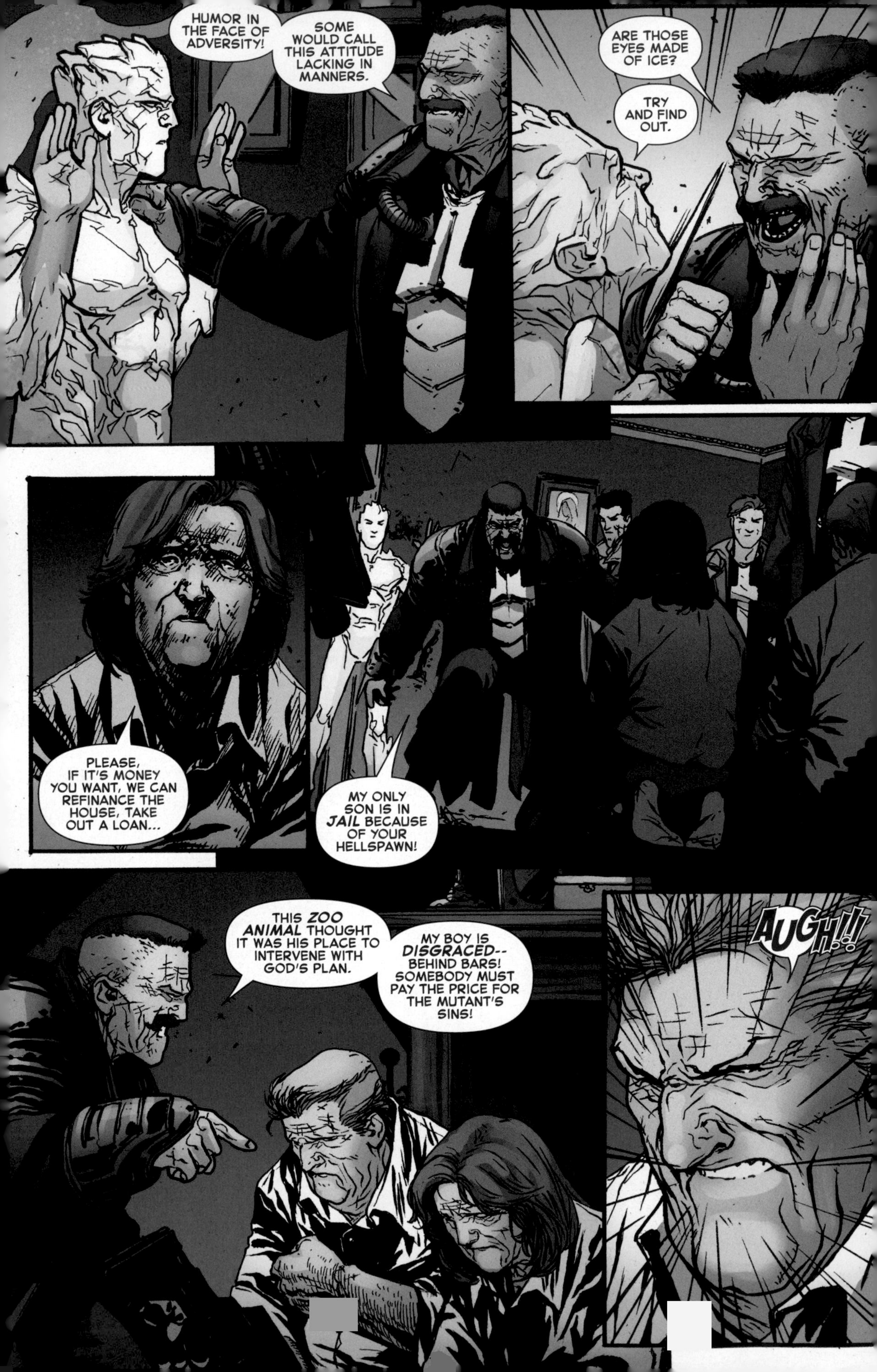
HUMOR IN THE FACE OF ADVERSITY!
SOME WOULD CALL THIS ATTITUDE LACKING IN MANNERS.
ARE THOSE EYES MADE OF ICE?
TRY AND FIND OUT.
PLEASE, IF IT'S MONEY YOU WANT, WE CAN REFINANCE THE HOUSE, TAKE OUT A LOAN...
MY ONLY SON IS IN *JAIL* BECAUSE OF YOUR HELLSPAWN!
THIS *ZOO ANIMAL* THOUGHT IT WAS HIS PLACE TO INTERVENE WITH GOD'S PLAN.
MY BOY IS *DISGRACED*-- BEHIND BARS! SOMEBODY MUST PAY THE PRICE FOR THE MUTANT'S SINS!
AUGH!!!

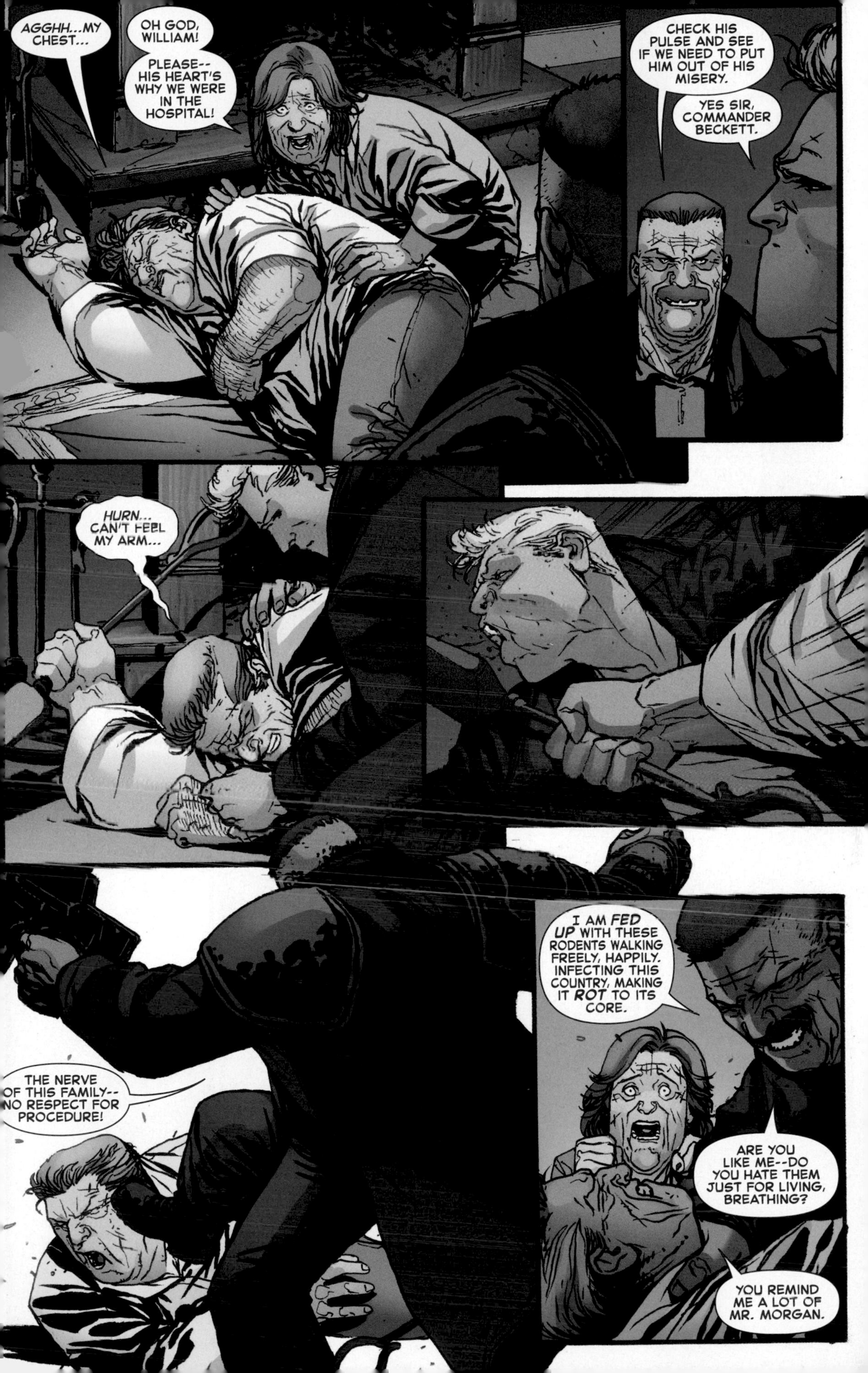
AGGHH...MY CHEST...
OH GOD, WILLIAM!
PLEASE-- HIS HEART'S WHY WE WERE IN THE HOSPITAL!
CHECK HIS PULSE AND SEE IF WE NEED TO PUT HIM OUT OF HIS MISERY.
YES SIR, COMMANDER BECKETT.
HURN... CAN'T FEEL MY ARM...
I AM FED UP WITH THESE RODENTS WALKING FREELY, HAPPILY. INFECTING THIS COUNTRY, MAKING IT ROT TO ITS CORE.
THE NERVE OF THIS FAMILY-- NO RESPECT FOR PROCEDURE!
ARE YOU LIKE ME--DO YOU HATE THEM JUST FOR LIVING, BREATHING?
YOU REMIND ME A LOT OF MR. MORGAN.

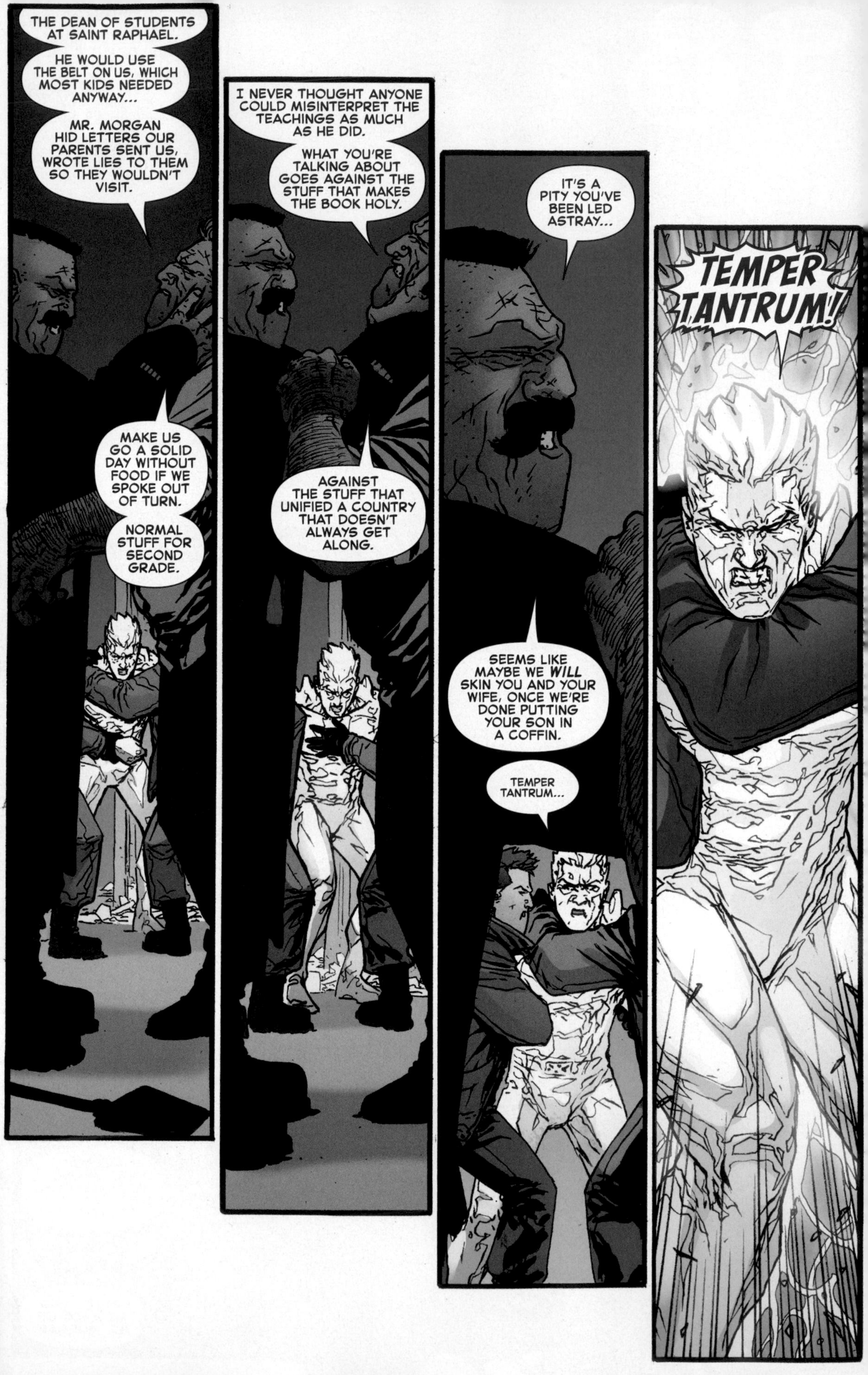
THE DEAN OF STUDENTS AT SAINT RAPHAEL.
HE WOULD USE THE BELT ON US, WHICH MOST KIDS NEEDED ANYWAY...
MR. MORGAN HID LETTERS OUR PARENTS SENT US, WROTE LIES TO THEM SO THEY WOULDN'T VISIT.
MAKE US GO A SOLID DAY WITHOUT FOOD IF WE SPOKE OUT OF TURN.
NORMAL STUFF FOR SECOND GRADE.
I NEVER THOUGHT ANYONE COULD MISINTERPRET THE TEACHINGS AS MUCH AS HE DID.
WHAT YOU'RE TALKING ABOUT GOES AGAINST THE STUFF THAT MAKES THE BOOK HOLY.
AGAINST THE STUFF THAT UNIFIED A COUNTRY THAT DOESN'T ALWAYS GET ALONG.
IT'S A PITY YOU'VE BEEN LED ASTRAY...
SEEMS LIKE MAYBE WE *WILL* SKIN YOU AND YOUR WIFE, ONCE WE'RE DONE PUTTING YOUR SON IN A COFFIN.
TEMPER TANTRUM...
TEMPER TANTRUM!

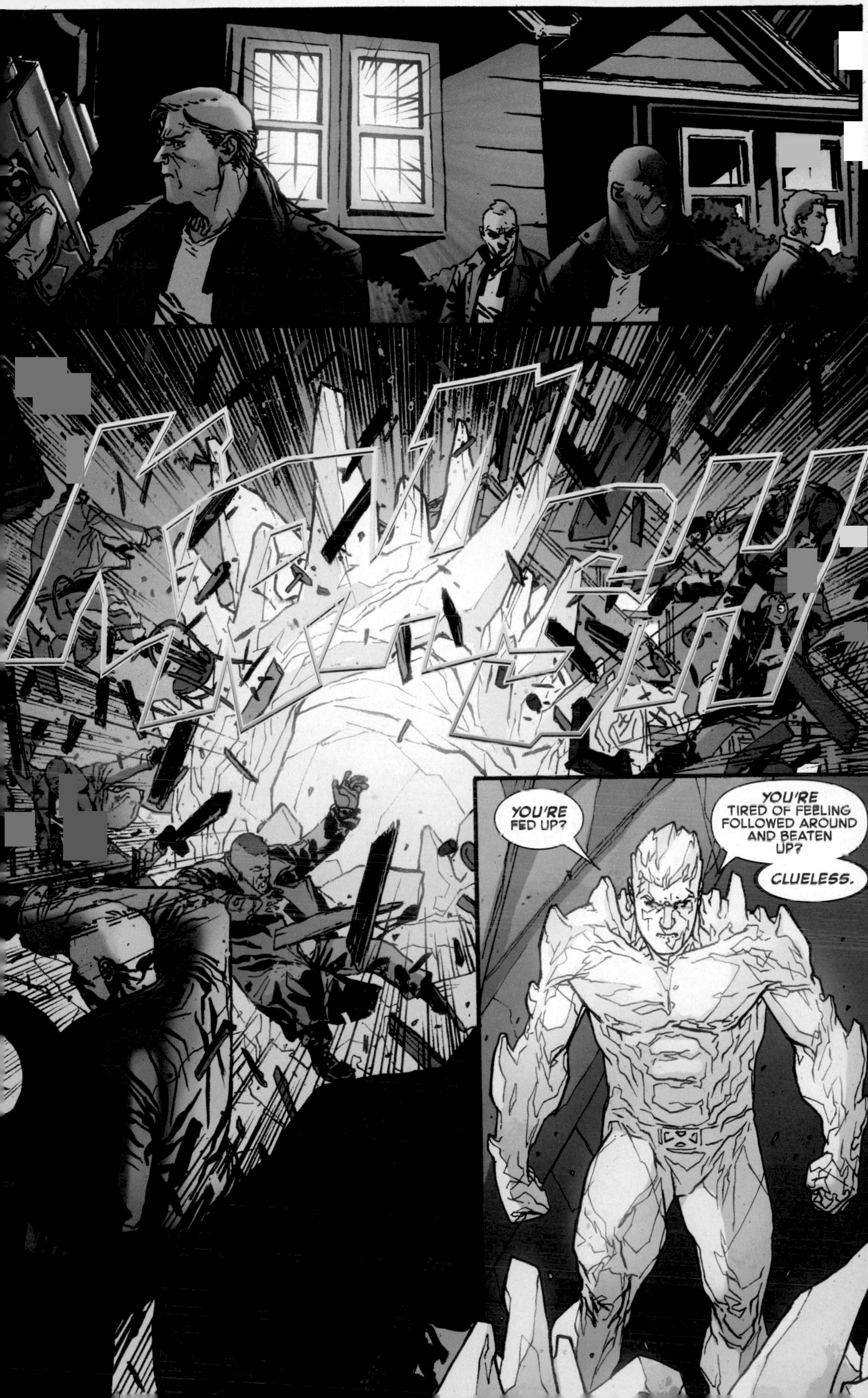
YOU'RE FED UP?
YOU'RE TIRED OF FEELING FOLLOWED AROUND AND BEATEN UP?
CLUELESS.

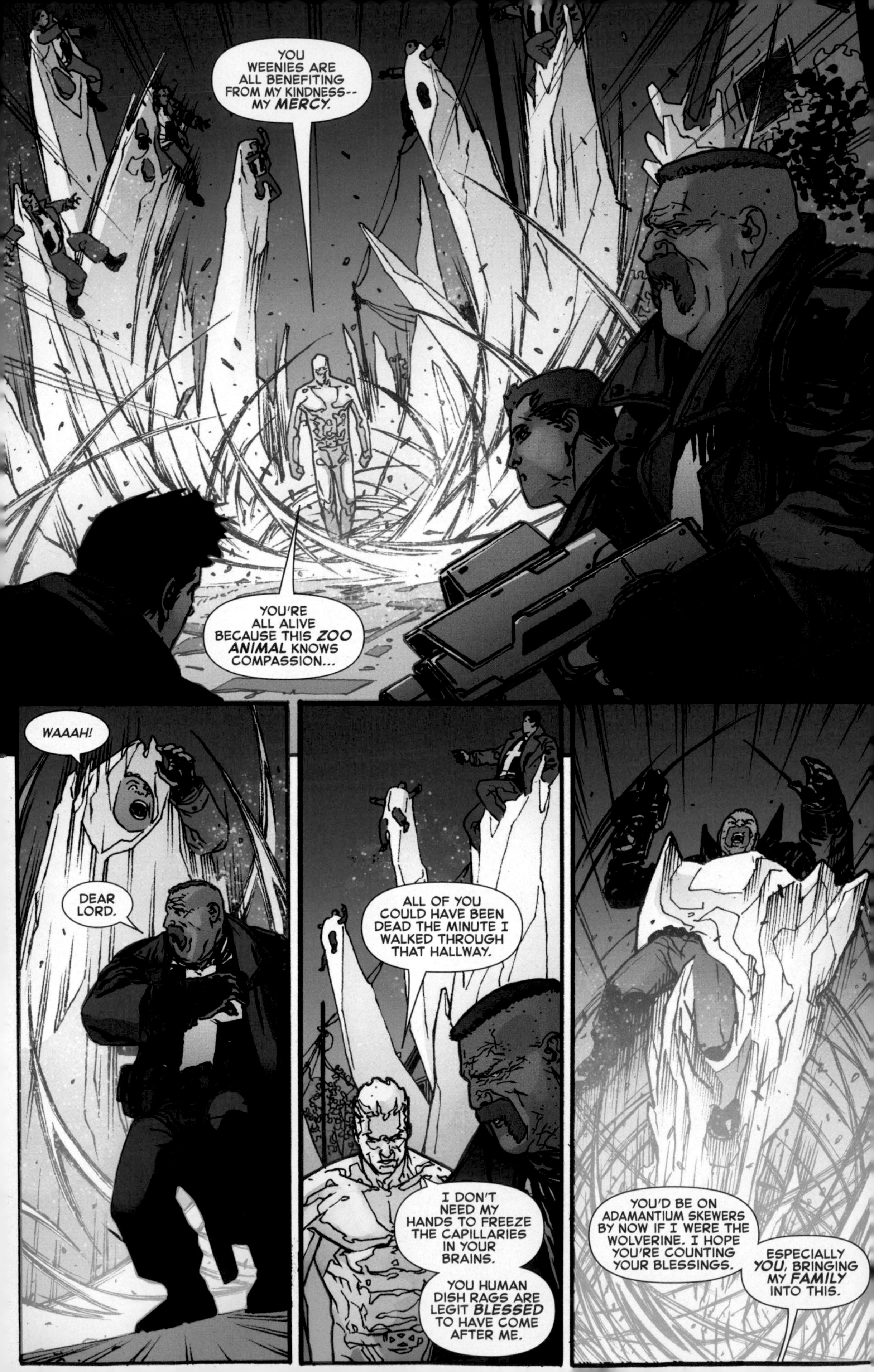
YOU WEENIES ARE ALL BENEFITING FROM MY KINDNESS-- MY MERCY.
YOU'RE ALL ALIVE BECAUSE THIS ZOO ANIMAL KNOWS COMPASSION...
WAAAH!
DEAR LORD.
ALL OF YOU COULD HAVE BEEN DEAD THE MINUTE I WALKED THROUGH THAT HALLWAY.
I DON'T NEED MY HANDS TO FREEZE THE CAPILLARIES IN YOUR BRAINS.
YOU HUMAN DISH RAGS ARE LEGIT BLESSED TO HAVE COME AFTER ME.
YOU'D BE ON ADAMANTIUM SKEWERS BY NOW IF I WERE THE WOLVERINE. I HOPE YOU'RE COUNTING YOUR BLESSINGS.
ESPECIALLY YOU, BRINGING MY FAMILY INTO THIS.

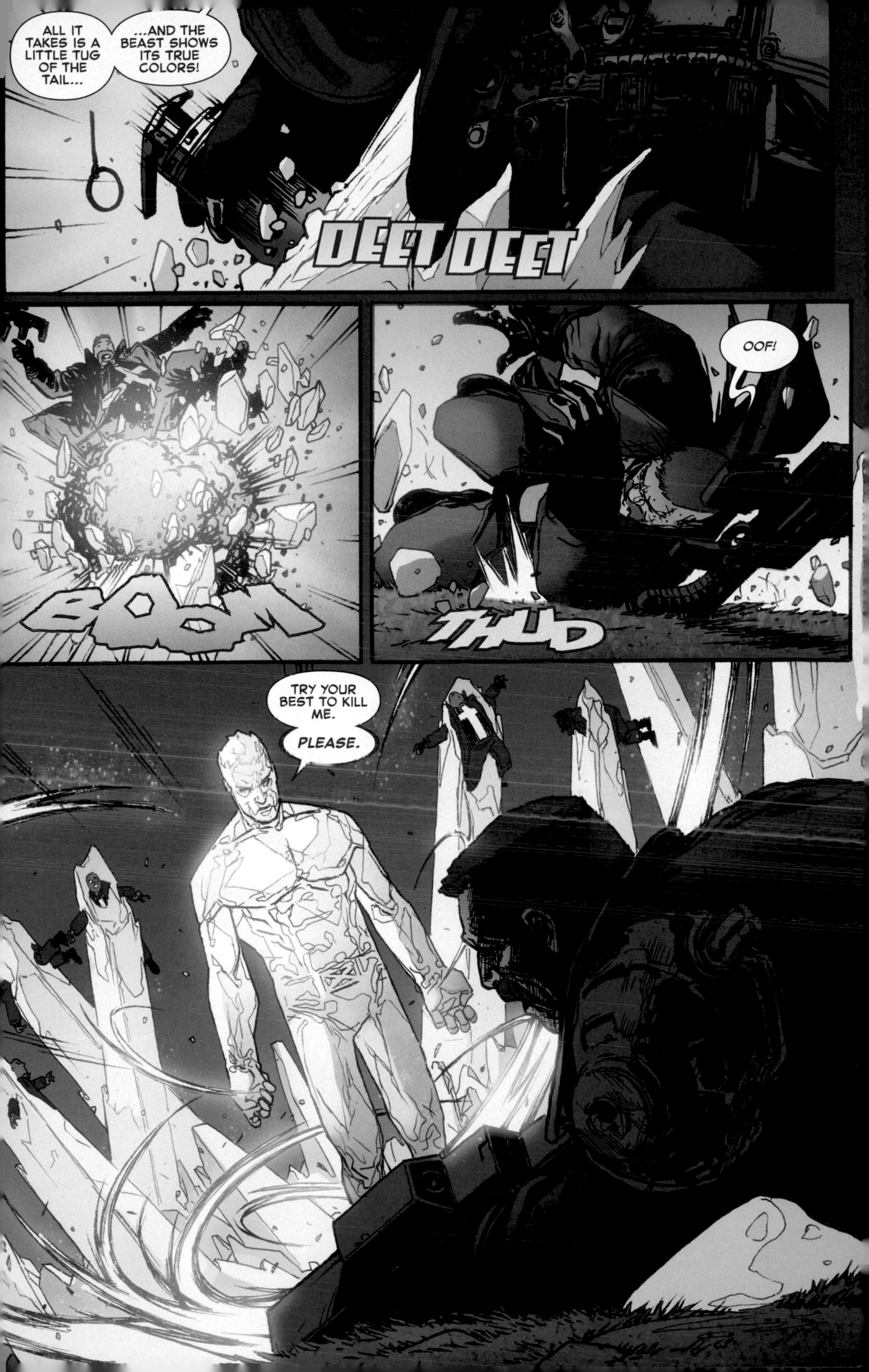
ALL IT TAKES IS A LITTLE TUG OF THE TAIL...
...AND THE BEAST SHOWS ITS TRUE COLORS!
DEET DEET
BOOM
OOF!
THUD
TRY YOUR BEST TO KILL ME.
PLEASE.

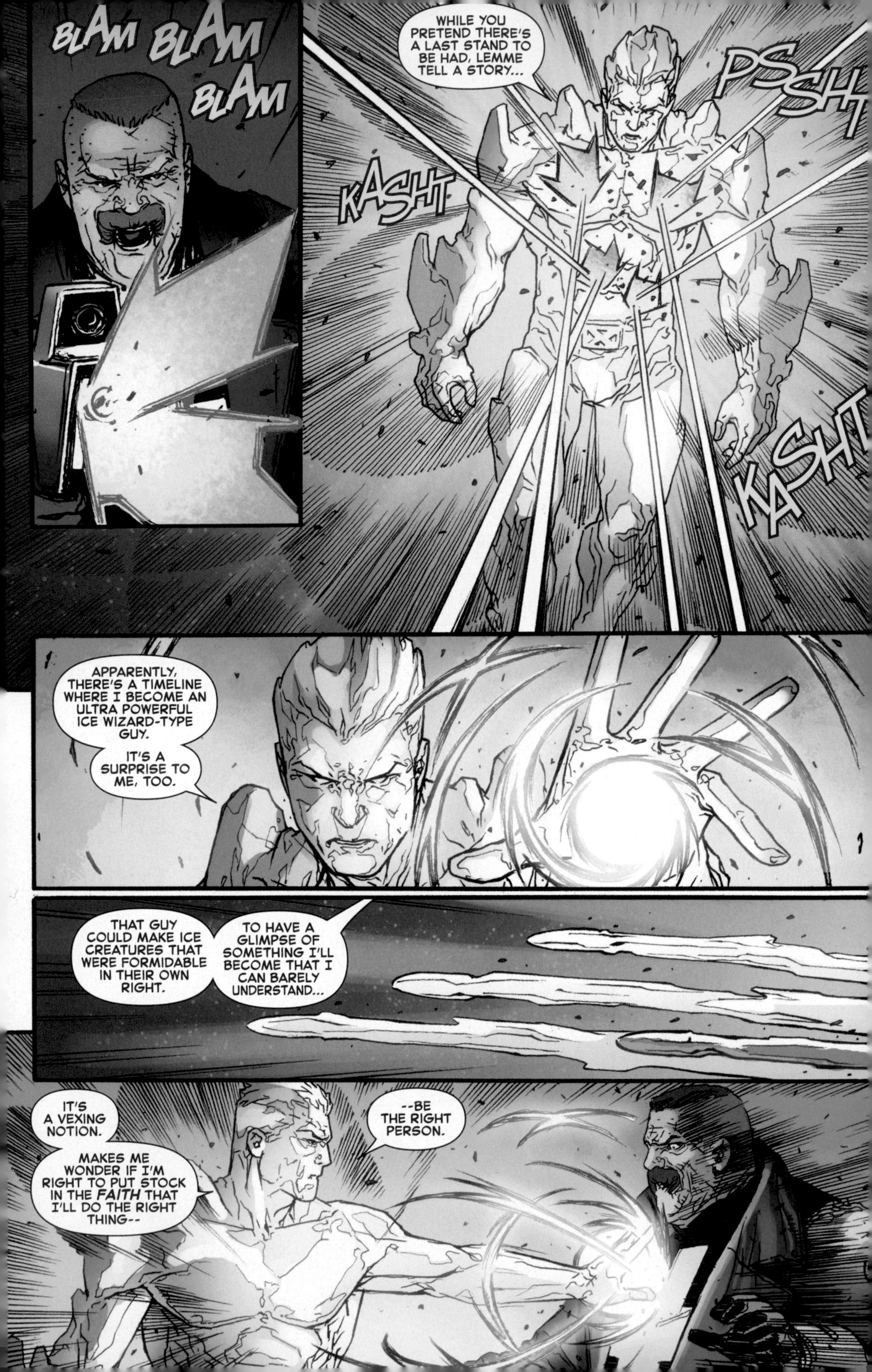
BLAM BLAM BLAM
WHILE YOU PRETEND THERE'S A LAST STAND TO BE HAD, LEMME TELL A STORY...
PSSHT
KASHT
KASHT
APPARENTLY, THERE'S A TIMELINE WHERE I BECOME AN ULTRA POWERFUL ICE WIZARD-TYPE GUY.
IT'S A SURPRISE TO ME, TOO.
THAT GUY COULD MAKE ICE CREATURES THAT WERE FORMIDABLE IN THEIR OWN RIGHT.
TO HAVE A GLIMPSE OF SOMETHING I'LL BECOME THAT I CAN BARELY UNDERSTAND...
IT'S A VEXING NOTION.
MAKES ME WONDER IF I'M RIGHT TO PUT STOCK IN THE FAITH THAT I'LL DO THE RIGHT THING--
--BE THE RIGHT PERSON.

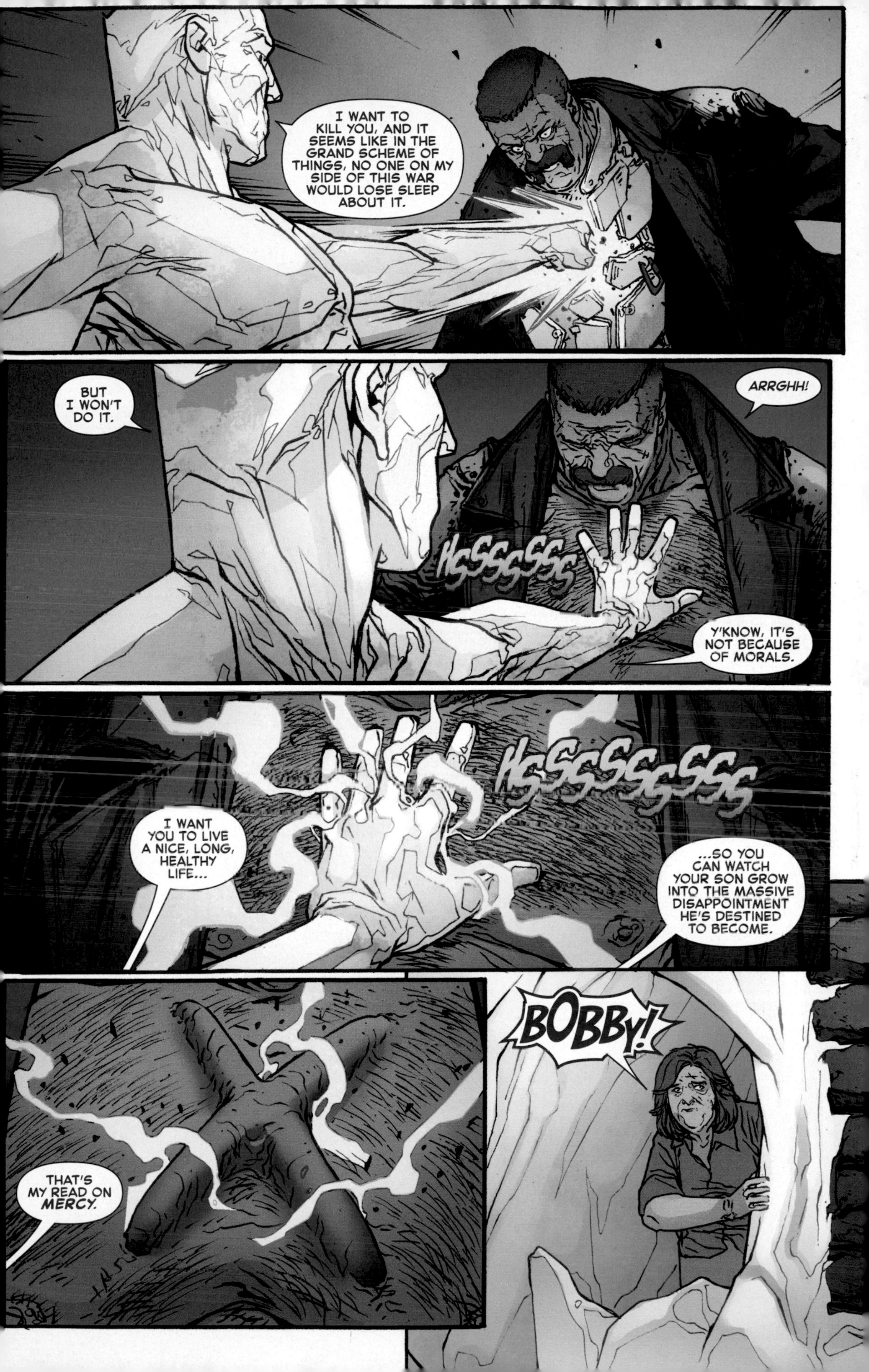

I WANT TO KILL YOU, AND IT SEEMS LIKE IN THE GRAND SCHEME OF THINGS, NO ONE ON MY SIDE OF THIS WAR WOULD LOSE SLEEP ABOUT IT.
BUT I WON'T DO IT.
ARRGHH!
HSSSSSSS
Y'KNOW, IT'S NOT BECAUSE OF MORALS.
HSSSSSSSSS
I WANT YOU TO LIVE A NICE, LONG, HEALTHY LIFE...
...SO YOU CAN WATCH YOUR SON GROW INTO THE MASSIVE DISAPPOINTMENT HE'S DESTINED TO BECOME.
BOBBY!
THAT'S MY READ ON MERCY.

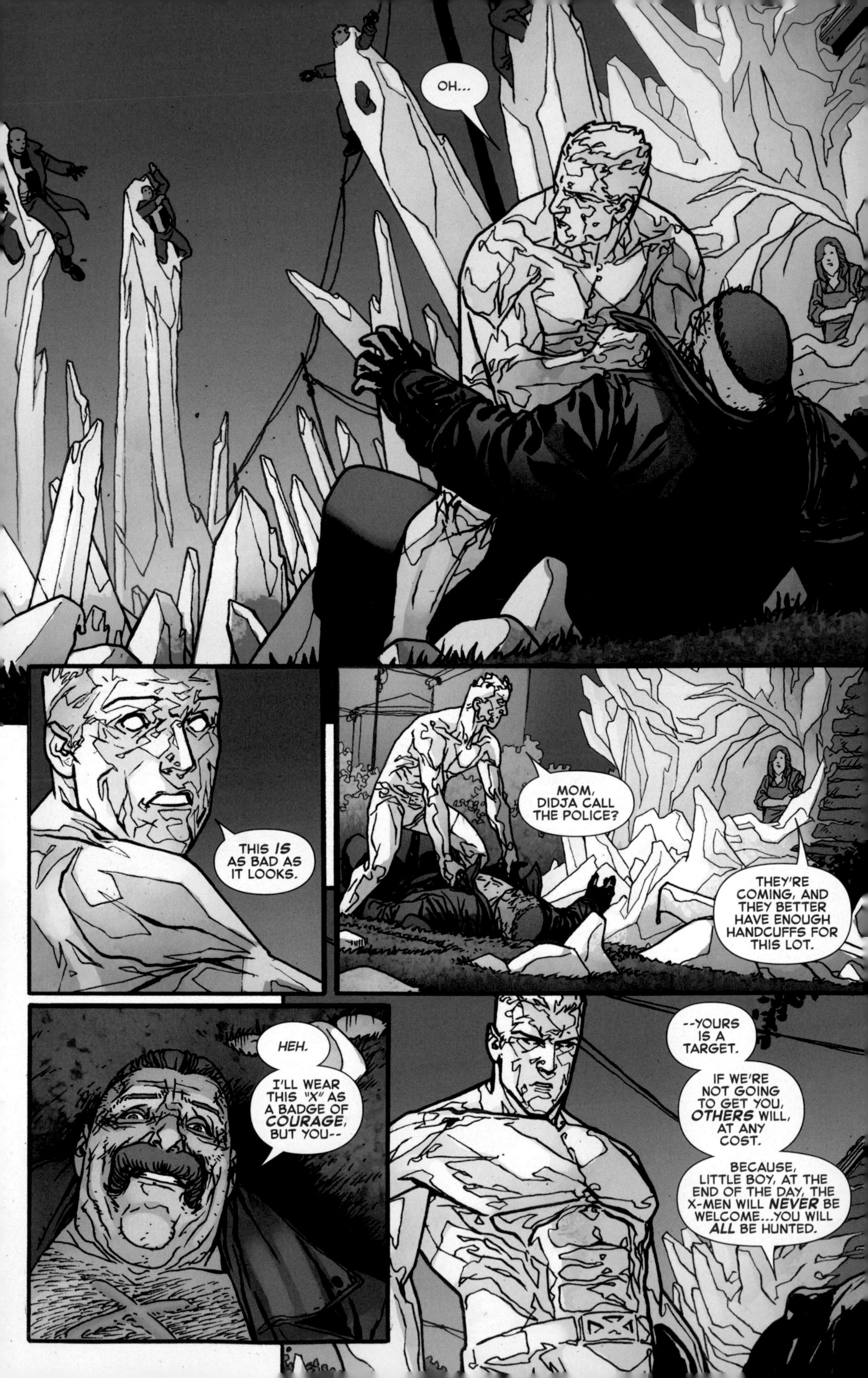
OH...
THIS *IS* AS BAD AS IT LOOKS.
MOM, DIDJA CALL THE POLICE?
THEY'RE COMING, AND THEY BETTER HAVE ENOUGH HANDCUFFS FOR THIS LOT.
HEH.
I'LL WEAR THIS "X" AS A BADGE OF *COURAGE*, BUT YOU--
--YOURS IS A TARGET.
IF WE'RE NOT GOING TO GET YOU, *OTHERS* WILL, AT ANY COST.
BECAUSE, LITTLE BOY, AT THE END OF THE DAY, THE X-MEN WILL *NEVER* BE WELCOME...YOU WILL *ALL* BE HUNTED.

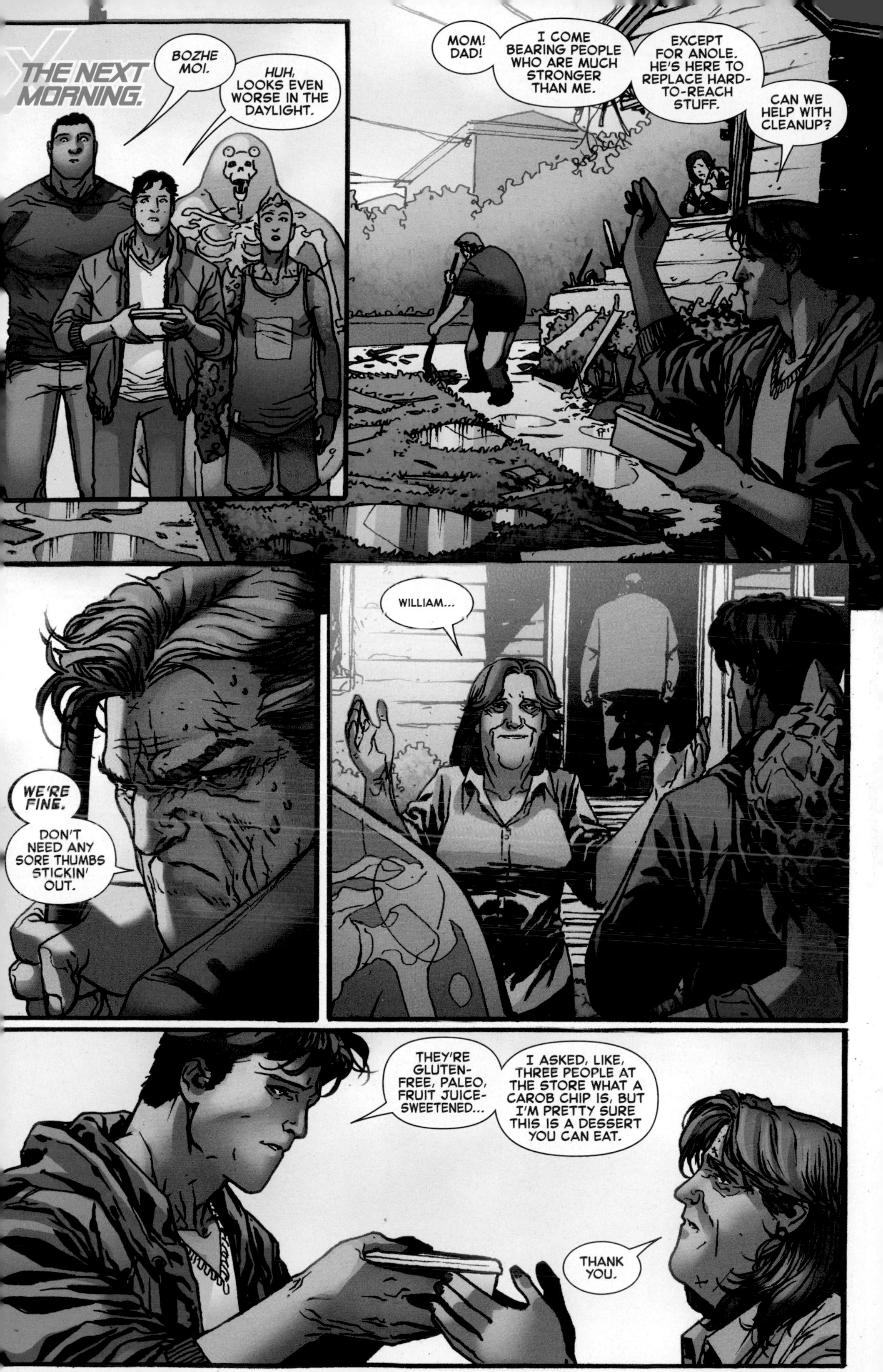
THE NEXT MORNING.
BOZHE MOI.
HUH, LOOKS EVEN WORSE IN THE DAYLIGHT.
MOM! DAD!
I COME BEARING PEOPLE WHO ARE MUCH STRONGER THAN ME.
EXCEPT FOR ANOLE. HE'S HERE TO REPLACE HARD-TO-REACH STUFF.
CAN WE HELP WITH CLEANUP?
WE'RE FINE.
DON'T NEED ANY SORE THUMBS STICKIN' OUT.
WILLIAM...
THEY'RE GLUTEN-FREE, PALEO, FRUIT JUICE-SWEETENED...
I ASKED, LIKE, THREE PEOPLE AT THE STORE WHAT A CAROB CHIP IS, BUT I'M PRETTY SURE THIS IS A DESSERT YOU CAN EAT.
THANK YOU.

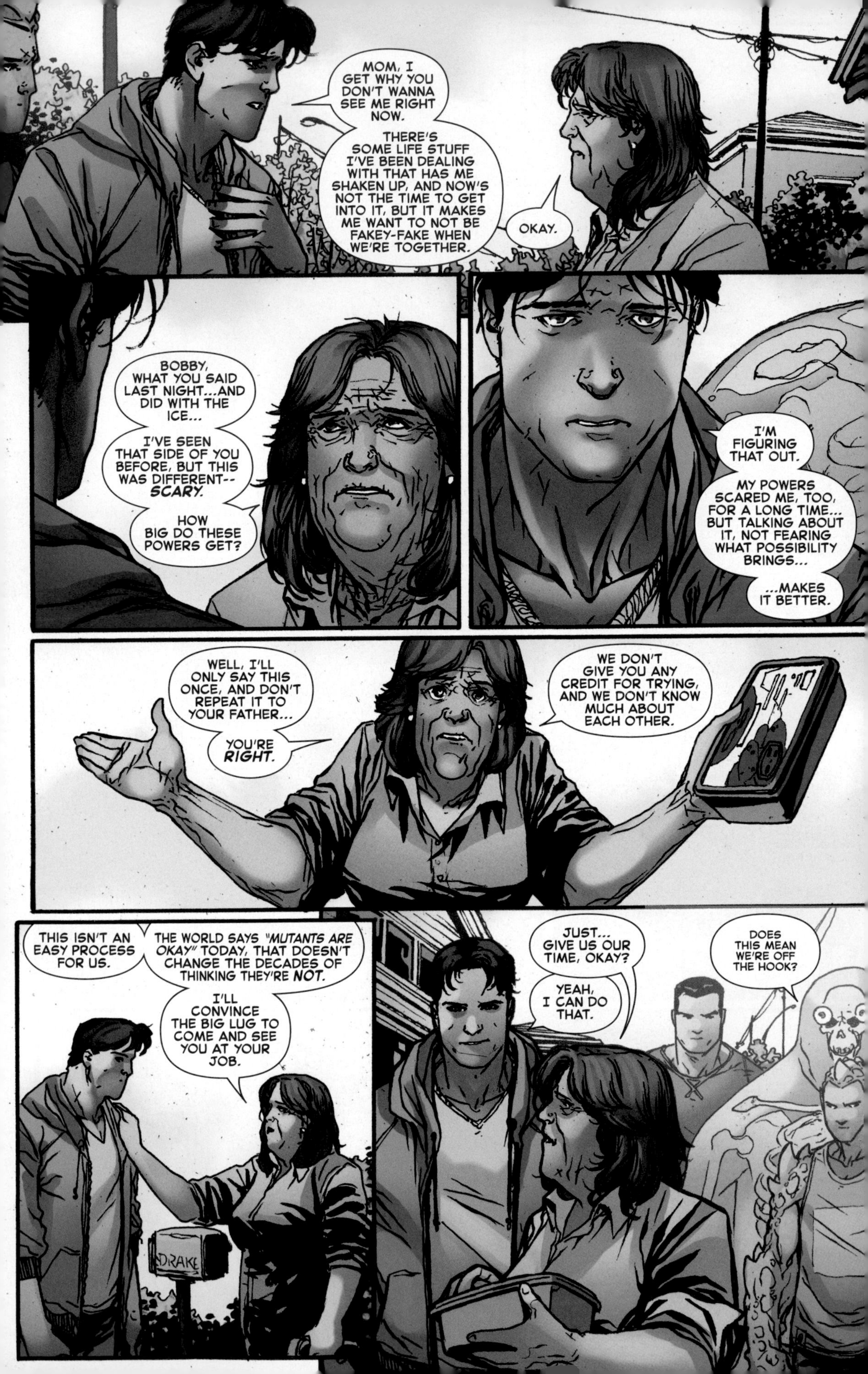
MOM, I GET WHY YOU DON'T WANNA SEE ME RIGHT NOW.
THERE'S SOME LIFE STUFF I'VE BEEN DEALING WITH THAT HAS ME SHAKEN UP, AND NOW'S NOT THE TIME TO GET INTO IT, BUT IT MAKES ME WANT TO NOT BE FAKEY-FAKE WHEN WE'RE TOGETHER.
OKAY.
BOBBY, WHAT YOU SAID LAST NIGHT...AND DID WITH THE ICE...
I'VE SEEN THAT SIDE OF YOU BEFORE, BUT THIS WAS DIFFERENT-- *SCARY.*
HOW BIG DO THESE POWERS GET?
I'M FIGURING THAT OUT.
MY POWERS SCARED ME, TOO, FOR A LONG TIME... BUT TALKING ABOUT IT, NOT FEARING WHAT POSSIBILITY BRINGS...
...MAKES IT BETTER.
WELL, I'LL ONLY SAY THIS ONCE, AND DON'T REPEAT IT TO YOUR FATHER...
YOU'RE *RIGHT.*
WE DON'T GIVE YOU ANY CREDIT FOR TRYING, AND WE DON'T KNOW MUCH ABOUT EACH OTHER.
THIS ISN'T AN EASY PROCESS FOR US.
THE WORLD SAYS *"MUTANTS ARE OKAY"* TODAY, THAT DOESN'T CHANGE THE DECADES OF THINKING THEY'RE *NOT.*
I'LL CONVINCE THE BIG LUG TO COME AND SEE YOU AT YOUR JOB.
DRAKE
JUST... GIVE US OUR TIME, OKAY?
YEAH, I CAN DO THAT.
DOES THIS MEAN WE'RE OFF THE HOOK?

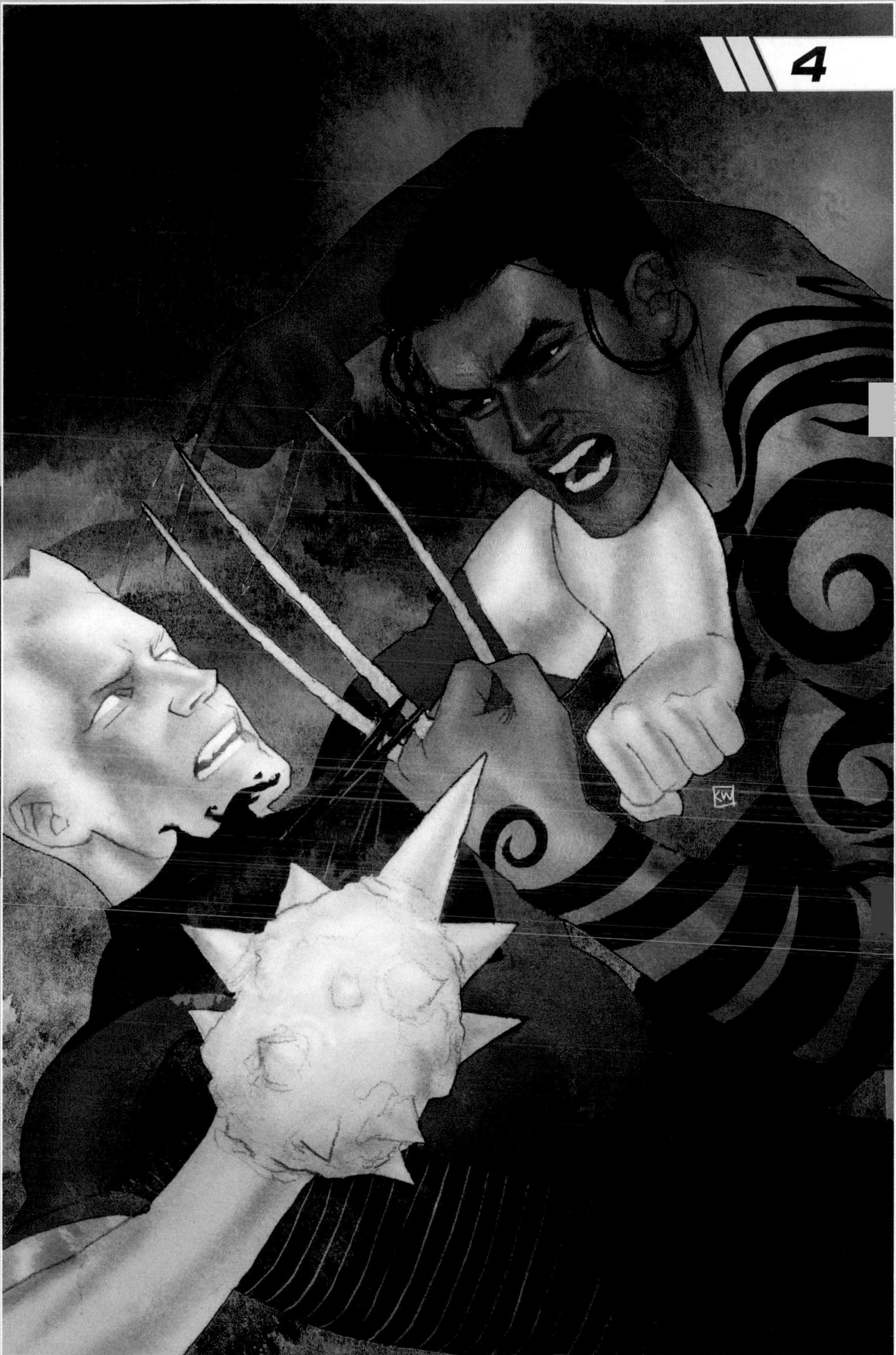
4

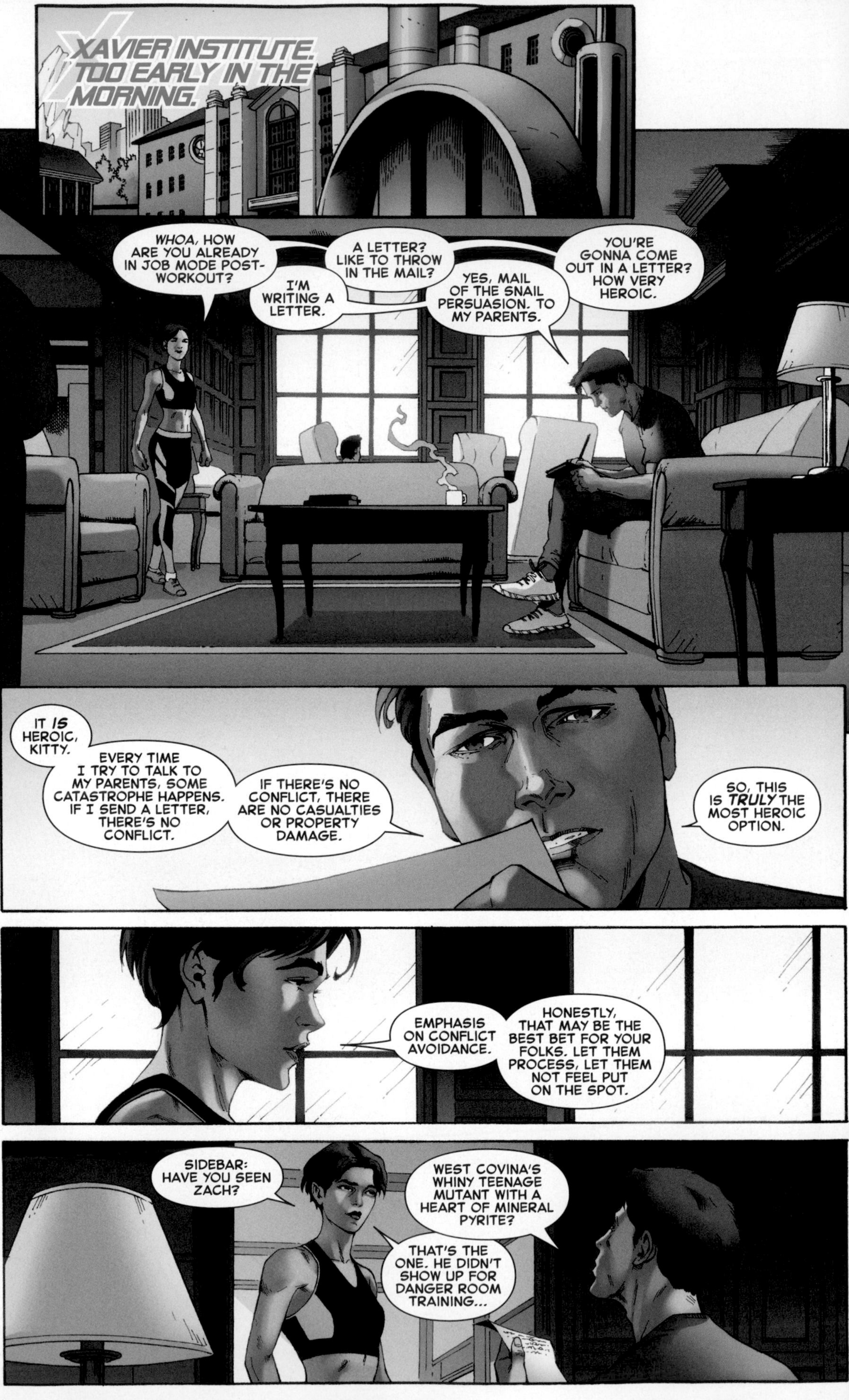

XAVIER INSTITUTE. TOO EARLY IN THE MORNING.
WHOA, HOW ARE YOU ALREADY IN JOB MODE POST-WORKOUT?
I'M WRITING A LETTER.
A LETTER? LIKE TO THROW IN THE MAIL?
YES, MAIL OF THE SNAIL PERSUASION. TO MY PARENTS.
YOU'RE GONNA COME OUT IN A LETTER? HOW VERY HEROIC.
IT IS HEROIC, KITTY.
EVERY TIME I TRY TO TALK TO MY PARENTS, SOME CATASTROPHE HAPPENS. IF I SEND A LETTER, THERE'S NO CONFLICT.
IF THERE'S NO CONFLICT, THERE ARE NO CASUALTIES OR PROPERTY DAMAGE.
SO, THIS IS TRULY THE MOST HEROIC OPTION.
EMPHASIS ON CONFLICT AVOIDANCE.
HONESTLY, THAT MAY BE THE BEST BET FOR YOUR FOLKS. LET THEM PROCESS, LET THEM NOT FEEL PUT ON THE SPOT.
SIDEBAR: HAVE YOU SEEN ZACH?
WEST COVINA'S WHINY TEENAGE MUTANT WITH A HEART OF MINERAL PYRITE?
THAT'S THE ONE. HE DIDN'T SHOW UP FOR DANGER ROOM TRAINING...

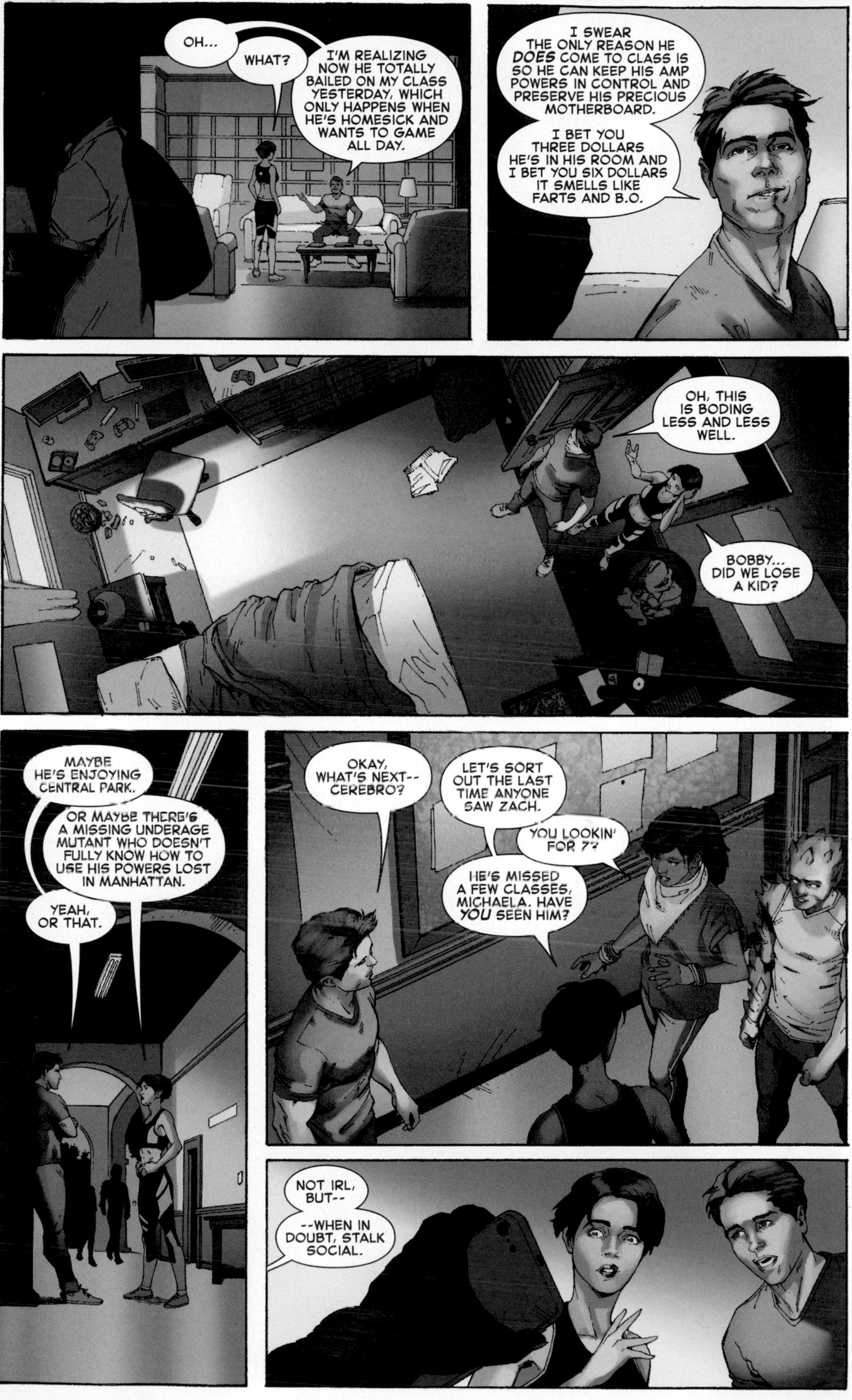
OH...
WHAT?
I'M REALIZING NOW HE TOTALLY BAILED ON MY CLASS YESTERDAY, WHICH ONLY HAPPENS WHEN HE'S HOMESICK AND WANTS TO GAME ALL DAY.
I SWEAR THE ONLY REASON HE DOES COME TO CLASS IS SO HE CAN KEEP HIS AMP POWERS IN CONTROL AND PRESERVE HIS PRECIOUS MOTHERBOARD.
I BET YOU THREE DOLLARS HE'S IN HIS ROOM AND I BET YOU SIX DOLLARS IT SMELLS LIKE FARTS AND B.O.
OH, THIS IS BODING LESS AND LESS WELL.
BOBBY... DID WE LOSE A KID?
MAYBE HE'S ENJOYING CENTRAL PARK.
OR MAYBE THERE'S A MISSING UNDERAGE MUTANT WHO DOESN'T FULLY KNOW HOW TO USE HIS POWERS LOST IN MANHATTAN.
YEAH, OR THAT.
OKAY, WHAT'S NEXT-- CEREBRO?
LET'S SORT OUT THE LAST TIME ANYONE SAW ZACH.
YOU LOOKIN' FOR 7?
HE'S MISSED A FEW CLASSES, MICHAELA. HAVE YOU SEEN HIM?
NOT IRL, BUT--
--WHEN IN DOUBT, STALK SOCIAL.

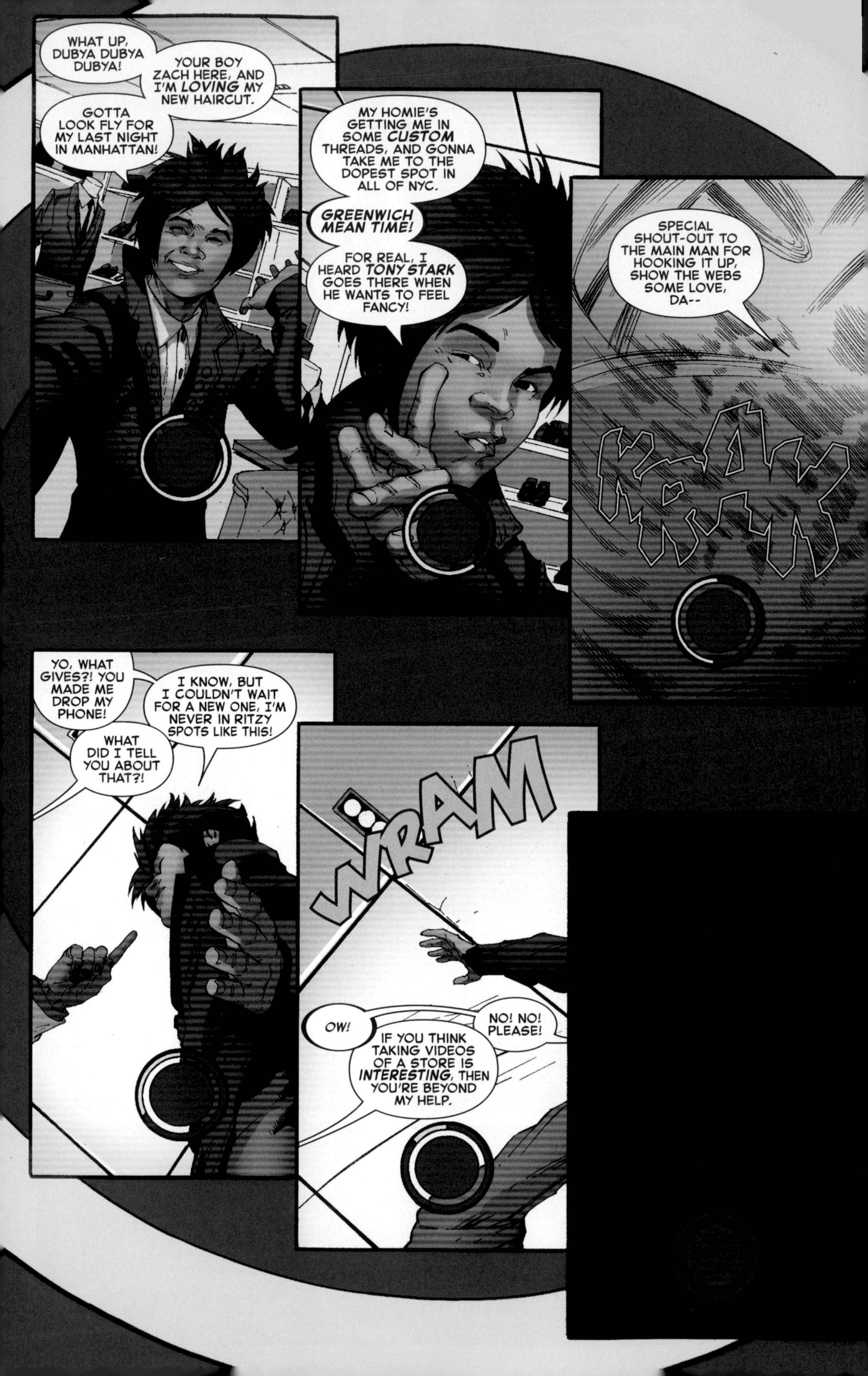
WHAT UP, DUBYA DUBYA DUBYA!
YOUR BOY ZACH HERE, AND I'M LOVING MY NEW HAIRCUT.
GOTTA LOOK FLY FOR MY LAST NIGHT IN MANHATTAN!
MY HOMIE'S GETTING ME IN SOME CUSTOM THREADS, AND GONNA TAKE ME TO THE DOPEST SPOT IN ALL OF NYC.
GREENWICH MEAN TIME!
FOR REAL, I HEARD TONY STARK GOES THERE WHEN HE WANTS TO FEEL FANCY!
SPECIAL SHOUT-OUT TO THE MAIN MAN FOR HOOKING IT UP, SHOW THE WEBS SOME LOVE, DA--
KRAK
YO, WHAT GIVES?! YOU MADE ME DROP MY PHONE!
I KNOW, BUT I COULDN'T WAIT FOR A NEW ONE, I'M NEVER IN RITZY SPOTS LIKE THIS!
WHAT DID I TELL YOU ABOUT THAT?!
WRAM
OW!
NO! NO! PLEASE!
IF YOU THINK TAKING VIDEOS OF A STORE IS INTERESTING, THEN YOU'RE BEYOND MY HELP.

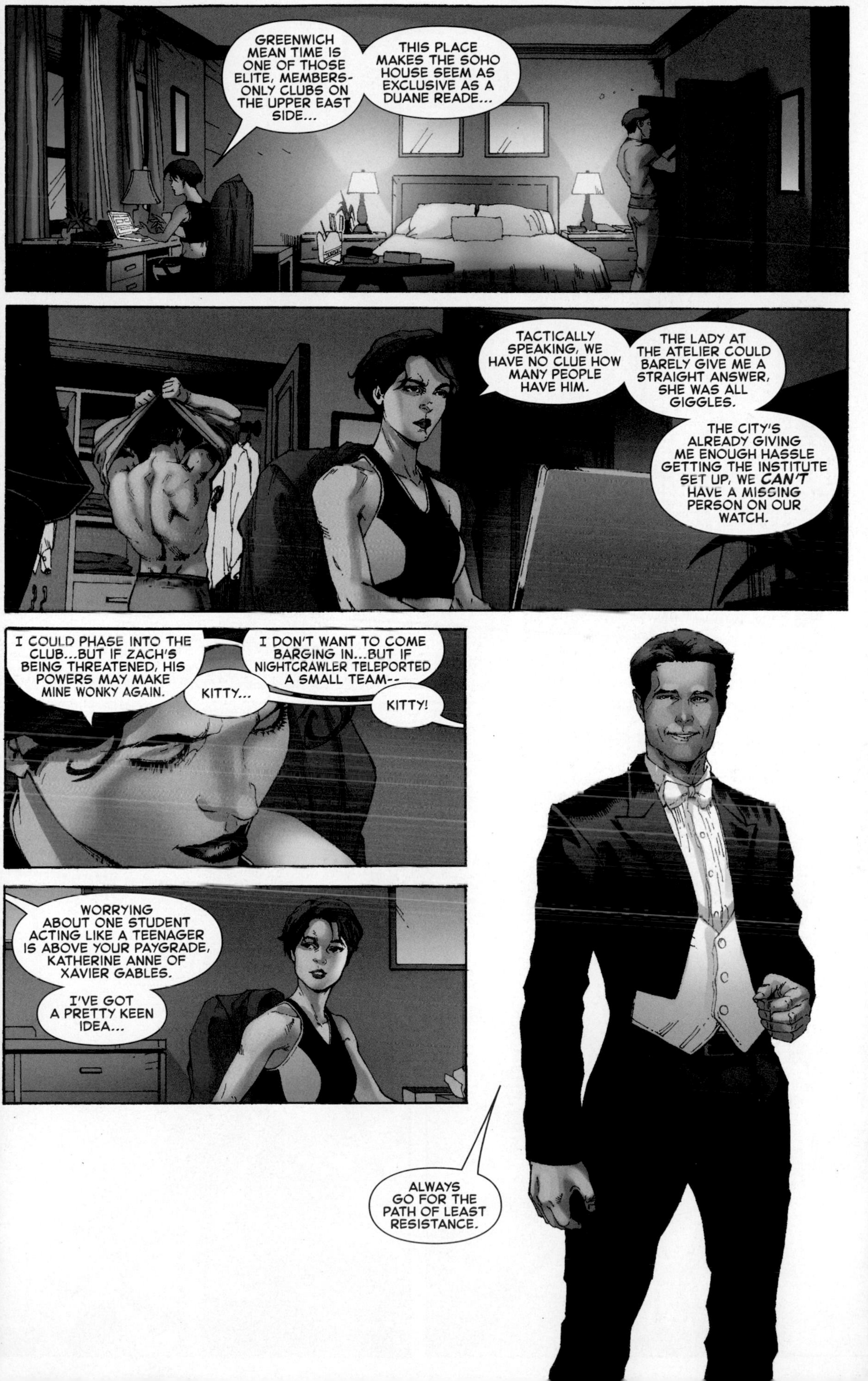
GREENWICH MEAN TIME IS ONE OF THOSE ELITE, MEMBERS-ONLY CLUBS ON THE UPPER EAST SIDE...
THIS PLACE MAKES THE SOHO HOUSE SEEM AS EXCLUSIVE AS A DUANE READE...
TACTICALLY SPEAKING, WE HAVE NO CLUE HOW MANY PEOPLE HAVE HIM.
THE LADY AT THE ATELIER COULD BARELY GIVE ME A STRAIGHT ANSWER, SHE WAS ALL GIGGLES.
THE CITY'S ALREADY GIVING ME ENOUGH HASSLE GETTING THE INSTITUTE SET UP, WE CAN'T HAVE A MISSING PERSON ON OUR WATCH.
I COULD PHASE INTO THE CLUB...BUT IF ZACH'S BEING THREATENED, HIS POWERS MAY MAKE MINE WONKY AGAIN.
I DON'T WANT TO COME BARGING IN...BUT IF NIGHTCRAWLER TELEPORTED A SMALL TEAM--
KITTY...
KITTY!
WORRYING ABOUT ONE STUDENT ACTING LIKE A TEENAGER IS ABOVE YOUR PAYGRADE, KATHERINE ANNE OF XAVIER GABLES.
I'VE GOT A PRETTY KEEN IDEA...
ALWAYS GO FOR THE PATH OF LEAST RESISTANCE.

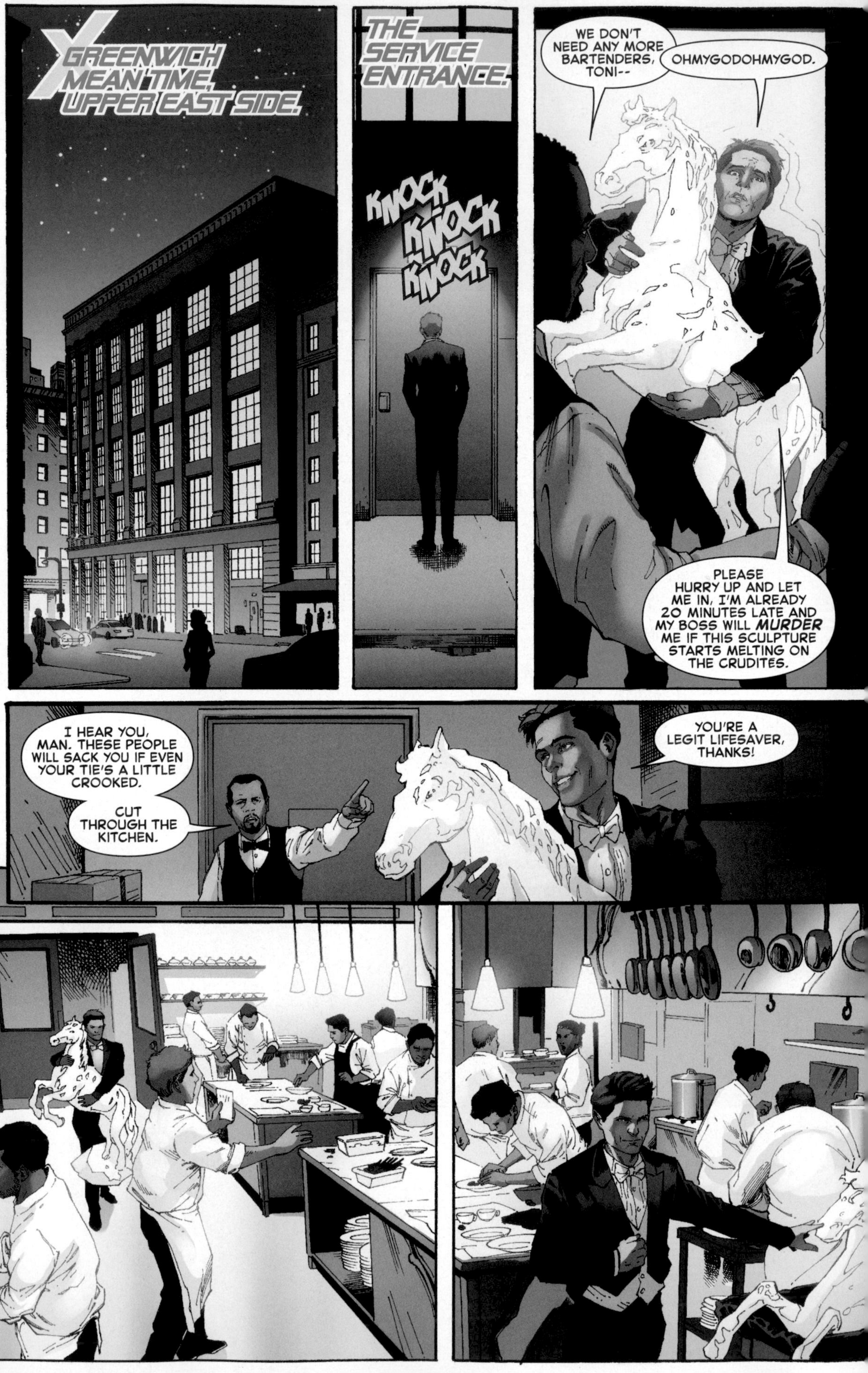
GREENWICH MEAN TIME, UPPER EAST SIDE.
THE SERVICE ENTRANCE.
KNOCK KNOCK KNOCK
WE DON'T NEED ANY MORE BARTENDERS, TONI--
OHMYGODOHMYGOD.
PLEASE HURRY UP AND LET ME IN, I'M ALREADY 20 MINUTES LATE AND MY BOSS WILL MURDER ME IF THIS SCULPTURE STARTS MELTING ON THE CRUDITES.
I HEAR YOU, MAN. THESE PEOPLE WILL SACK YOU IF EVEN YOUR TIE'S A LITTLE CROOKED.
CUT THROUGH THE KITCHEN.
YOU'RE A LEGIT LIFESAVER, THANKS!

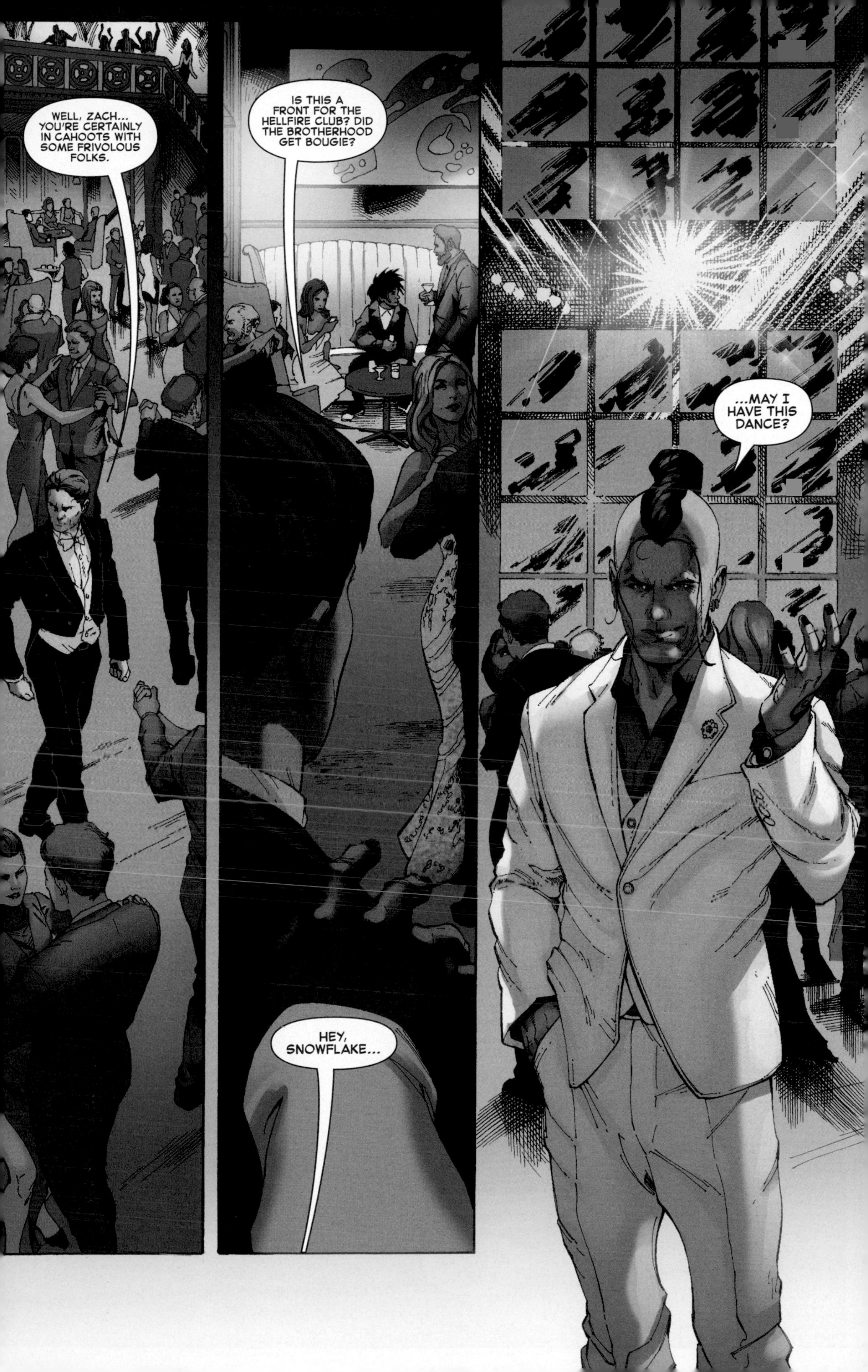
WELL, ZACH... YOU'RE CERTAINLY IN CAHOOTS WITH SOME FRIVOLOUS FOLKS.
IS THIS A FRONT FOR THE HELLFIRE CLUB? DID THE BROTHERHOOD GET BOUGIE?
HEY, SNOWFLAKE...
...MAY I HAVE THIS DANCE?

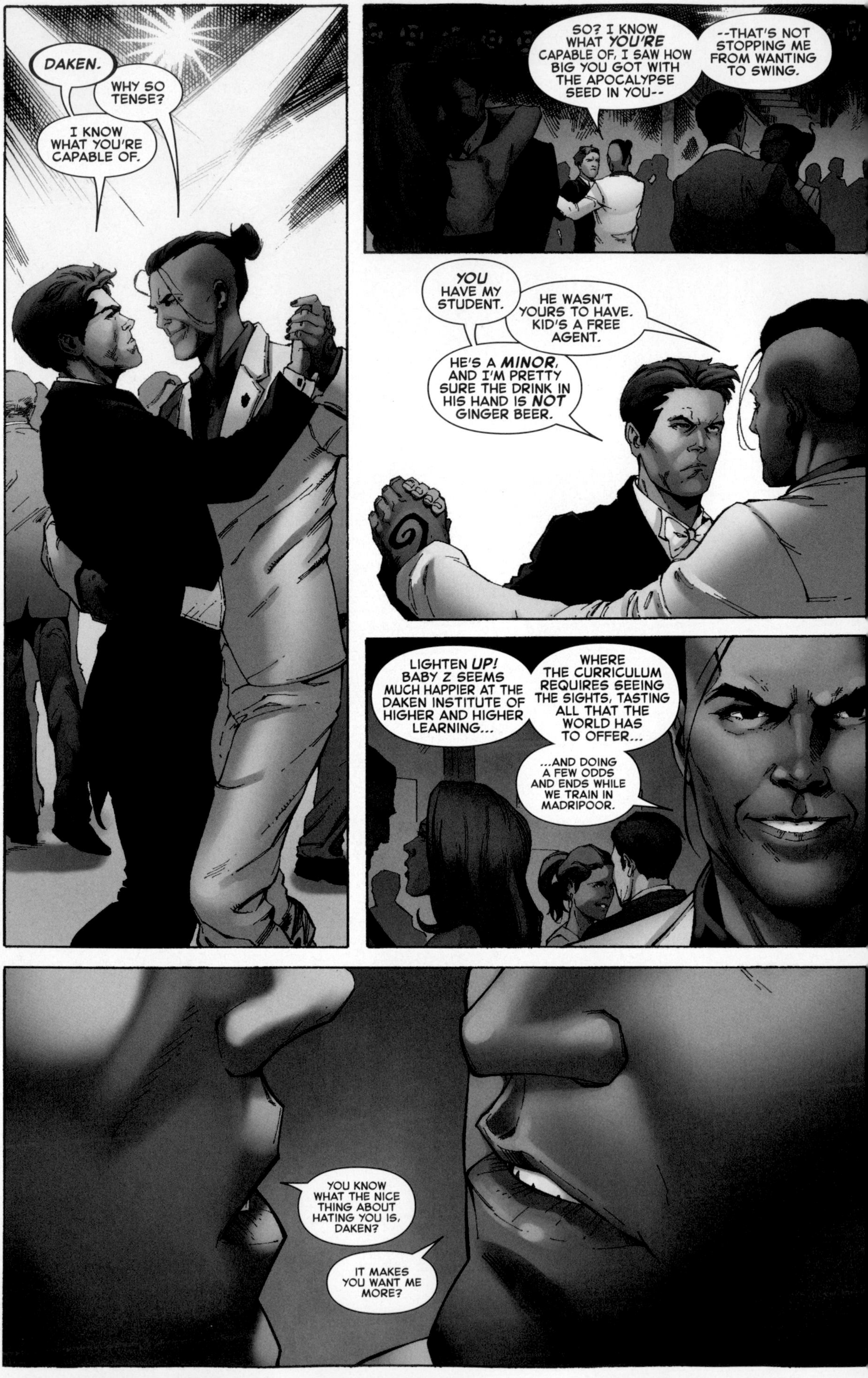
DAKEN.
WHY SO TENSE?
I KNOW WHAT YOU'RE CAPABLE OF.
SO? I KNOW WHAT YOU'RE CAPABLE OF, I SAW HOW BIG YOU GOT WITH THE APOCALYPSE SEED IN YOU--
--THAT'S NOT STOPPING ME FROM WANTING TO SWING.
YOU HAVE MY STUDENT.
HE WASN'T YOURS TO HAVE. KID'S A FREE AGENT.
HE'S A MINOR, AND I'M PRETTY SURE THE DRINK IN HIS HAND IS NOT GINGER BEER.
LIGHTEN UP! BABY Z SEEMS MUCH HAPPIER AT THE DAKEN INSTITUTE OF HIGHER AND HIGHER LEARNING...
WHERE THE CURRICULUM REQUIRES SEEING THE SIGHTS, TASTING ALL THAT THE WORLD HAS TO OFFER...
...AND DOING A FEW ODDS AND ENDS WHILE WE TRAIN IN MADRIPOOR.
YOU KNOW WHAT THE NICE THING ABOUT HATING YOU IS, DAKEN?
IT MAKES YOU WANT ME MORE?

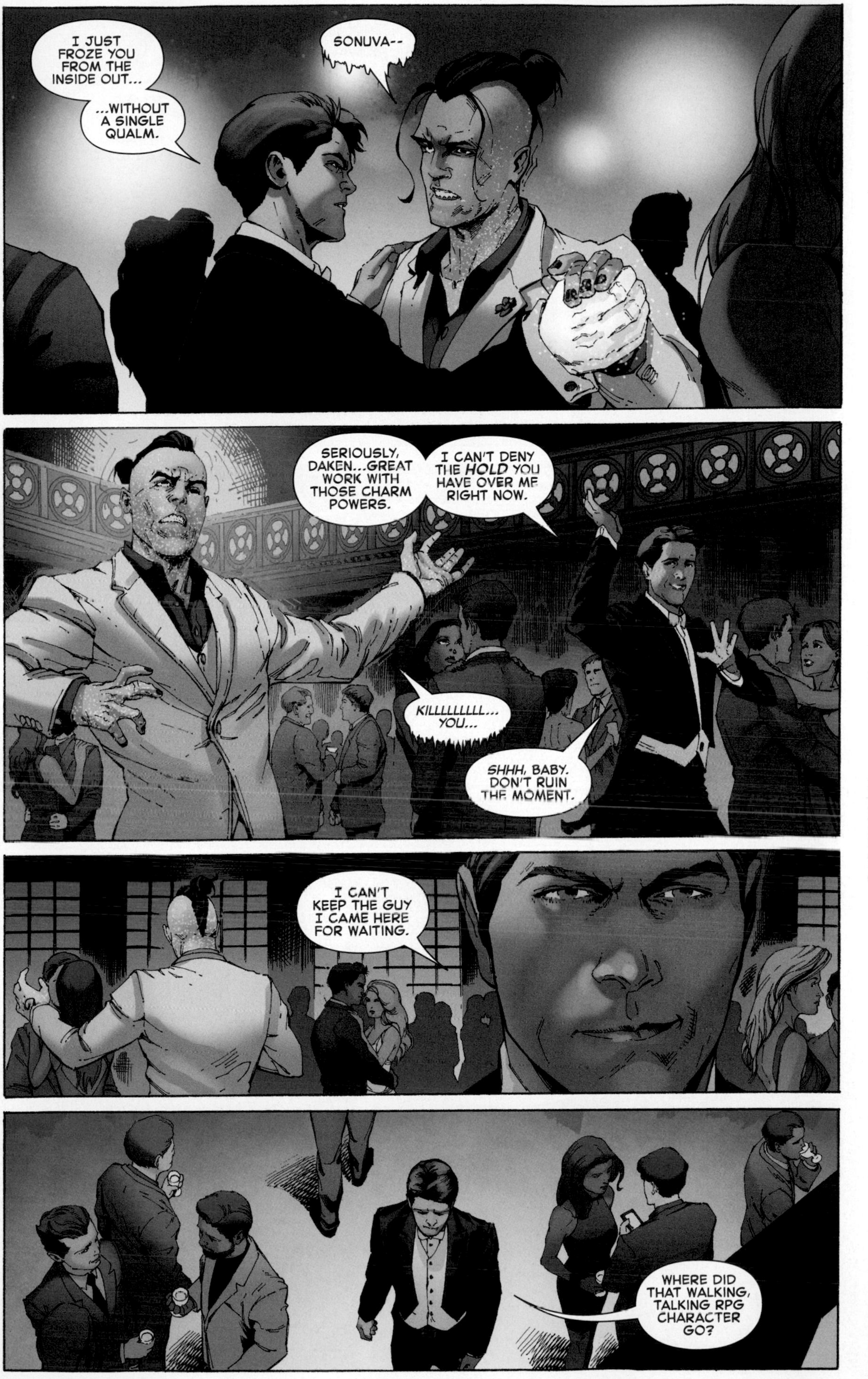
I JUST FROZE YOU FROM THE INSIDE OUT...
...WITHOUT A SINGLE QUALM.
SONUVA--
SERIOUSLY, DAKEN...GREAT WORK WITH THOSE CHARM POWERS.
I CAN'T DENY THE HOLD YOU HAVE OVER ME RIGHT NOW.
KILLLLLLLLL... YOU...
SHHH, BABY. DON'T RUIN THE MOMENT.
I CAN'T KEEP THE GUY I CAME HERE FOR WAITING.
WHERE DID THAT WALKING, TALKING RPG CHARACTER GO?

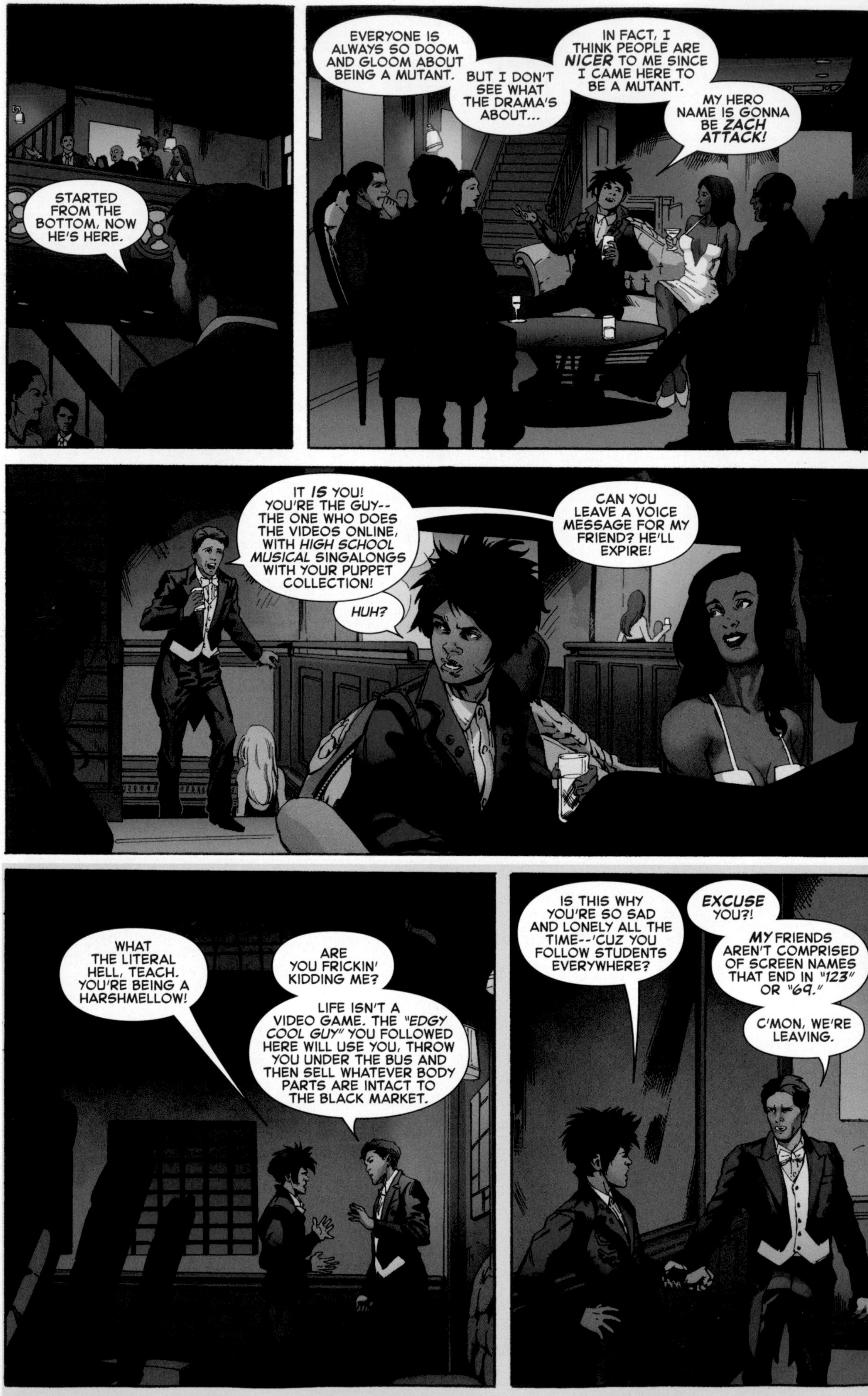
STARTED FROM THE BOTTOM, NOW HE'S HERE.
EVERYONE IS ALWAYS SO DOOM AND GLOOM ABOUT BEING A MUTANT.
BUT I DON'T SEE WHAT THE DRAMA'S ABOUT...
IN FACT, I THINK PEOPLE ARE *NICER* TO ME SINCE I CAME HERE TO BE A MUTANT.
MY HERO NAME IS GONNA BE *ZACH ATTACK!*
IT *IS* YOU! YOU'RE THE GUY-- THE ONE WHO DOES THE VIDEOS ONLINE, WITH *HIGH SCHOOL MUSICAL* SINGALONGS WITH YOUR PUPPET COLLECTION!
CAN YOU LEAVE A VOICE MESSAGE FOR MY FRIEND? HE'LL EXPIRE!
HUH?
WHAT THE LITERAL HELL, TEACH. YOU'RE BEING A HARSHMELLOW!
ARE YOU FRICKIN' KIDDING ME?
LIFE ISN'T A VIDEO GAME. THE *"EDGY COOL GUY"* YOU FOLLOWED HERE WILL USE YOU, THROW YOU UNDER THE BUS AND THEN SELL WHATEVER BODY PARTS ARE INTACT TO THE BLACK MARKET.
IS THIS WHY YOU'RE SO SAD AND LONELY ALL THE TIME--'CUZ YOU FOLLOW STUDENTS EVERYWHERE?
EXCUSE YOU?!
MY FRIENDS AREN'T COMPRISED OF SCREEN NAMES THAT END IN *"123"* OR *"69."*
C'MON, WE'RE LEAVING.

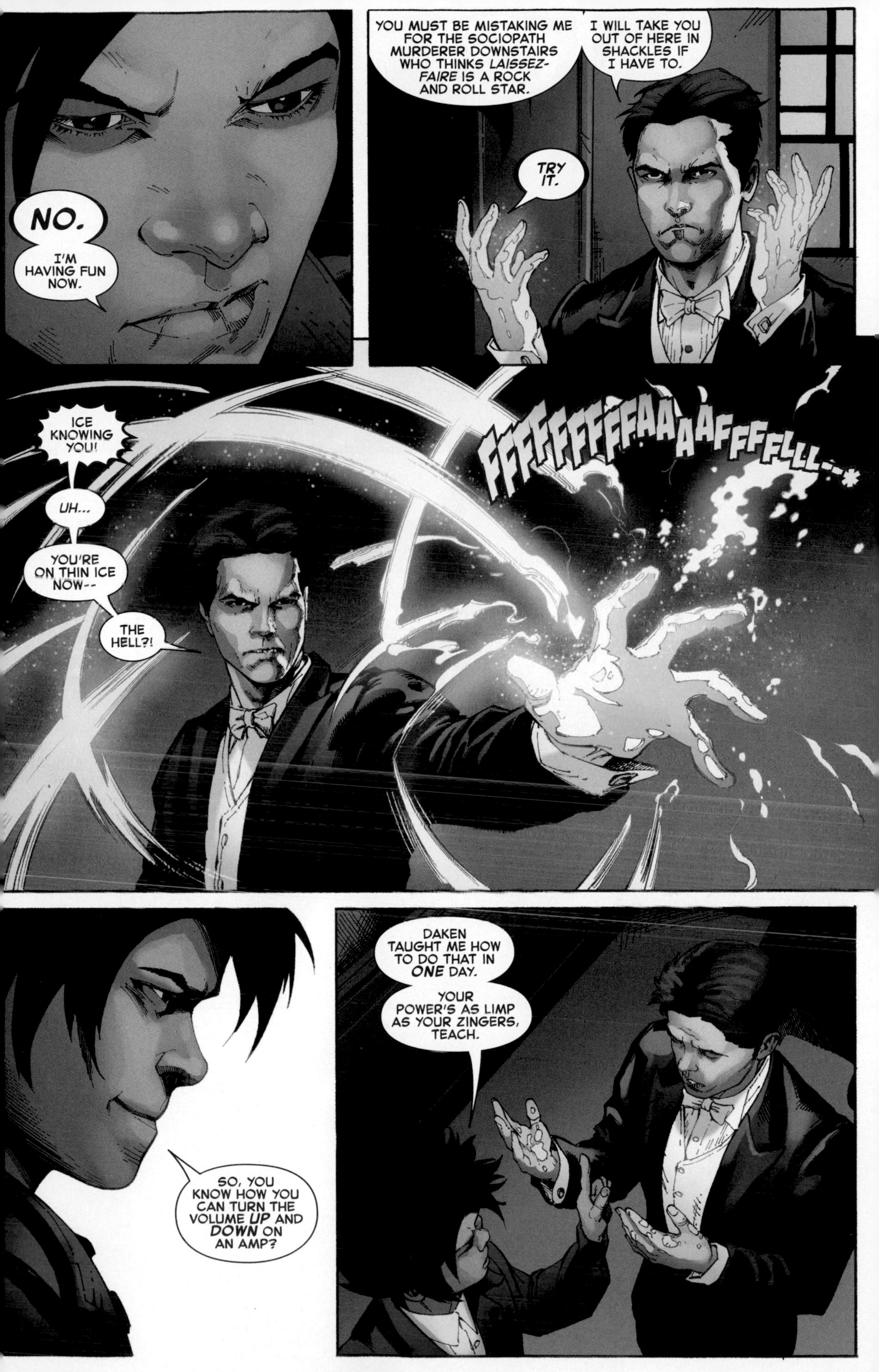
YOU MUST BE MISTAKING ME FOR THE SOCIOPATH MURDERER DOWNSTAIRS WHO THINKS LAISSEZ-FAIRE IS A ROCK AND ROLL STAR.
I WILL TAKE YOU OUT OF HERE IN SHACKLES IF I HAVE TO.
NO.
I'M HAVING FUN NOW.
TRY IT.
ICE KNOWING YOU!
UH...
YOU'RE ON THIN ICE NOW--
THE HELL?!
FFFFFFFFFAAAAFFFFLLL--*
DAKEN TAUGHT ME HOW TO DO THAT IN ONE DAY.
YOUR POWER'S AS LIMP AS YOUR ZINGERS, TEACH.
SO, YOU KNOW HOW YOU CAN TURN THE VOLUME UP AND DOWN ON AN AMP?

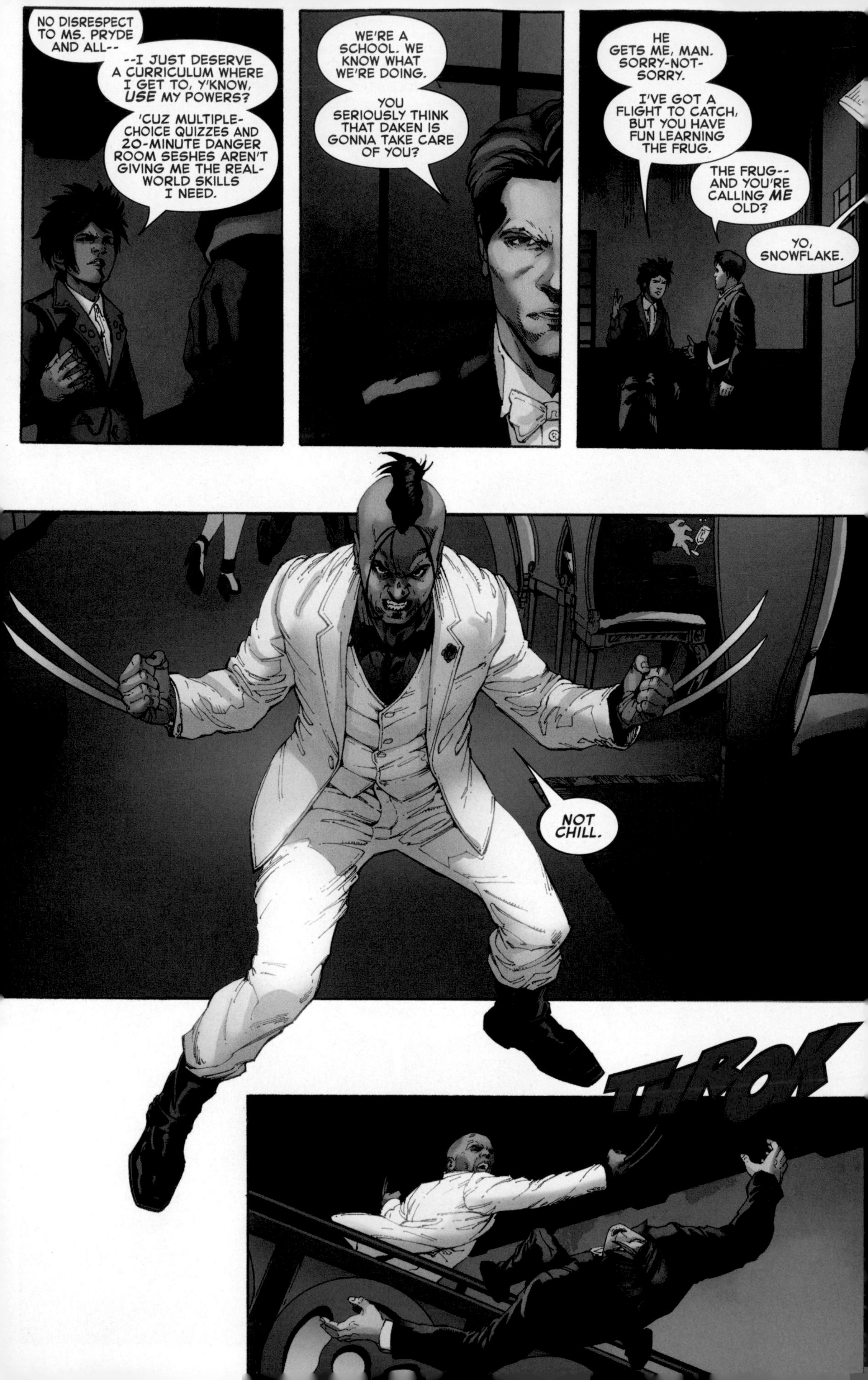
NO DISRESPECT TO MS. PRYDE AND ALL--
--I JUST DESERVE A CURRICULUM WHERE I GET TO, Y'KNOW, USE MY POWERS?
'CUZ MULTIPLE-CHOICE QUIZZES AND 20-MINUTE DANGER ROOM SESHES AREN'T GIVING ME THE REAL-WORLD SKILLS I NEED.
WE'RE A SCHOOL. WE KNOW WHAT WE'RE DOING.
YOU SERIOUSLY THINK THAT DAKEN IS GONNA TAKE CARE OF YOU?
HE GETS ME, MAN. SORRY-NOT-SORRY.
I'VE GOT A FLIGHT TO CATCH, BUT YOU HAVE FUN LEARNING THE FRUG.
THE FRUG--AND YOU'RE CALLING ME OLD?
YO, SNOWFLAKE.
NOT CHILL.
THROK

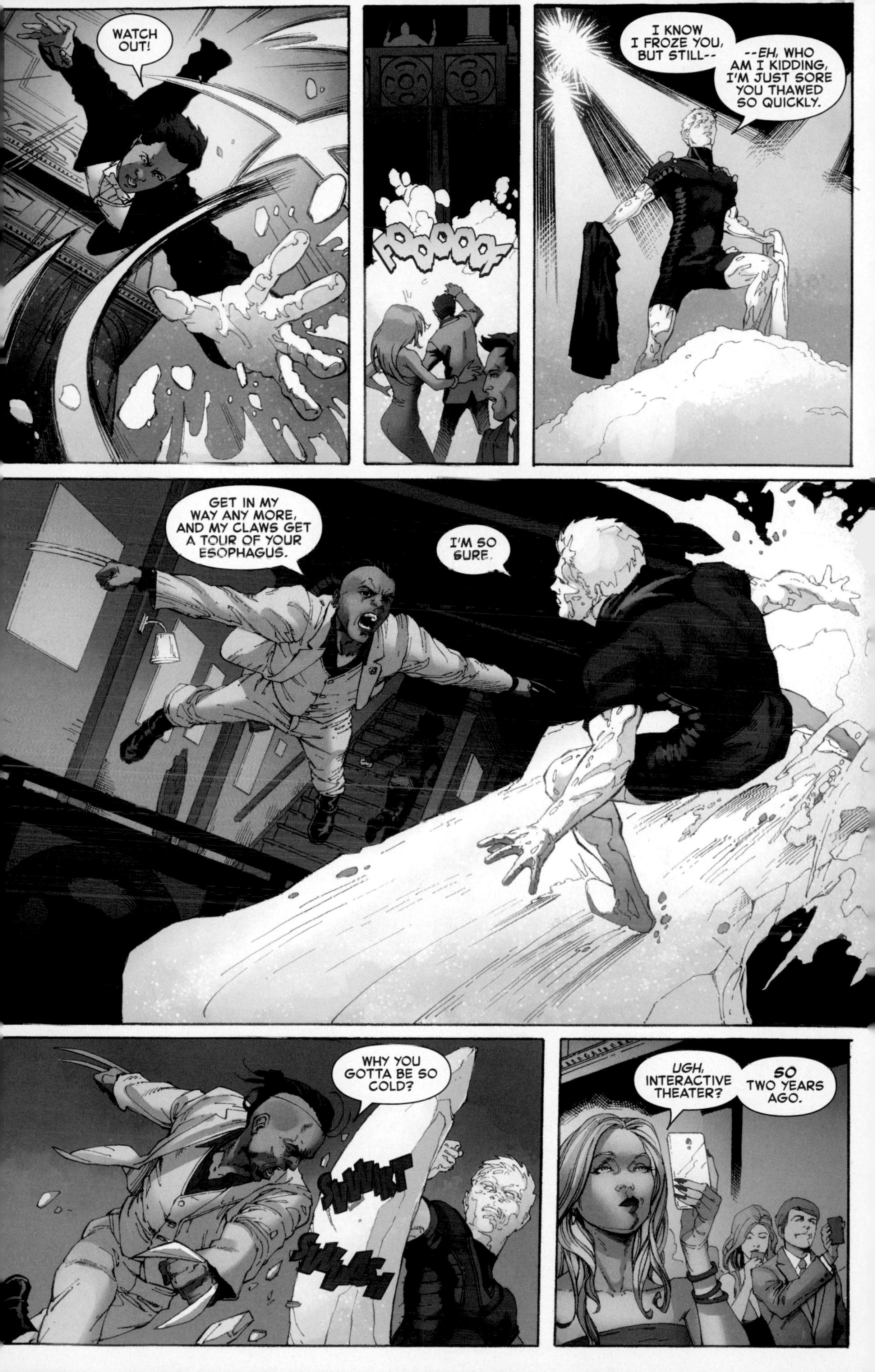
WATCH OUT!
FOOOOM
I KNOW I FROZE YOU, BUT STILL--
--EH, WHO AM I KIDDING, I'M JUST SORE YOU THAWED SO QUICKLY.
GET IN MY WAY ANY MORE, AND MY CLAWS GET A TOUR OF YOUR ESOPHAGUS.
I'M SO SURE.
WHY YOU GOTTA BE SO COLD?
SNIKT
SHLAK
UGH, INTERACTIVE THEATER?
SO TWO YEARS AGO.

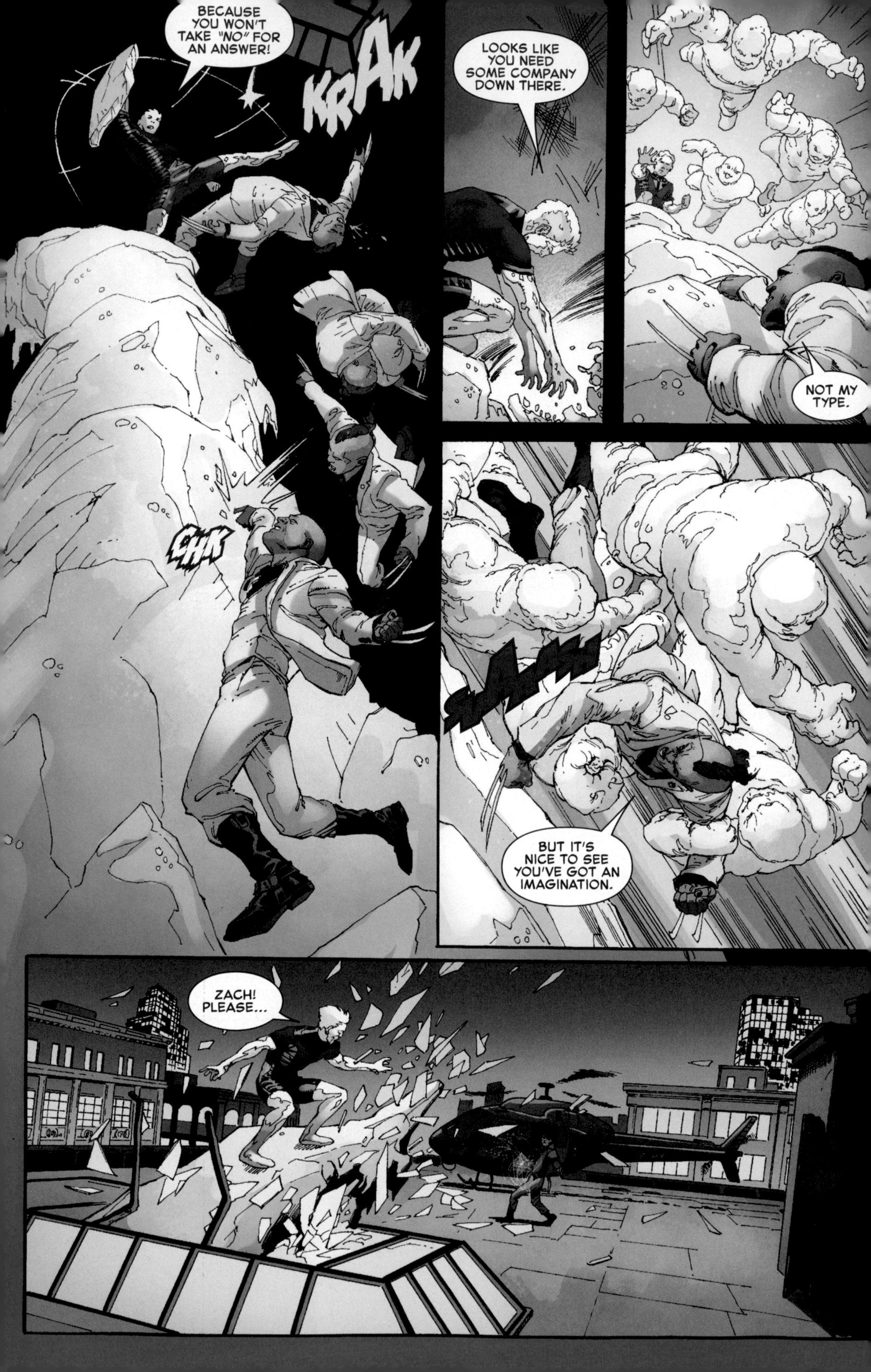
BECAUSE YOU WON'T TAKE "NO" FOR AN ANSWER!
KRAK
CHK
LOOKS LIKE YOU NEED SOME COMPANY DOWN THERE.
NOT MY TYPE.
BUT IT'S NICE TO SEE YOU'VE GOT AN IMAGINATION.
ZACH! PLEASE...

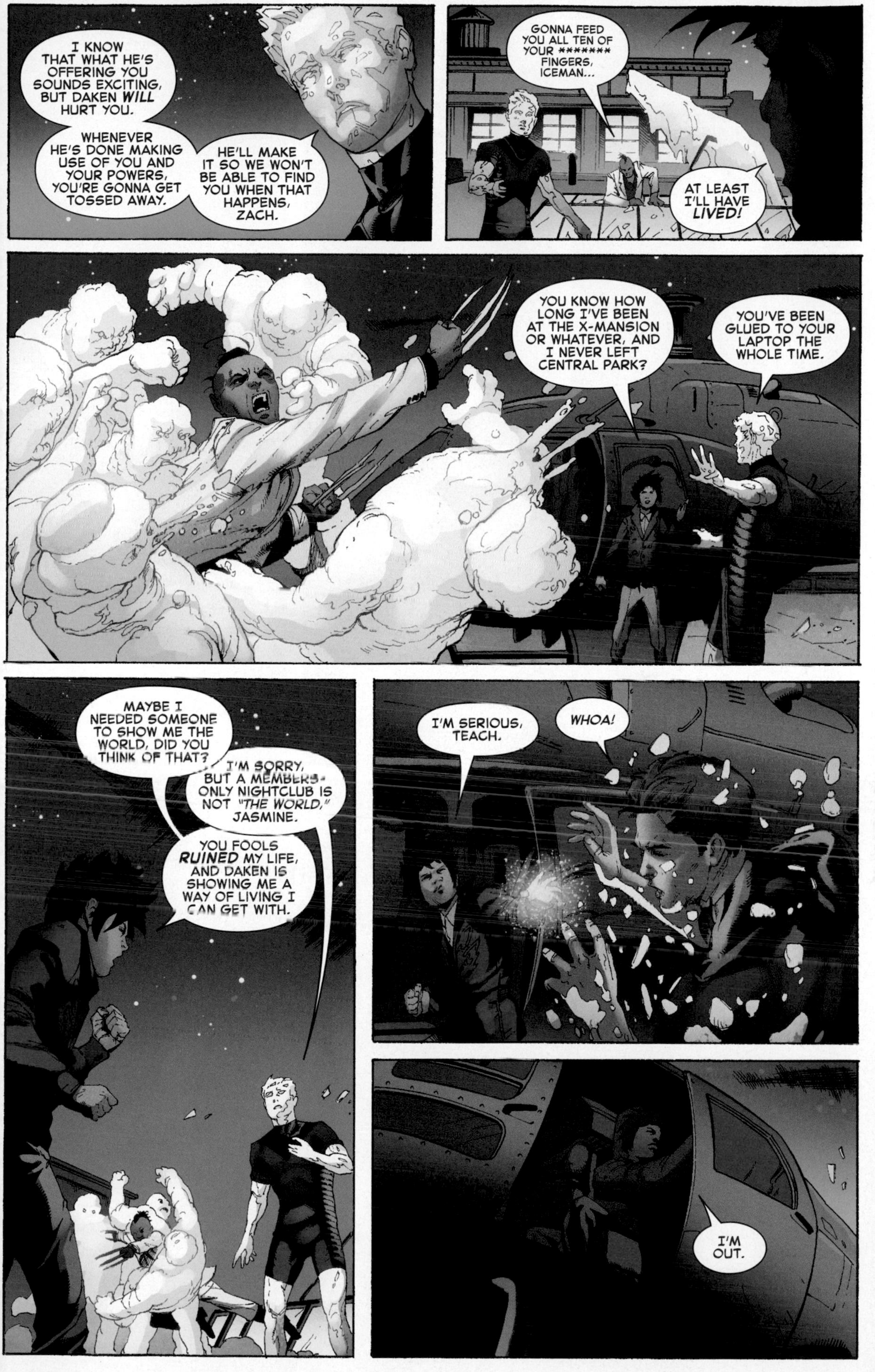
I KNOW THAT WHAT HE'S OFFERING YOU SOUNDS EXCITING, BUT DAKEN *WILL* HURT YOU.
WHENEVER HE'S DONE MAKING USE OF YOU AND YOUR POWERS, YOU'RE GONNA GET TOSSED AWAY.
HE'LL MAKE IT SO WE WON'T BE ABLE TO FIND YOU WHEN THAT HAPPENS, ZACH.
GONNA FEED YOU ALL TEN OF YOUR ******* FINGERS, ICEMAN...
AT LEAST I'LL HAVE *LIVED!*
YOU KNOW HOW LONG I'VE BEEN AT THE X-MANSION OR WHATEVER, AND I NEVER LEFT CENTRAL PARK?
YOU'VE BEEN GLUED TO YOUR LAPTOP THE WHOLE TIME.
MAYBE I NEEDED SOMEONE TO SHOW ME THE WORLD, DID YOU THINK OF THAT?
I'M SORRY, BUT A MEMBERS-ONLY NIGHTCLUB IS NOT *"THE WORLD,"* JASMINE.
YOU FOOLS ***RUINED*** MY LIFE, AND DAKEN IS SHOWING ME A WAY OF LIVING I CAN GET WITH.
I'M SERIOUS, TEACH.
WHOA!
I'M OUT.

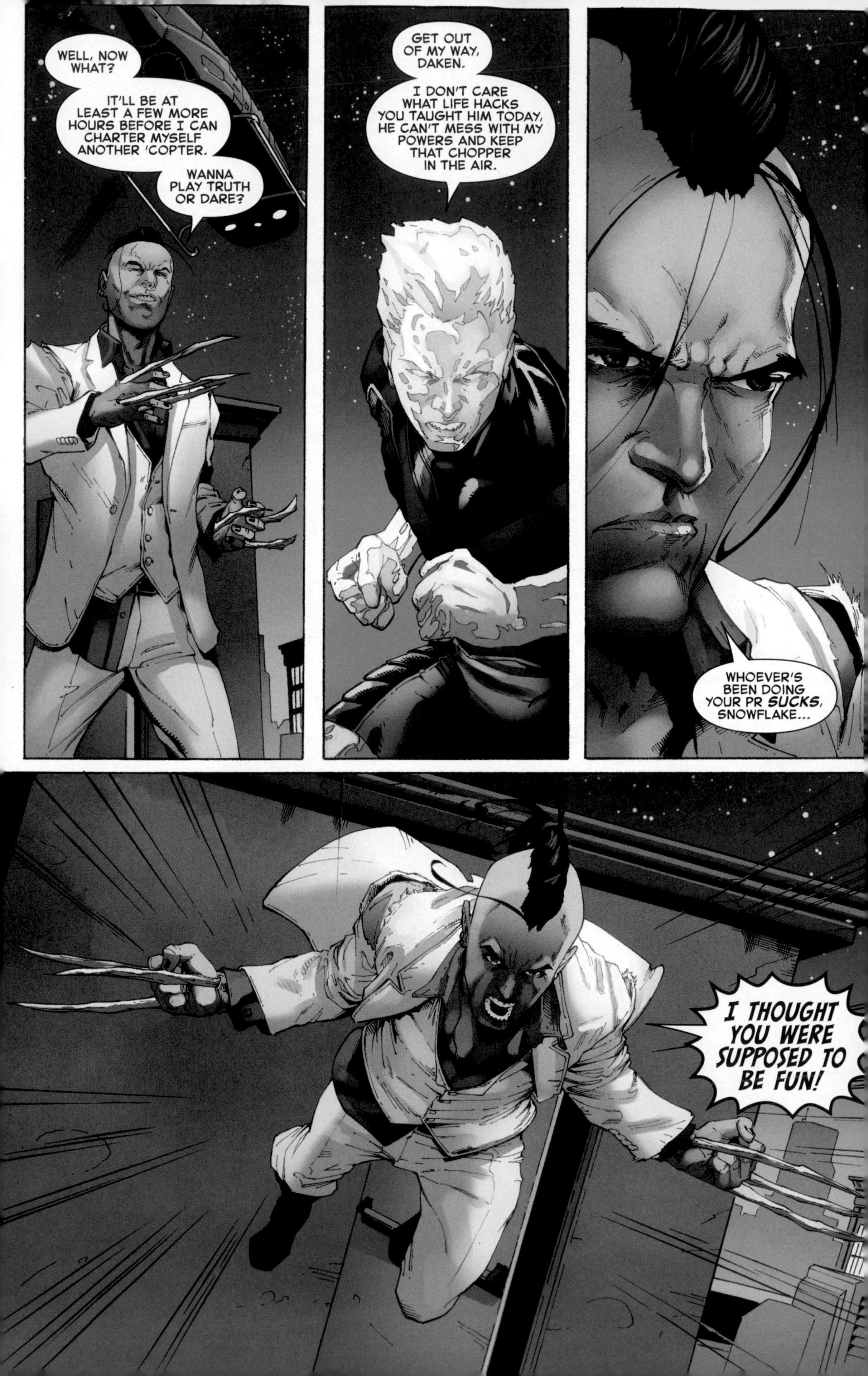
WELL, NOW WHAT?
IT'LL BE AT LEAST A FEW MORE HOURS BEFORE I CAN CHARTER MYSELF ANOTHER 'COPTER.
WANNA PLAY TRUTH OR DARE?
GET OUT OF MY WAY, DAKEN.
I DON'T CARE WHAT LIFE HACKS YOU TAUGHT HIM TODAY, HE CAN'T MESS WITH MY POWERS AND KEEP THAT CHOPPER IN THE AIR.
WHOEVER'S BEEN DOING YOUR PR SUCKS, SNOWFLAKE...
I THOUGHT YOU WERE SUPPOSED TO BE FUN!

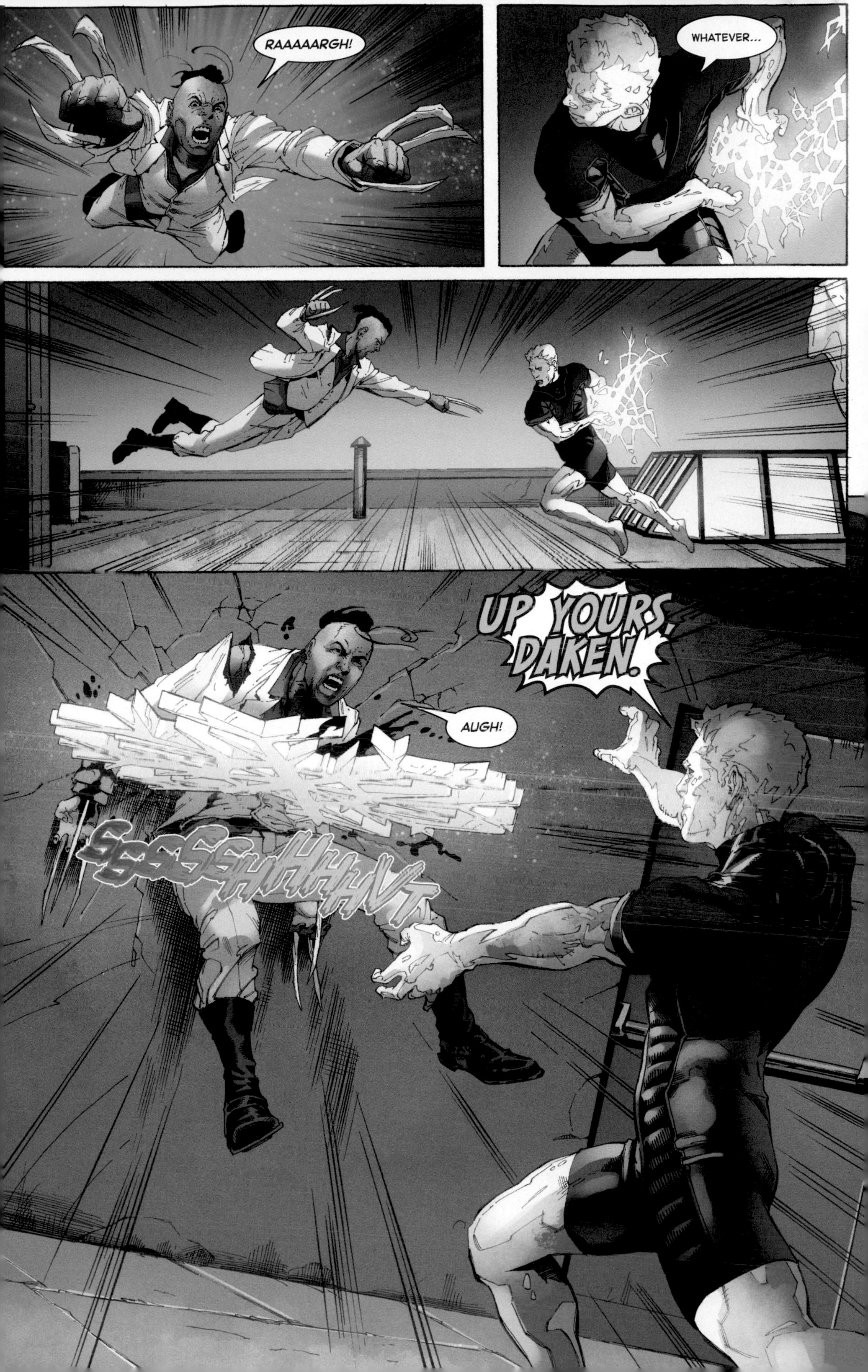
RAAAAARGH!
WHATEVER...
UP YOURS, DAKEN.
AUGH!
SSSSSHHHHVT

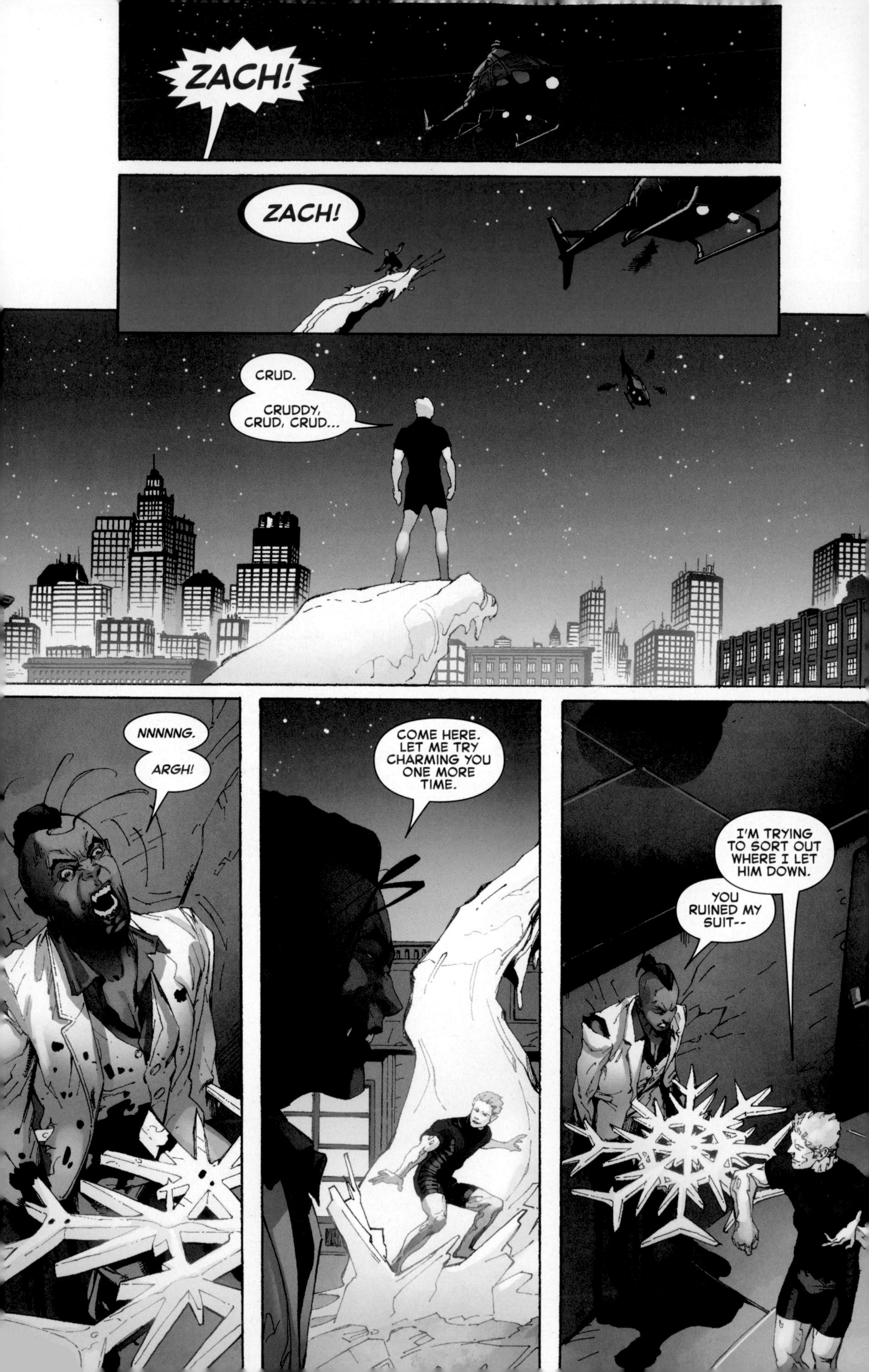
ZACH!
ZACH!
CRUD.
CRUDDY, CRUD, CRUD...
NNNNNG.
ARGH!
COME HERE. LET ME TRY CHARMING YOU ONE MORE TIME.
I'M TRYING TO SORT OUT WHERE I LET HIM DOWN.
YOU RUINED MY SUIT--

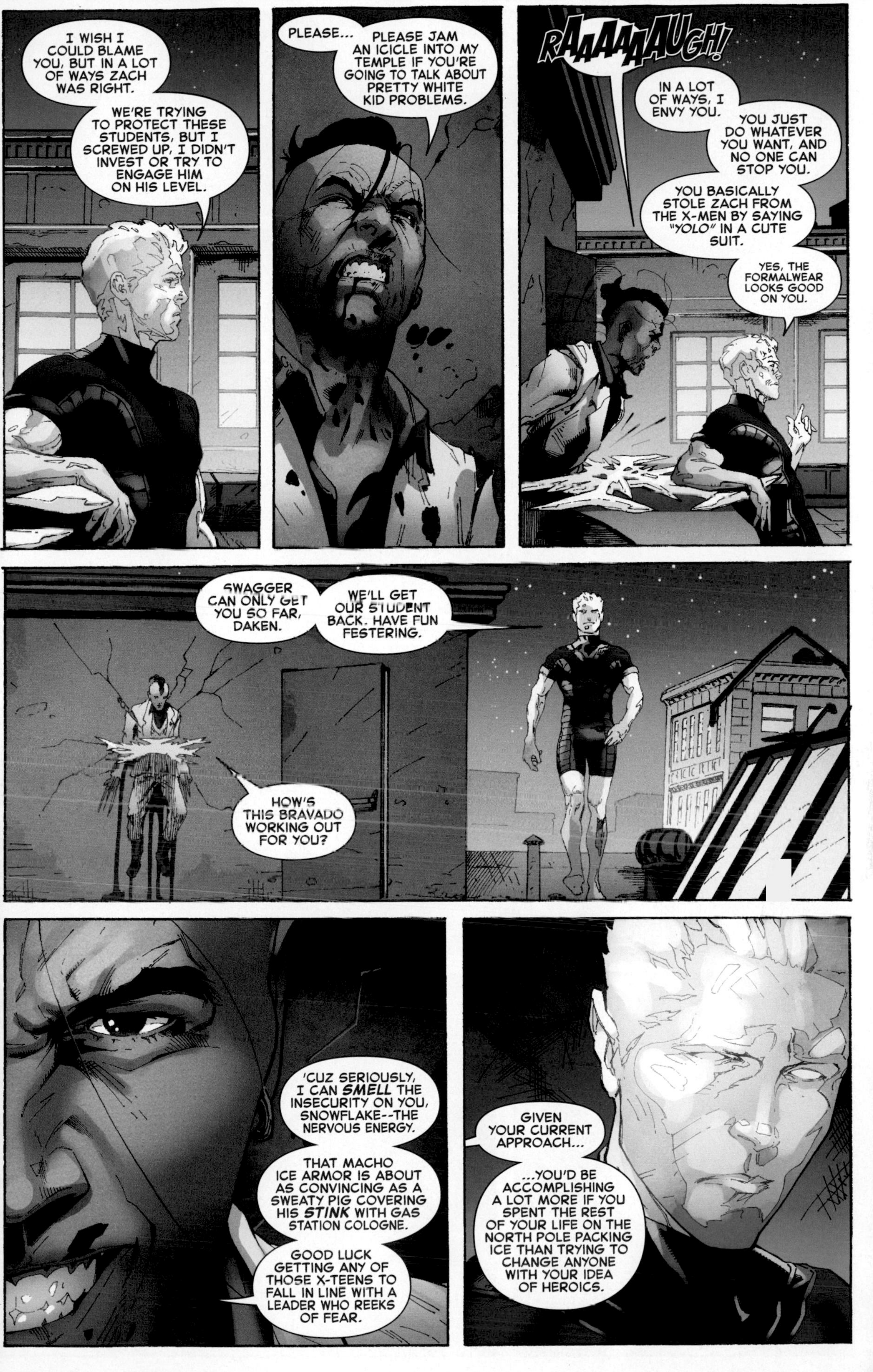
I WISH I COULD BLAME YOU, BUT IN A LOT OF WAYS ZACH WAS RIGHT.
WE'RE TRYING TO PROTECT THESE STUDENTS, BUT I SCREWED UP, I DIDN'T INVEST OR TRY TO ENGAGE HIM ON HIS LEVEL.
PLEASE...
PLEASE JAM AN ICICLE INTO MY TEMPLE IF YOU'RE GOING TO TALK ABOUT PRETTY WHITE KID PROBLEMS.
RAAAAAAAUGH!
IN A LOT OF WAYS, I ENVY YOU.
YOU JUST DO WHATEVER YOU WANT, AND NO ONE CAN STOP YOU.
YOU BASICALLY STOLE ZACH FROM THE X-MEN BY SAYING "YOLO" IN A CUTE SUIT.
YES, THE FORMALWEAR LOOKS GOOD ON YOU.
SWAGGER CAN ONLY GET YOU SO FAR, DAKEN.
WE'LL GET OUR STUDENT BACK. HAVE FUN FESTERING.
HOW'S THIS BRAVADO WORKING OUT FOR YOU?
'CUZ SERIOUSLY, I CAN SMELL THE INSECURITY ON YOU, SNOWFLAKE--THE NERVOUS ENERGY.
THAT MACHO ICE ARMOR IS ABOUT AS CONVINCING AS A SWEATY PIG COVERING HIS STINK WITH GAS STATION COLOGNE.
GOOD LUCK GETTING ANY OF THOSE X-TEENS TO FALL IN LINE WITH A LEADER WHO REEKS OF FEAR.
GIVEN YOUR CURRENT APPROACH...
...YOU'D BE ACCOMPLISHING A LOT MORE IF YOU SPENT THE REST OF YOUR LIFE ON THE NORTH POLE PACKING ICE THAN TRYING TO CHANGE ANYONE WITH YOUR IDEA OF HEROICS.

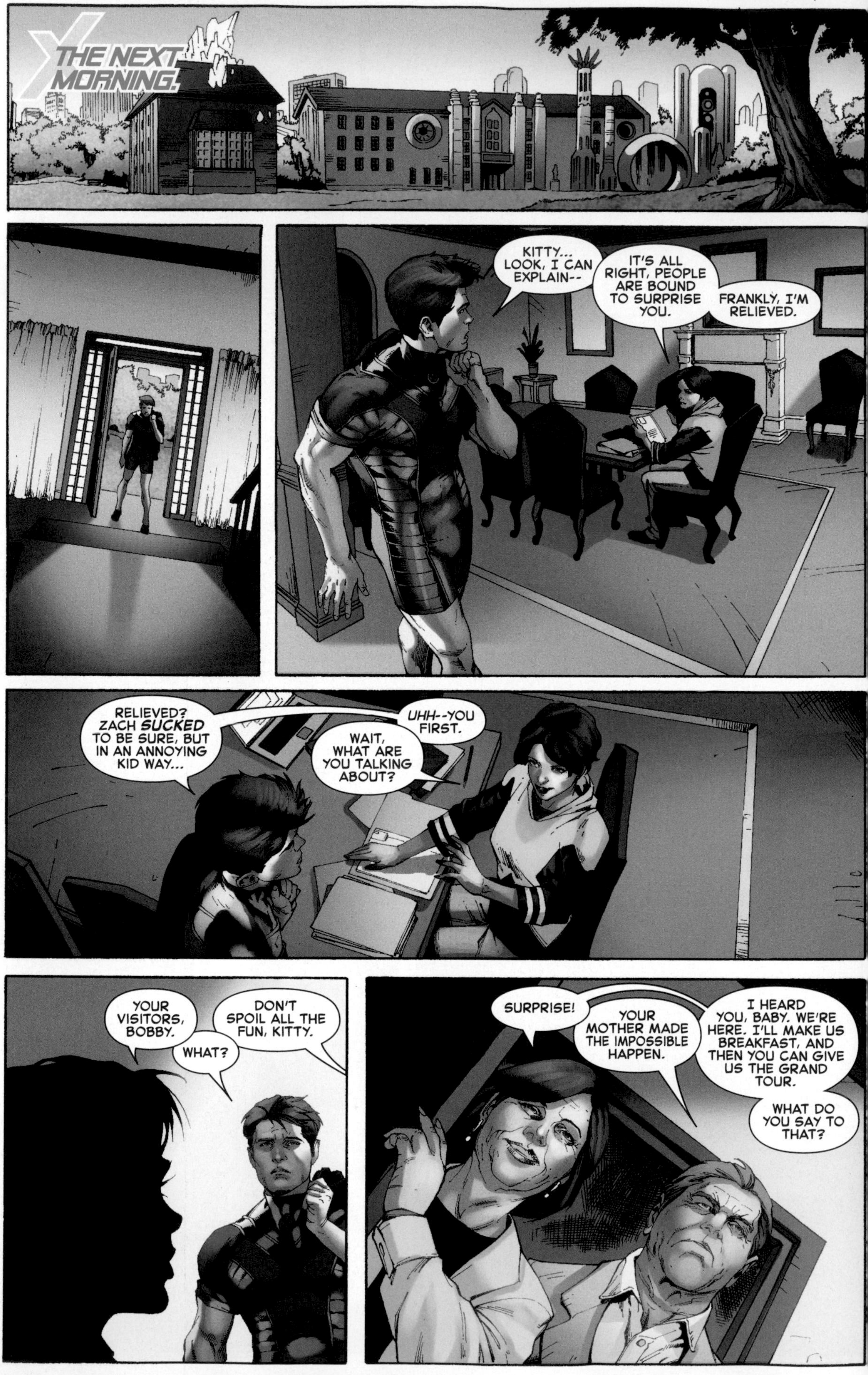
THE NEXT MORNING.
KITTY... LOOK, I CAN EXPLAIN--
IT'S ALL RIGHT, PEOPLE ARE BOUND TO SURPRISE YOU.
FRANKLY, I'M RELIEVED.
RELIEVED? ZACH SUCKED TO BE SURE, BUT IN AN ANNOYING KID WAY...
UHH--YOU FIRST.
WAIT, WHAT ARE YOU TALKING ABOUT?
YOUR VISITORS, BOBBY.
WHAT?
DON'T SPOIL ALL THE FUN, KITTY.
SURPRISE!
YOUR MOTHER MADE THE IMPOSSIBLE HAPPEN.
I HEARD YOU, BABY. WE'RE HERE. I'LL MAKE US BREAKFAST, AND THEN YOU CAN GIVE US THE GRAND TOUR.
WHAT DO YOU SAY TO THAT?

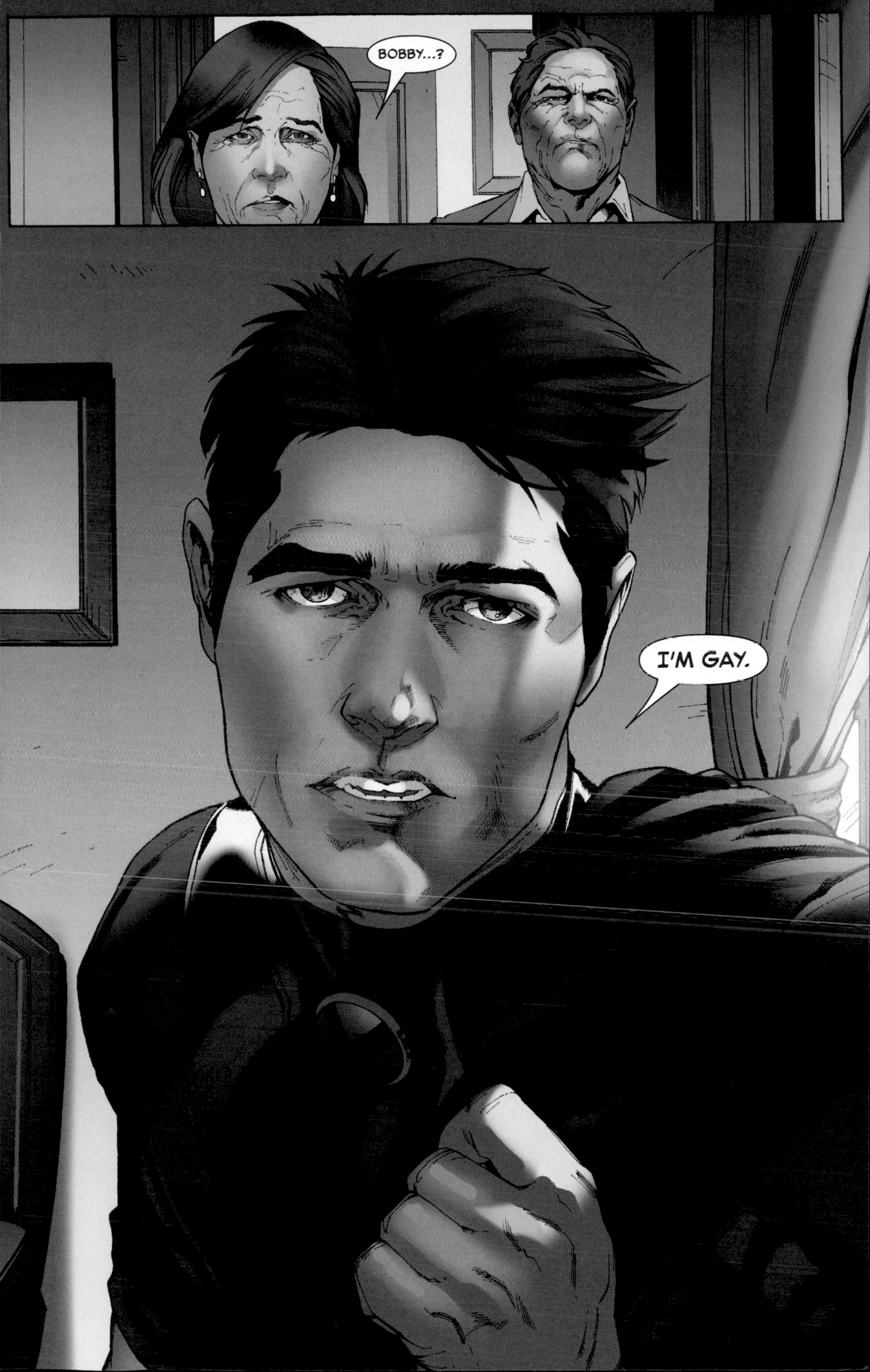
BOBBY...?
I'M GAY.

5

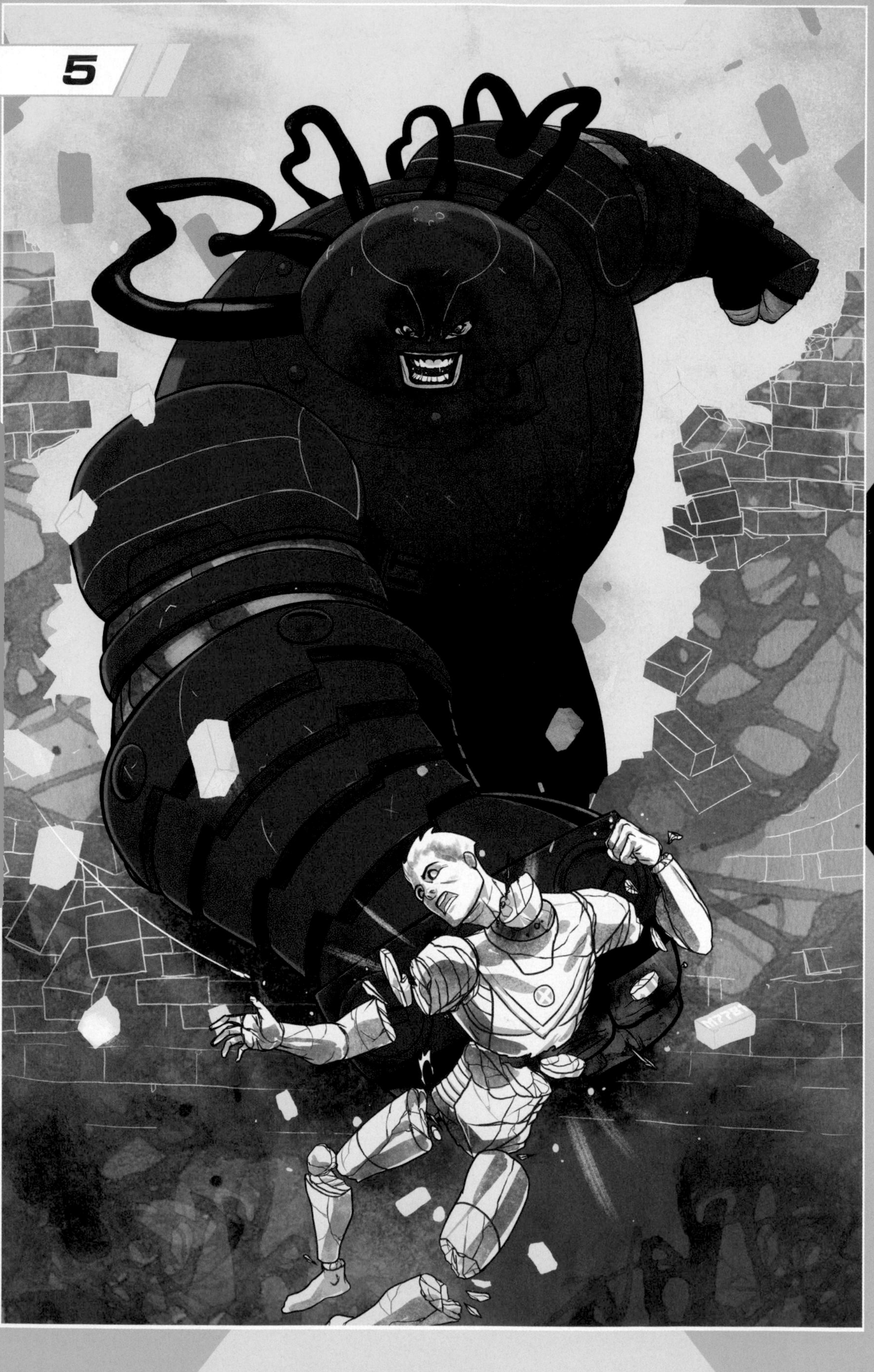

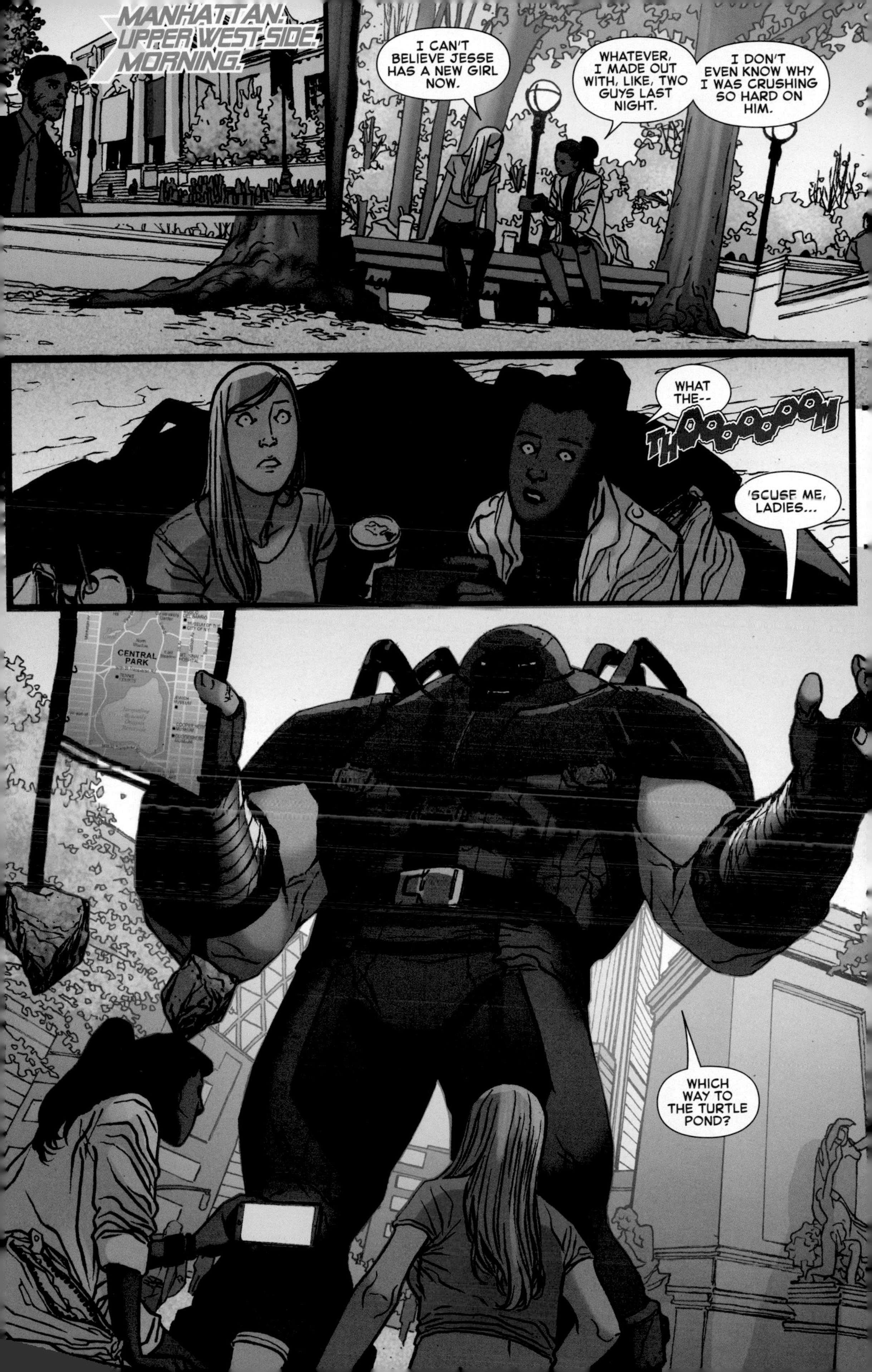

MANHATTAN. UPPER WEST SIDE. MORNING.
I CAN'T BELIEVE JESSE HAS A NEW GIRL NOW.
WHATEVER, I MADE OUT WITH, LIKE, TWO GUYS LAST NIGHT.
I DON'T EVEN KNOW WHY I WAS CRUSHING SO HARD ON HIM.
WHAT THE--
THOOOOOOOM
'SCUSE ME, LADIES...
CENTRAL PARK
WHICH WAY TO THE TURTLE POND?

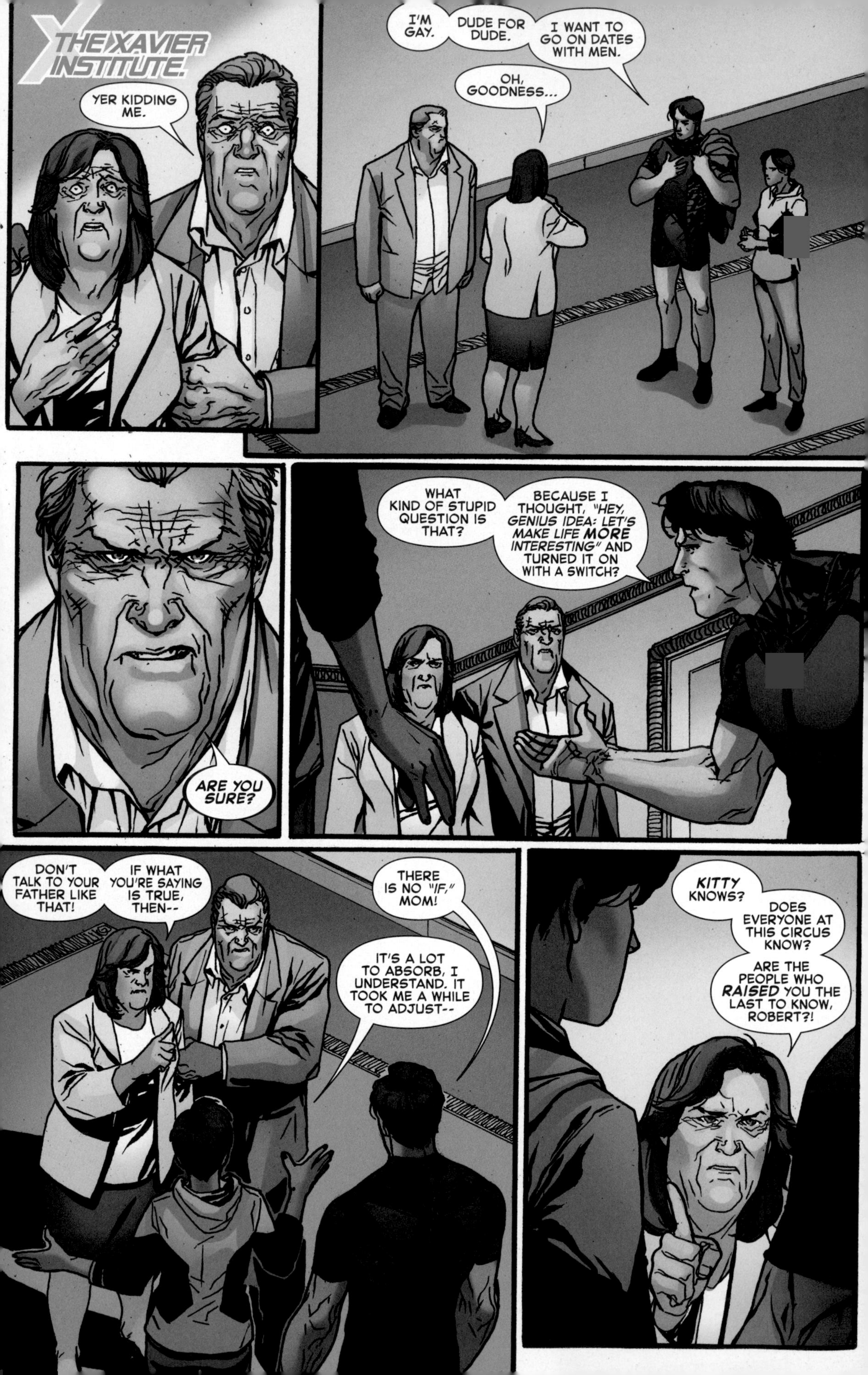
THE XAVIER INSTITUTE.
YER KIDDING ME.
I'M GAY.
DUDE FOR DUDE.
I WANT TO GO ON DATES WITH MEN.
OH, GOODNESS...
ARE YOU SURE?
WHAT KIND OF STUPID QUESTION IS THAT?
BECAUSE I THOUGHT, "HEY, GENIUS IDEA: LET'S MAKE LIFE MORE INTERESTING" AND TURNED IT ON WITH A SWITCH?
DON'T TALK TO YOUR FATHER LIKE THAT!
IF WHAT YOU'RE SAYING IS TRUE, THEN--
THERE IS NO "IF," MOM!
IT'S A LOT TO ABSORB, I UNDERSTAND. IT TOOK ME A WHILE TO ADJUST--
KITTY KNOWS?
DOES EVERYONE AT THIS CIRCUS KNOW?
ARE THE PEOPLE WHO RAISED YOU THE LAST TO KNOW, ROBERT?!

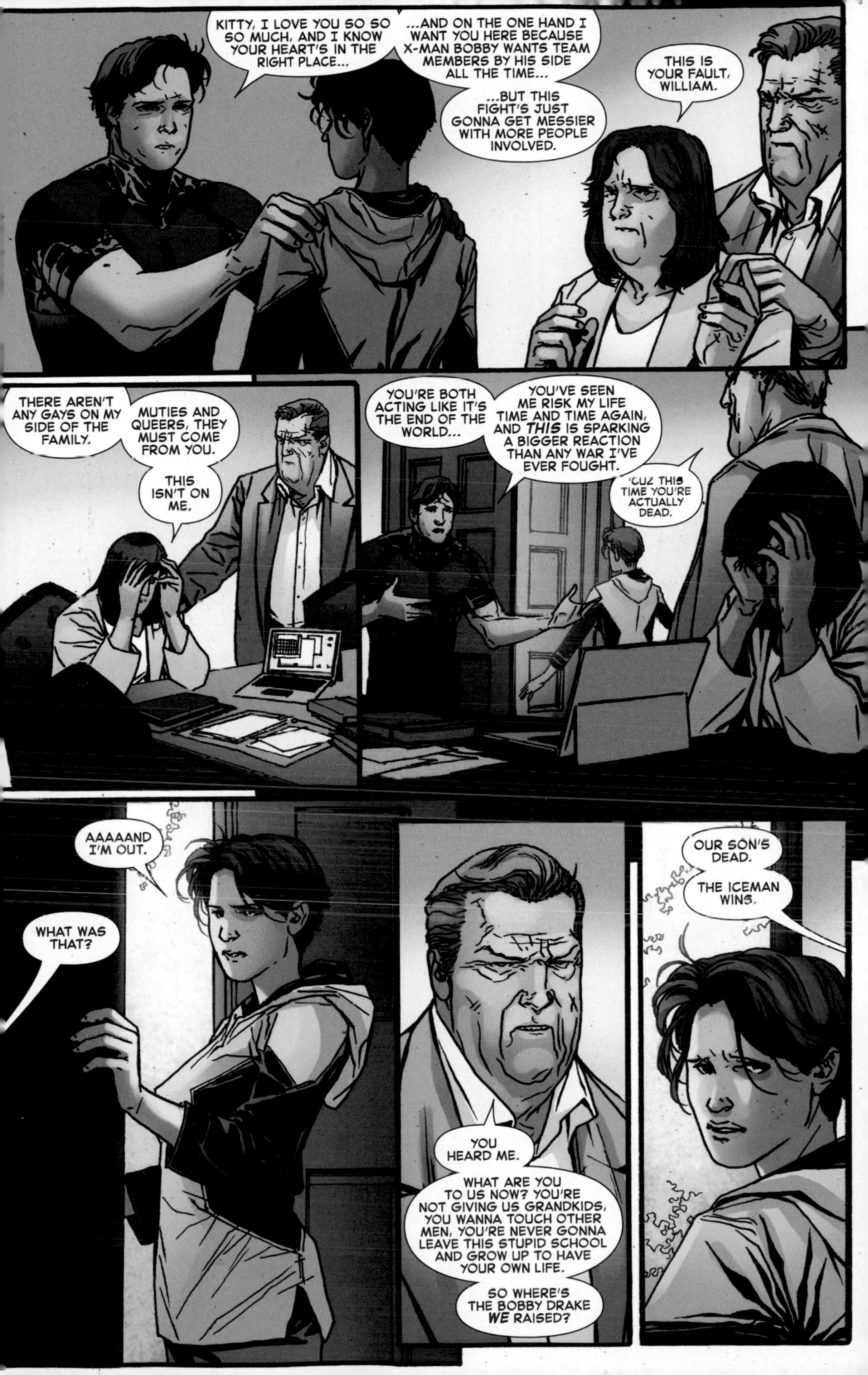
KITTY, I LOVE YOU SO SO SO MUCH, AND I KNOW YOUR HEART'S IN THE RIGHT PLACE...
...AND ON THE ONE HAND I WANT YOU HERE BECAUSE X-MAN BOBBY WANTS TEAM MEMBERS BY HIS SIDE ALL THE TIME...
...BUT THIS FIGHT'S JUST GONNA GET MESSIER WITH MORE PEOPLE INVOLVED.
THIS IS YOUR FAULT, WILLIAM.
THERE AREN'T ANY GAYS ON MY SIDE OF THE FAMILY.
MUTIES AND QUEERS, THEY MUST COME FROM YOU.
THIS ISN'T ON ME.
YOU'RE BOTH ACTING LIKE IT'S THE END OF THE WORLD...
YOU'VE SEEN ME RISK MY LIFE TIME AND TIME AGAIN, AND THIS IS SPARKING A BIGGER REACTION THAN ANY WAR I'VE EVER FOUGHT.
'CUZ THIS TIME YOU'RE ACTUALLY DEAD.
AAAAAND I'M OUT.
WHAT WAS THAT?
YOU HEARD ME.
WHAT ARE YOU TO US NOW? YOU'RE NOT GIVING US GRANDKIDS, YOU WANNA TOUCH OTHER MEN, YOU'RE NEVER GONNA LEAVE THIS STUPID SCHOOL AND GROW UP TO HAVE YOUR OWN LIFE.
SO WHERE'S THE BOBBY DRAKE WE RAISED?
OUR SON'S DEAD.
THE ICEMAN WINS.

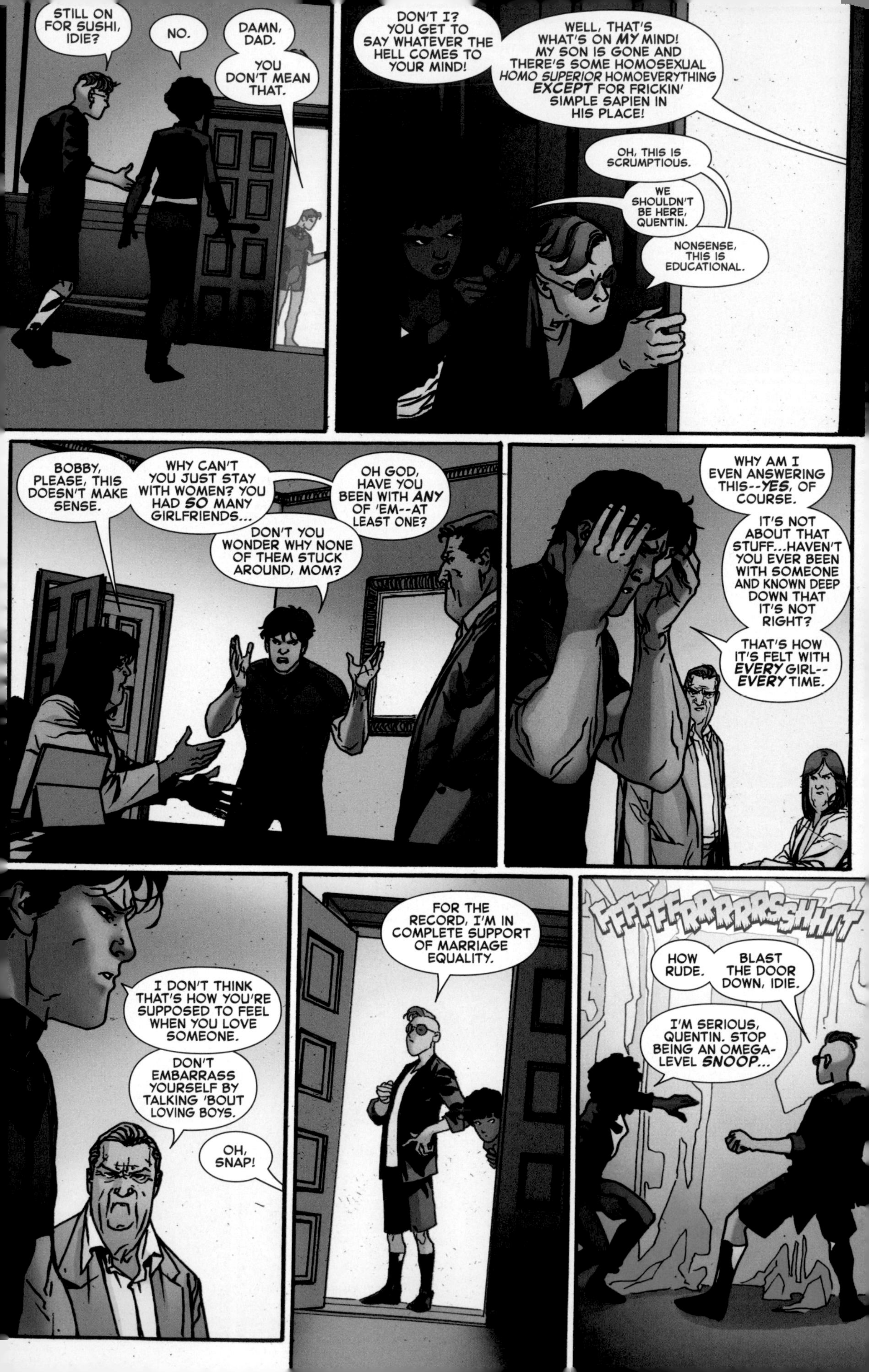
STILL ON FOR SUSHI, IDIE?
NO.
DAMN, DAD.
YOU DON'T MEAN THAT.
DON'T I? YOU GET TO SAY WHATEVER THE HELL COMES TO YOUR MIND!
WELL, THAT'S WHAT'S ON MY MIND! MY SON IS GONE AND THERE'S SOME HOMOSEXUAL HOMO SUPERIOR HOMOEVERYTHING EXCEPT FOR FRICKIN' SIMPLE SAPIEN IN HIS PLACE!
OH, THIS IS SCRUMPTIOUS.
WE SHOULDN'T BE HERE, QUENTIN.
NONSENSE, THIS IS EDUCATIONAL.
BOBBY, PLEASE, THIS DOESN'T MAKE SENSE.
WHY CAN'T YOU JUST STAY WITH WOMEN? YOU HAD SO MANY GIRLFRIENDS...
OH GOD, HAVE YOU BEEN WITH ANY OF 'EM--AT LEAST ONE?
DON'T YOU WONDER WHY NONE OF THEM STUCK AROUND, MOM?
WHY AM I EVEN ANSWERING THIS--YES, OF COURSE.
IT'S NOT ABOUT THAT STUFF...HAVEN'T YOU EVER BEEN WITH SOMEONE AND KNOWN DEEP DOWN THAT IT'S NOT RIGHT?
THAT'S HOW IT'S FELT WITH EVERY GIRL--EVERY TIME.
I DON'T THINK THAT'S HOW YOU'RE SUPPOSED TO FEEL WHEN YOU LOVE SOMEONE.
DON'T EMBARRASS YOURSELF BY TALKING 'BOUT LOVING BOYS.
OH, SNAP!
FOR THE RECORD, I'M IN COMPLETE SUPPORT OF MARRIAGE EQUALITY.
FFFFFFRRRRRRSSHHHT
HOW RUDE.
BLAST THE DOOR DOWN, IDIE.
I'M SERIOUS, QUENTIN. STOP BEING AN OMEGA-LEVEL SNOOP...

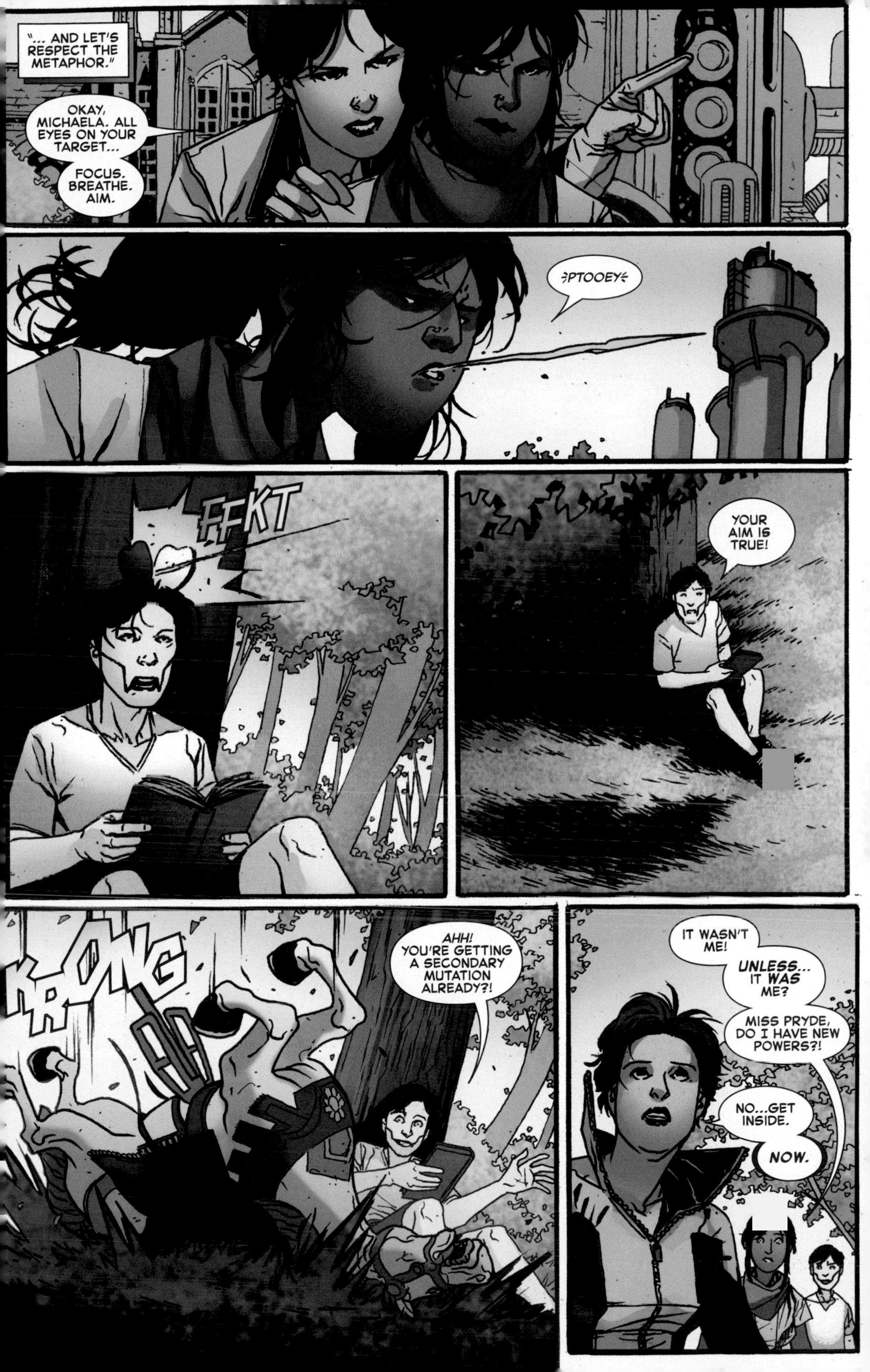
"... AND LET'S RESPECT THE METAPHOR."
OKAY, MICHAELA. ALL EYES ON YOUR TARGET...
FOCUS. BREATHE. AIM.
PTOOEY
FFKT
YOUR AIM IS TRUE!
KRONG
AHH! YOU'RE GETTING A SECONDARY MUTATION ALREADY?!
IT WASN'T ME!
UNLESS... IT WAS ME?
MISS PRYDE, DO I HAVE NEW POWERS?!
NO...GET INSIDE.
NOW.

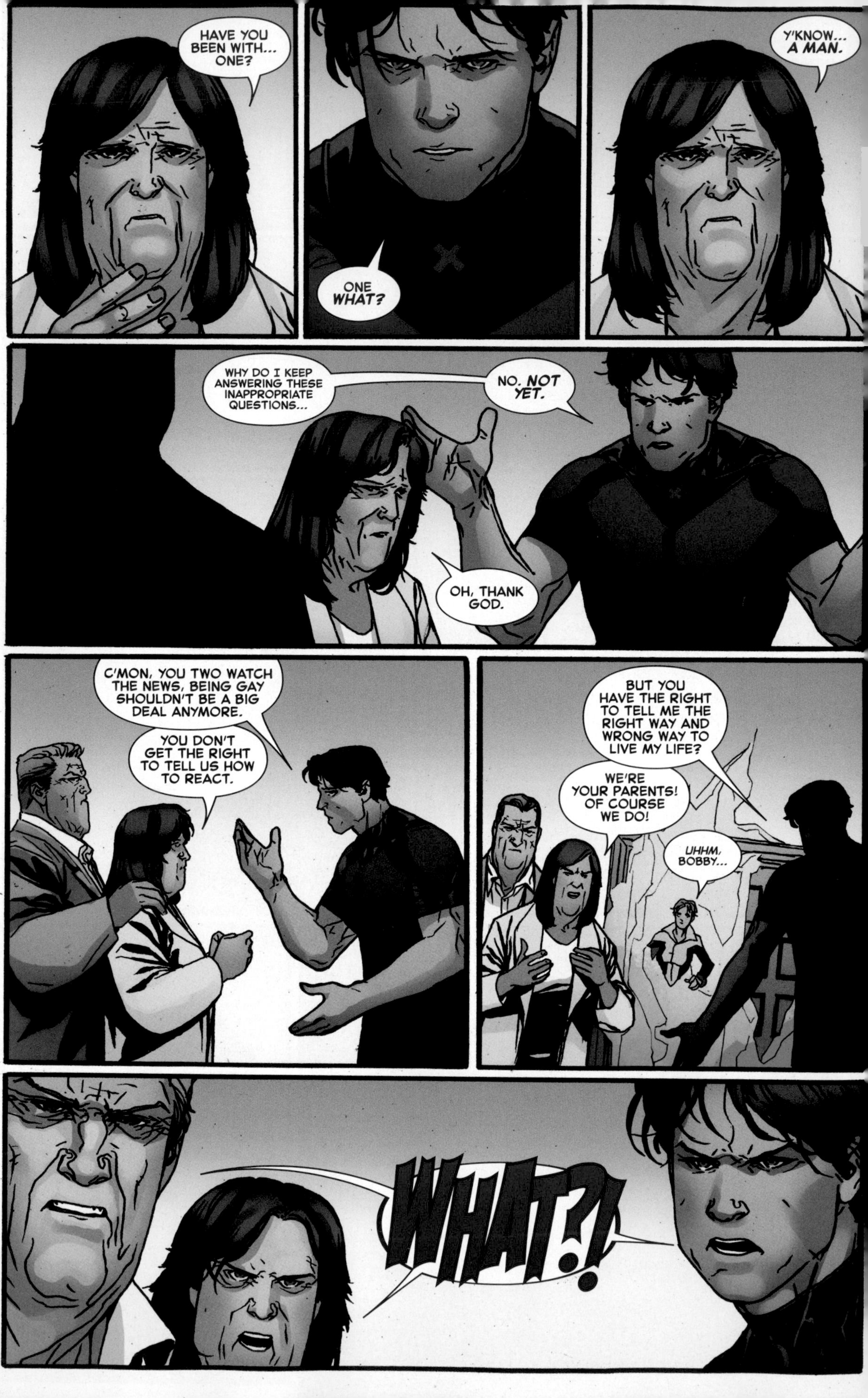
HAVE YOU BEEN WITH... ONE?
ONE WHAT?
Y'KNOW... A MAN.
WHY DO I KEEP ANSWERING THESE INAPPROPRIATE QUESTIONS...
NO. NOT YET.
OH, THANK GOD.
C'MON, YOU TWO WATCH THE NEWS, BEING GAY SHOULDN'T BE A BIG DEAL ANYMORE.
YOU DON'T GET THE RIGHT TO TELL US HOW TO REACT.
BUT YOU HAVE THE RIGHT TO TELL ME THE RIGHT WAY AND WRONG WAY TO LIVE MY LIFE?
WE'RE YOUR PARENTS! OF COURSE WE DO!
UHHM, BOBBY...
WHAT?!

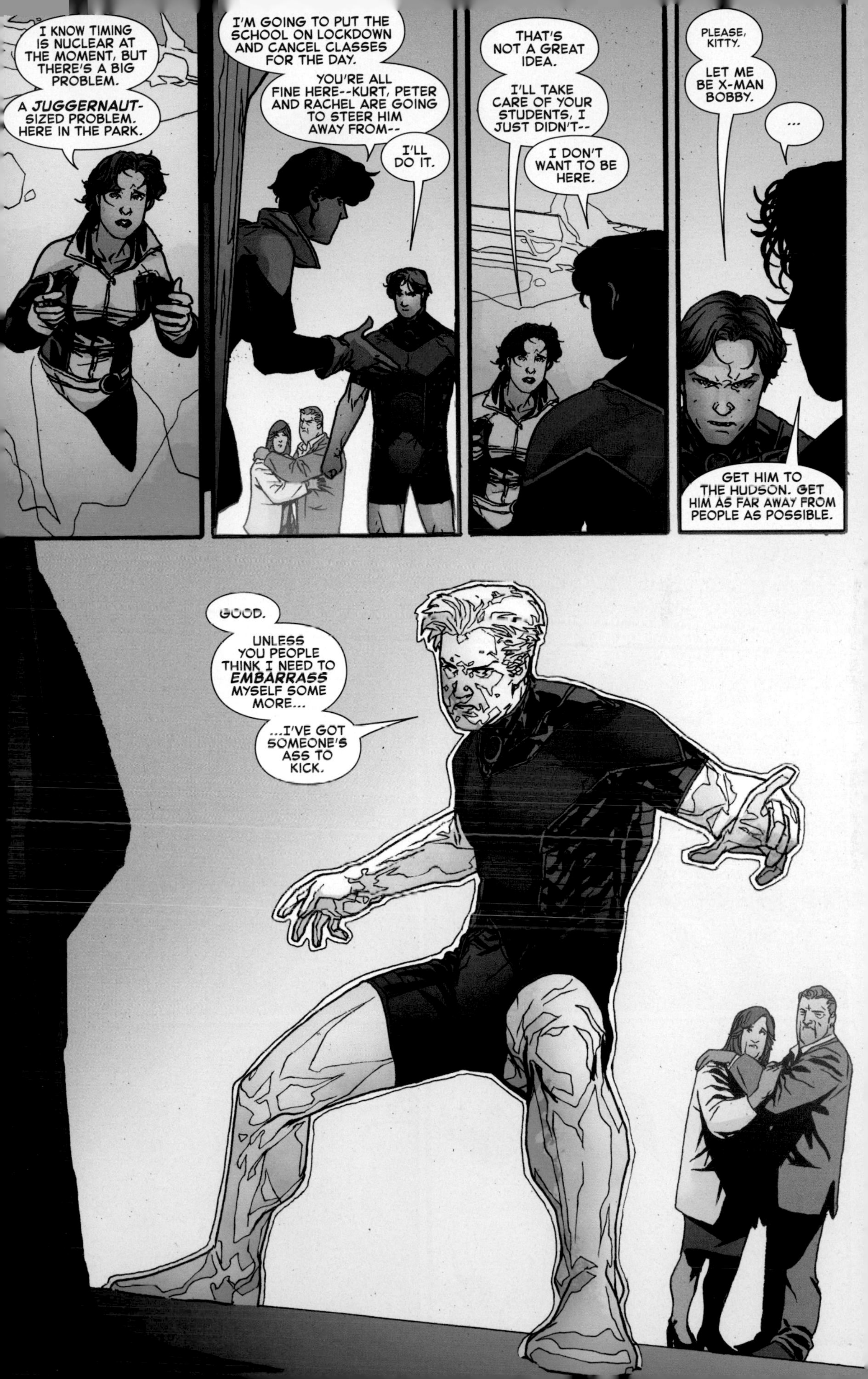
I KNOW TIMING IS NUCLEAR AT THE MOMENT, BUT THERE'S A BIG PROBLEM.
A JUGGERNAUT-SIZED PROBLEM. HERE IN THE PARK.
I'M GOING TO PUT THE SCHOOL ON LOCKDOWN AND CANCEL CLASSES FOR THE DAY.
YOU'RE ALL FINE HERE--KURT, PETER AND RACHEL ARE GOING TO STEER HIM AWAY FROM--
I'LL DO IT.
THAT'S NOT A GREAT IDEA.
I'LL TAKE CARE OF YOUR STUDENTS, I JUST DIDN'T--
I DON'T WANT TO BE HERE.
PLEASE, KITTY.
LET ME BE X-MAN BOBBY.
...
GET HIM TO THE HUDSON. GET HIM AS FAR AWAY FROM PEOPLE AS POSSIBLE.
GOOD.
UNLESS YOU PEOPLE THINK I NEED TO EMBARRASS MYSELF SOME MORE...
...I'VE GOT SOMEONE'S ASS TO KICK.

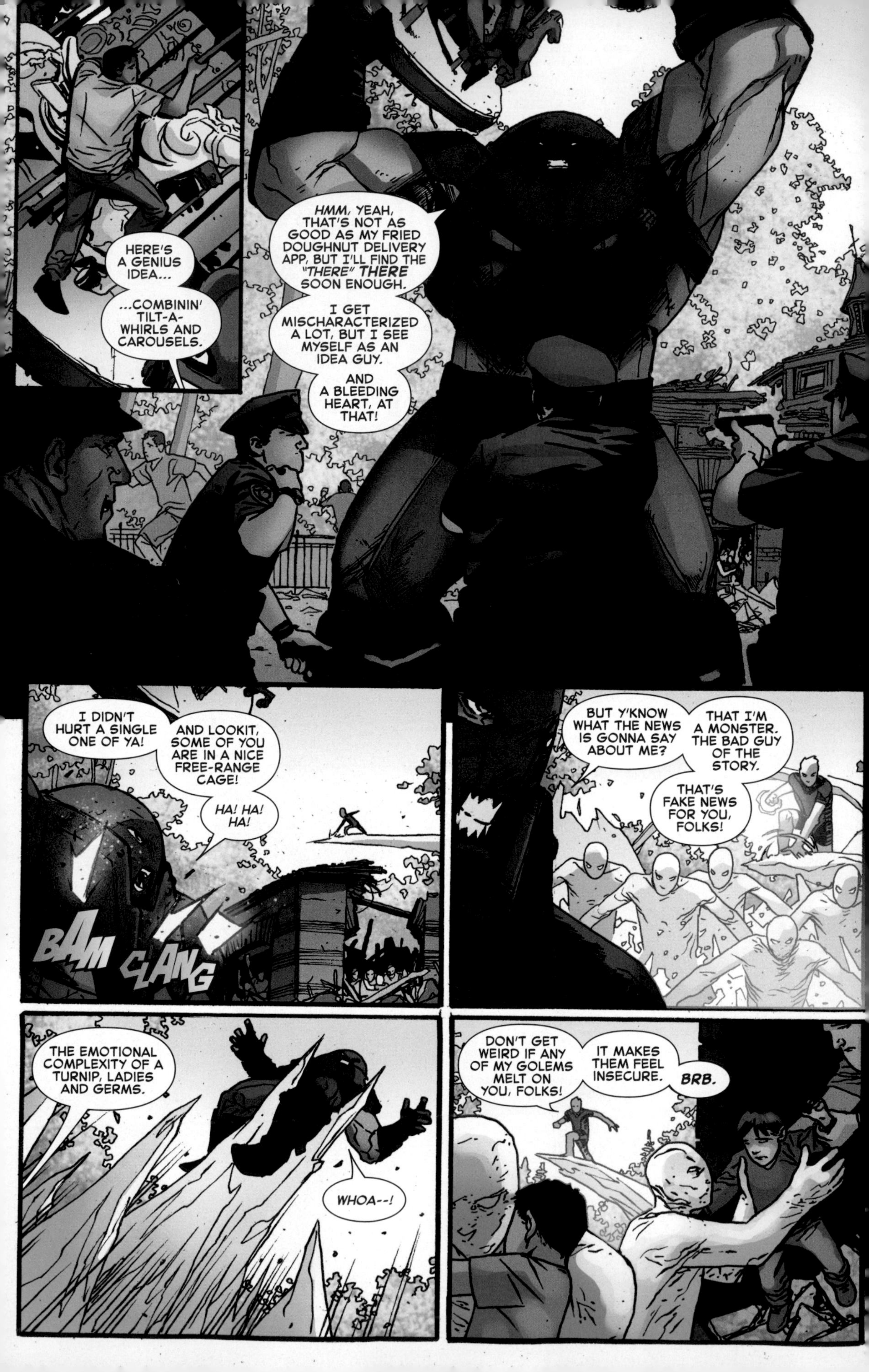
HERE'S A GENIUS IDEA...
...COMBININ' TILT-A-WHIRLS AND CAROUSELS.
HMM, YEAH, THAT'S NOT AS GOOD AS MY FRIED DOUGHNUT DELIVERY APP, BUT I'LL FIND THE "THERE" THERE SOON ENOUGH.
I GET MISCHARACTERIZED A LOT, BUT I SEE MYSELF AS AN IDEA GUY.
AND A BLEEDING HEART, AT THAT!
I DIDN'T HURT A SINGLE ONE OF YA!
AND LOOKIT, SOME OF YOU ARE IN A NICE FREE-RANGE CAGE!
HA! HA! HA!
BAM
CLANG
BUT Y'KNOW WHAT THE NEWS IS GONNA SAY ABOUT ME?
THAT I'M A MONSTER. THE BAD GUY OF THE STORY.
THAT'S FAKE NEWS FOR YOU, FOLKS!
THE EMOTIONAL COMPLEXITY OF A TURNIP, LADIES AND GERMS.
WHOA--!
DON'T GET WEIRD IF ANY OF MY GOLEMS MELT ON YOU, FOLKS!
IT MAKES THEM FEEL INSECURE.
BRB.

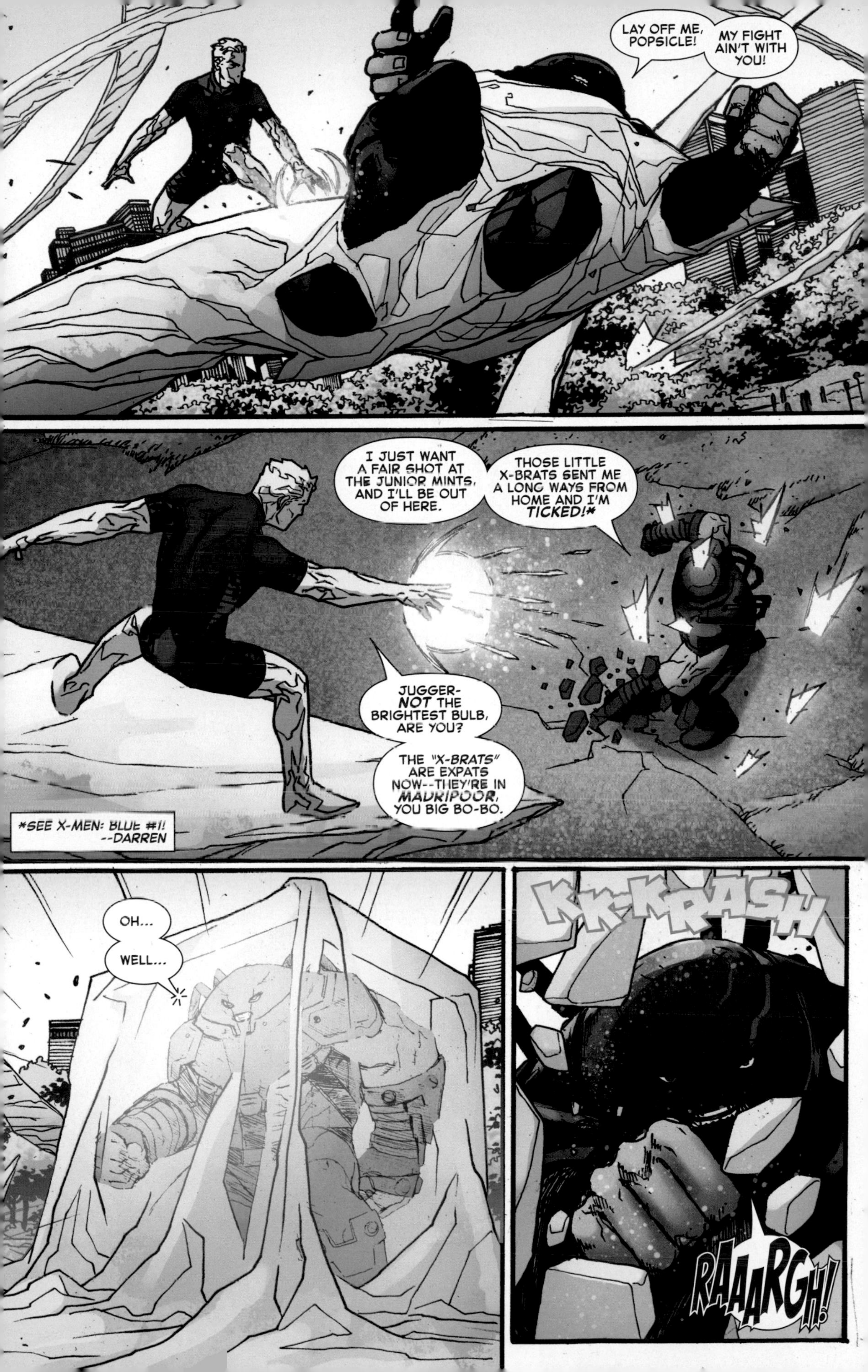
LAY OFF ME, POPSICLE!
MY FIGHT AIN'T WITH YOU!
I JUST WANT A FAIR SHOT AT THE JUNIOR MINTS, AND I'LL BE OUT OF HERE.
THOSE LITTLE X-BRATS SENT ME A LONG WAYS FROM HOME AND I'M *TICKED!**
JUGGER-*NOT* THE BRIGHTEST BULB, ARE YOU?
THE "*X-BRATS*" ARE EXPATS NOW--THEY'RE IN *MADRIPOOR*, YOU BIG BO-BO.
*SEE X-MEN: BLUE #1! --DARREN
OH...
WELL...
KK-KRASH
RAAARGH!

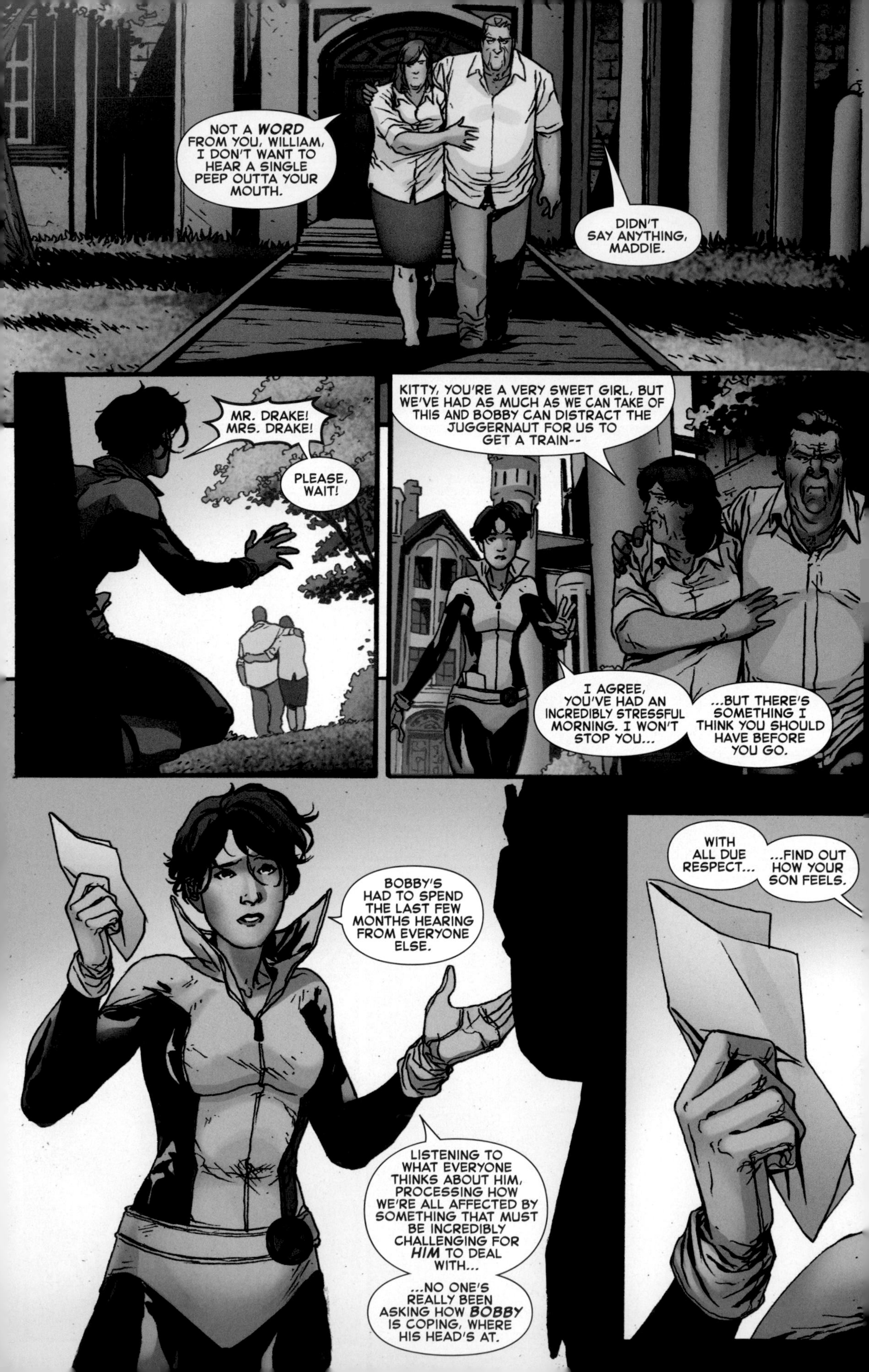
NOT A *WORD* FROM YOU, WILLIAM, I DON'T WANT TO HEAR A SINGLE PEEP OUTTA YOUR MOUTH.
DIDN'T SAY ANYTHING, MADDIE.
MR. DRAKE! MRS. DRAKE!
PLEASE, WAIT!
KITTY, YOU'RE A VERY SWEET GIRL, BUT WE'VE HAD AS MUCH AS WE CAN TAKE OF THIS AND BOBBY CAN DISTRACT THE JUGGERNAUT FOR US TO GET A TRAIN--
I AGREE, YOU'VE HAD AN INCREDIBLY STRESSFUL MORNING. I WON'T STOP YOU...
...BUT THERE'S SOMETHING I THINK YOU SHOULD HAVE BEFORE YOU GO.
BOBBY'S HAD TO SPEND THE LAST FEW MONTHS HEARING FROM EVERYONE ELSE.
LISTENING TO WHAT EVERYONE THINKS ABOUT HIM, PROCESSING HOW WE'RE ALL AFFECTED BY SOMETHING THAT MUST BE INCREDIBLY CHALLENGING FOR *HIM* TO DEAL WITH...
...NO ONE'S REALLY BEEN ASKING HOW *BOBBY* IS COPING, WHERE HIS HEAD'S AT.
WITH ALL DUE RESPECT...
...FIND OUT HOW YOUR SON FEELS.

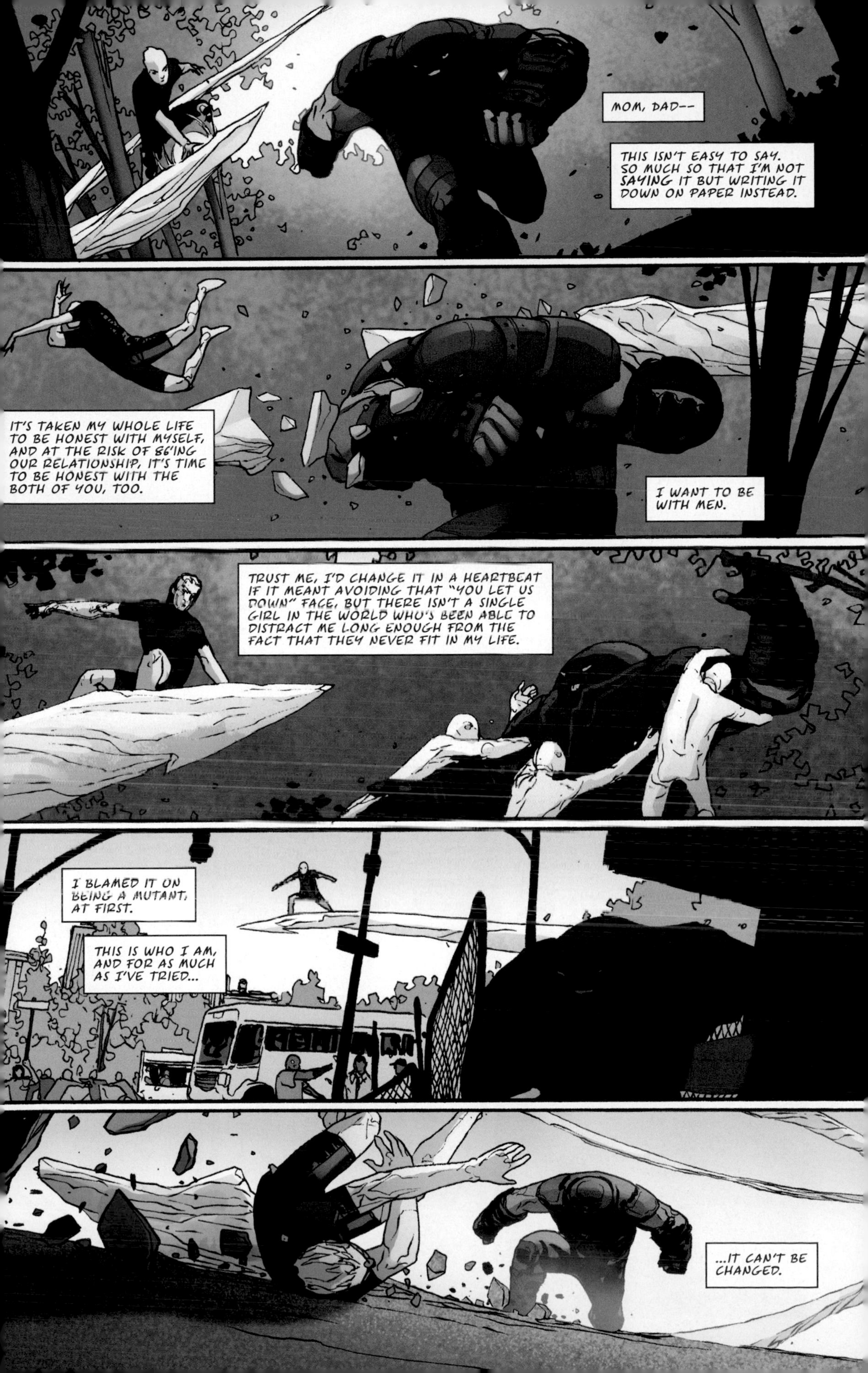
MOM, DAD--
THIS ISN'T EASY TO SAY. SO MUCH SO THAT I'M NOT SAYING IT BUT WRITING IT DOWN ON PAPER INSTEAD.
IT'S TAKEN MY WHOLE LIFE TO BE HONEST WITH MYSELF, AND AT THE RISK OF 86'ING OUR RELATIONSHIP, IT'S TIME TO BE HONEST WITH THE BOTH OF YOU, TOO.
I WANT TO BE WITH MEN.
TRUST ME, I'D CHANGE IT IN A HEARTBEAT IF IT MEANT AVOIDING THAT "YOU LET US DOWN" FACE, BUT THERE ISN'T A SINGLE GIRL IN THE WORLD WHO'S BEEN ABLE TO DISTRACT ME LONG ENOUGH FROM THE FACT THAT THEY NEVER FIT IN MY LIFE.
I BLAMED IT ON BEING A MUTANT, AT FIRST.
THIS IS WHO I AM, AND FOR AS MUCH AS I'VE TRIED...
...IT CAN'T BE CHANGED.

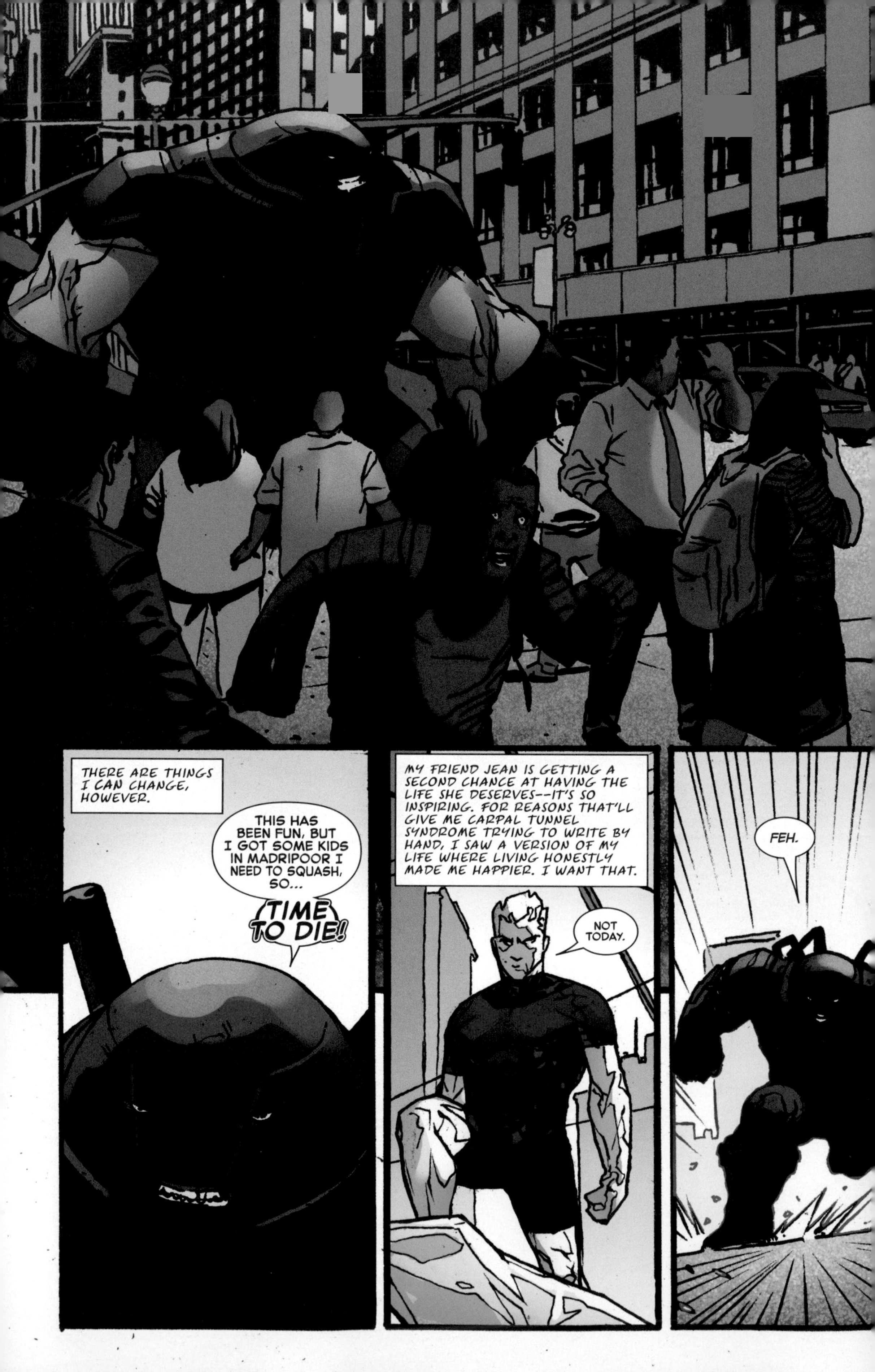
THERE ARE THINGS I CAN CHANGE, HOWEVER.
THIS HAS BEEN FUN, BUT I GOT SOME KIDS IN MADRIPOOR I NEED TO SQUASH, SO...
TIME TO DIE!
MY FRIEND JEAN IS GETTING A SECOND CHANCE AT HAVING THE LIFE SHE DESERVES--IT'S SO INSPIRING. FOR REASONS THAT'LL GIVE ME CARPAL TUNNEL SYNDROME TRYING TO WRITE BY HAND, I SAW A VERSION OF MY LIFE WHERE LIVING HONESTLY MADE ME HAPPIER. I WANT THAT.
NOT TODAY.
FEH.

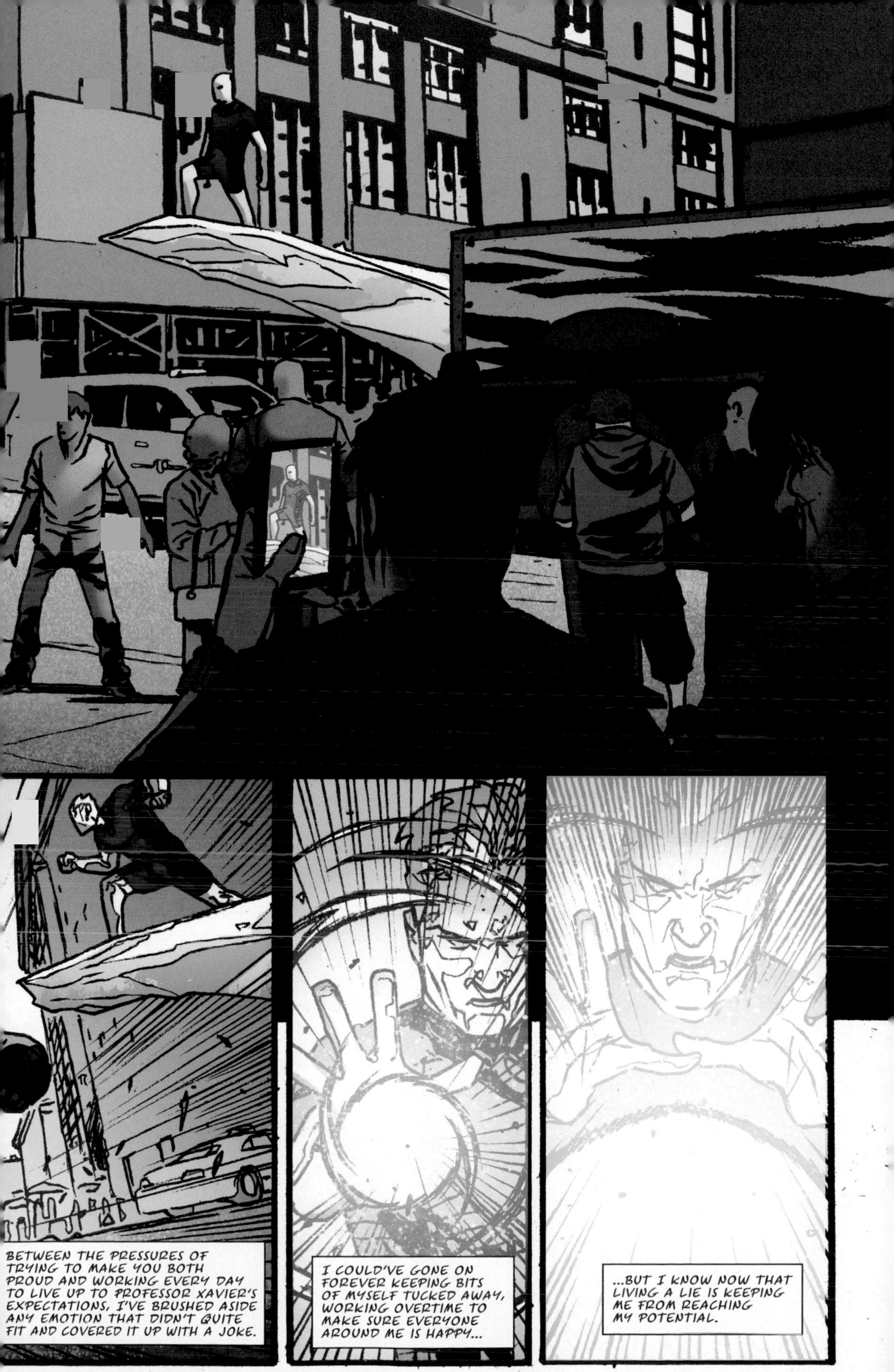
BETWEEN THE PRESSURES OF TRYING TO MAKE YOU BOTH PROUD AND WORKING EVERY DAY TO LIVE UP TO PROFESSOR XAVIER'S EXPECTATIONS, I'VE BRUSHED ASIDE ANY EMOTION THAT DIDN'T QUITE FIT AND COVERED IT UP WITH A JOKE.
I COULD'VE GONE ON FOREVER KEEPING BITS OF MYSELF TUCKED AWAY, WORKING OVERTIME TO MAKE SURE EVERYONE AROUND ME IS HAPPY...
...BUT I KNOW NOW THAT LIVING A LIE IS KEEPING ME FROM REACHING MY POTENTIAL.

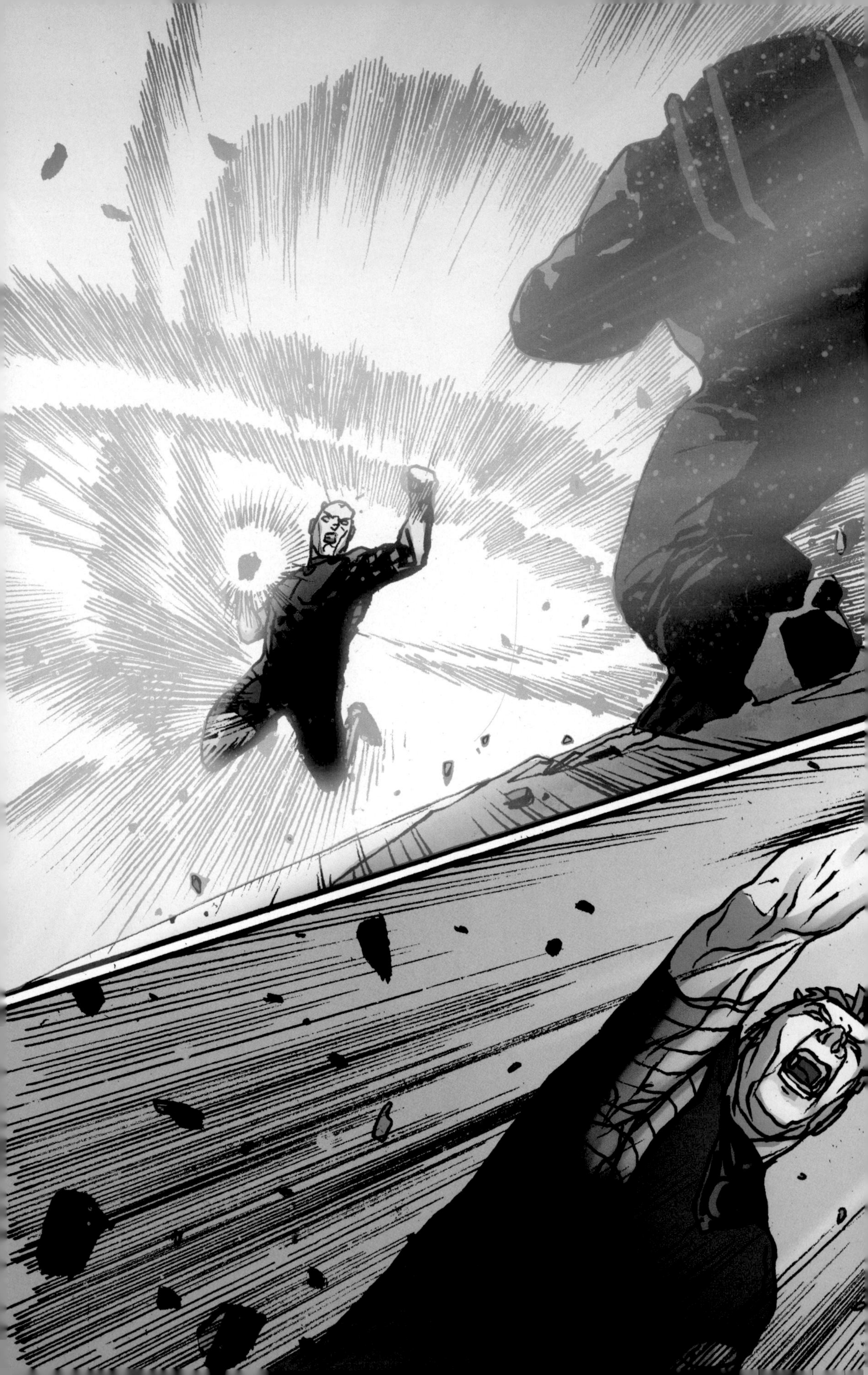

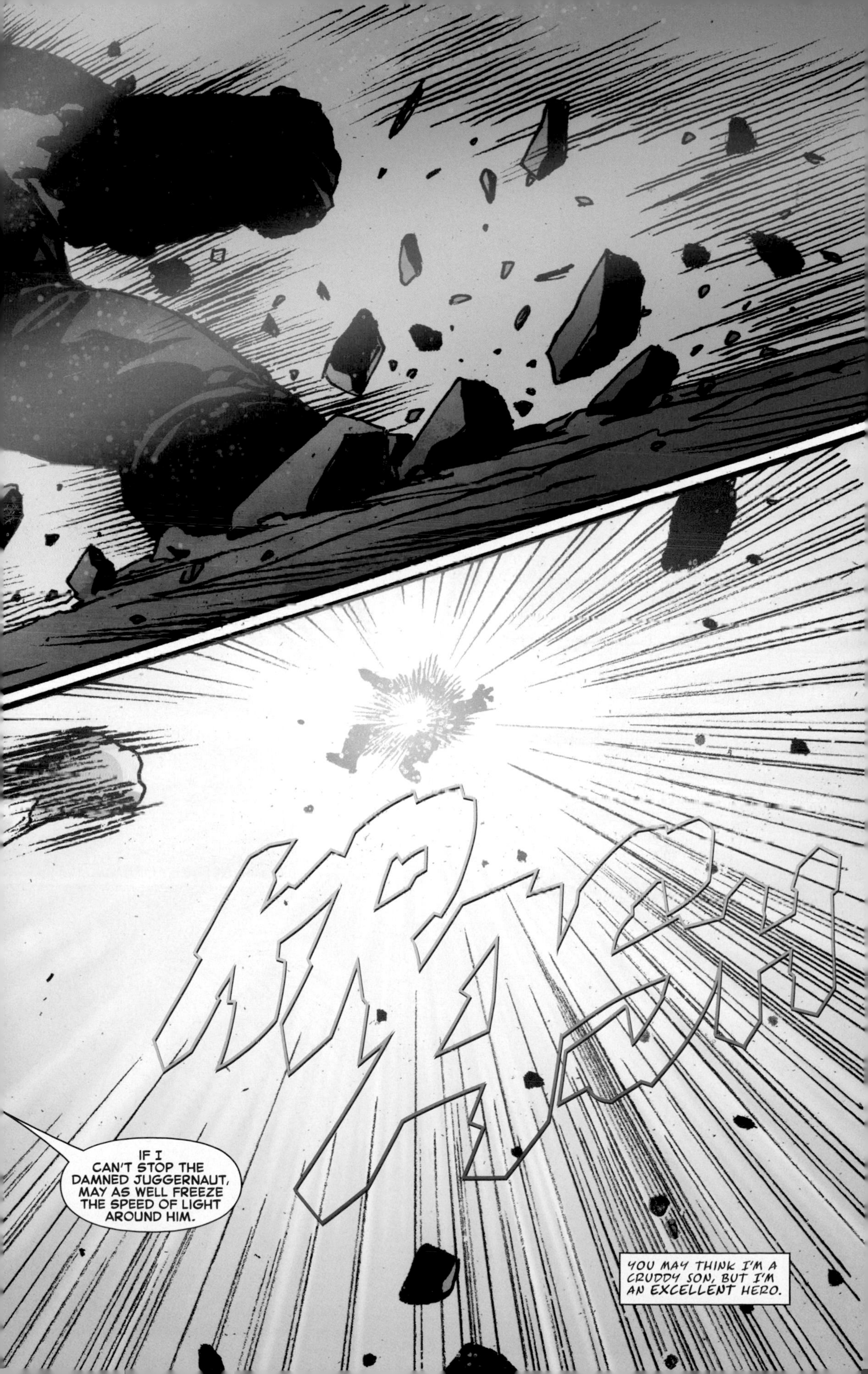
IF I CAN'T STOP THE DAMNED JUGGERNAUT, MAY AS WELL FREEZE THE SPEED OF LIGHT AROUND HIM.
YOU MAY THINK I'M A CRUDDY SON, BUT I'M AN EXCELLENT HERO.

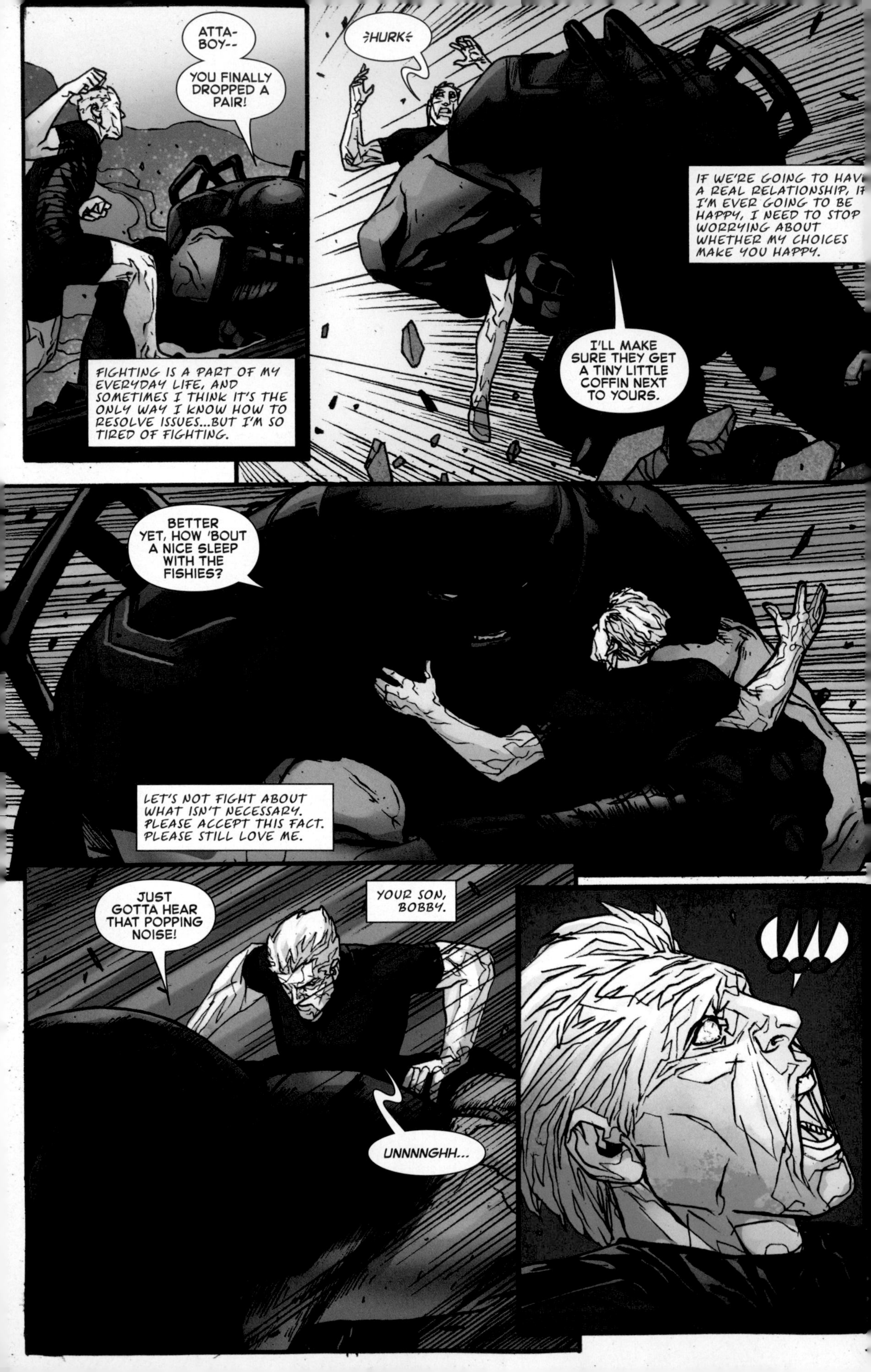
ATTA-BOY--
YOU FINALLY DROPPED A PAIR!
FIGHTING IS A PART OF MY EVERYDAY LIFE, AND SOMETIMES I THINK IT'S THE ONLY WAY I KNOW HOW TO RESOLVE ISSUES...BUT I'M SO TIRED OF FIGHTING.
HURK
IF WE'RE GOING TO HAV A REAL RELATIONSHIP, IF I'M EVER GOING TO BE HAPPY, I NEED TO STOP WORRYING ABOUT WHETHER MY CHOICES MAKE YOU HAPPY.
I'LL MAKE SURE THEY GET A TINY LITTLE COFFIN NEXT TO YOURS.
BETTER YET, HOW 'BOUT A NICE SLEEP WITH THE FISHIES?
LET'S NOT FIGHT ABOUT WHAT ISN'T NECESSARY. PLEASE ACCEPT THIS FACT. PLEASE STILL LOVE ME.
JUST GOTTA HEAR THAT POPPING NOISE!
YOUR SON, BOBBY.
UNNNNGHH...
!!!

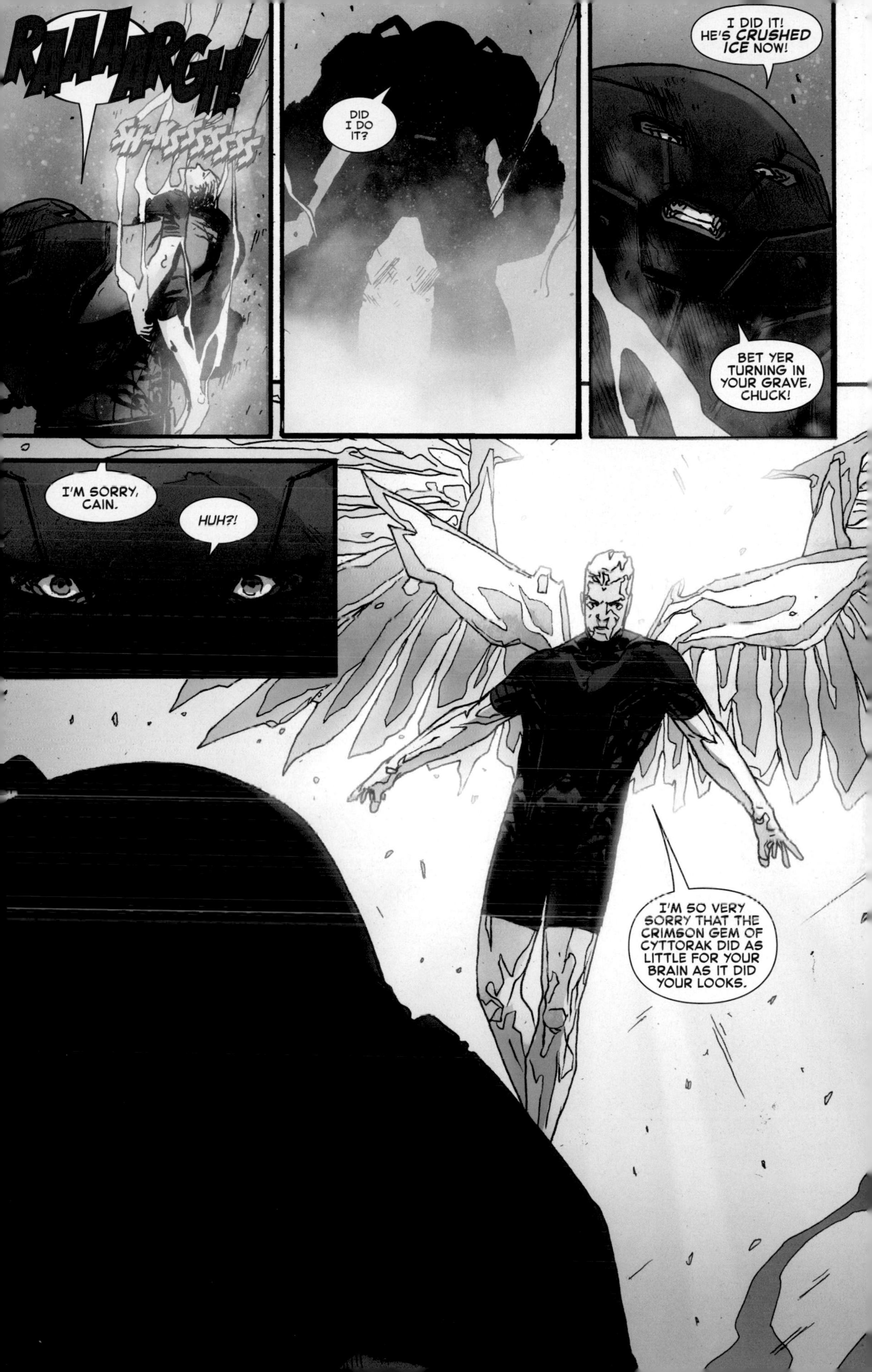
RAAAARGH!
SHKSSSSSS
DID I DO IT?
I DID IT! HE'S CRUSHED ICE NOW!
BET YER TURNING IN YOUR GRAVE, CHUCK!
I'M SORRY, CAIN.
HUH?!
I'M SO VERY SORRY THAT THE CRIMSON GEM OF CYTTORAK DID AS LITTLE FOR YOUR BRAIN AS IT DID YOUR LOOKS.

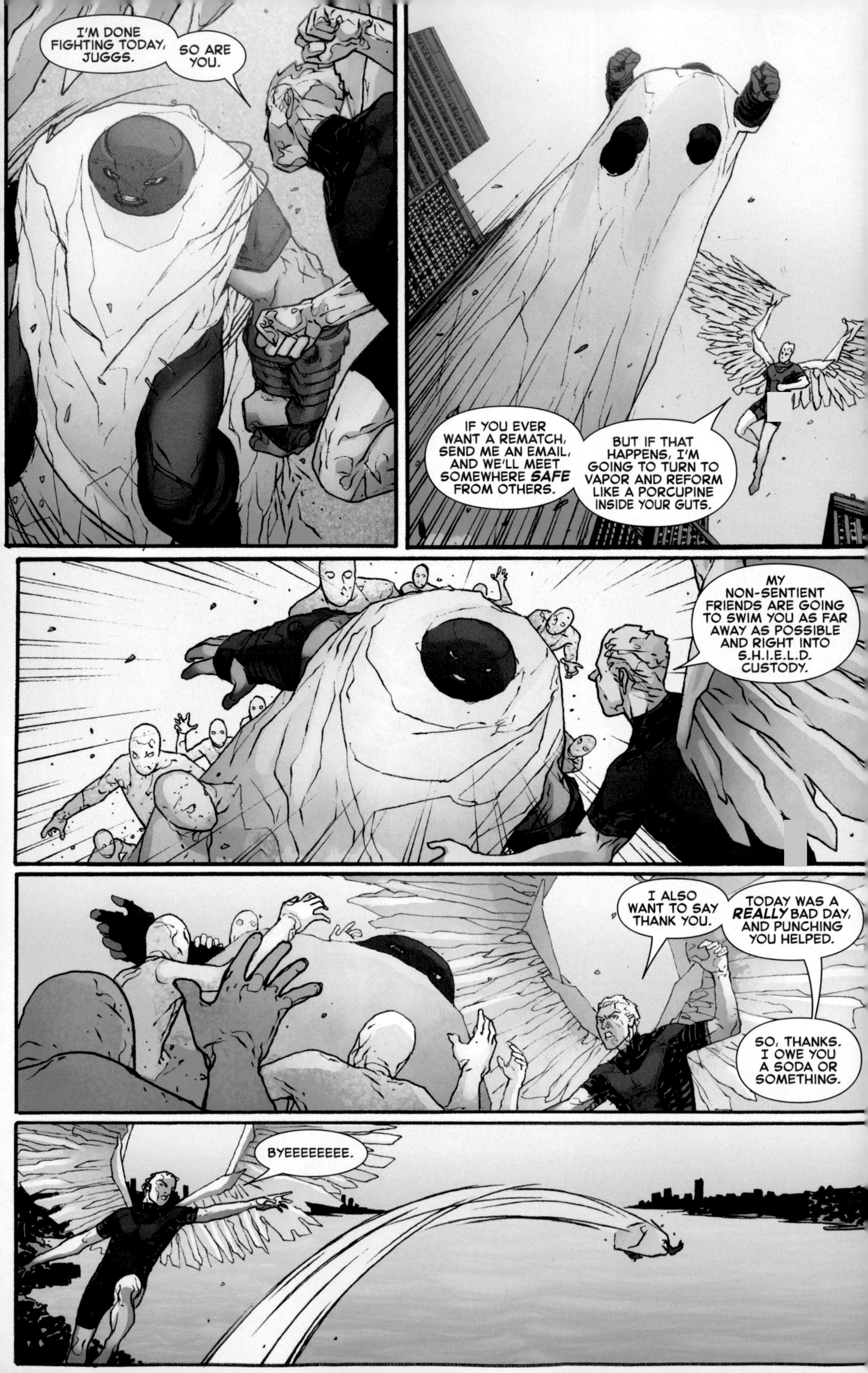
I'M DONE FIGHTING TODAY, JUGGS.
SO ARE YOU.
IF YOU EVER WANT A REMATCH, SEND ME AN EMAIL, AND WE'LL MEET SOMEWHERE *SAFE* FROM OTHERS.
BUT IF THAT HAPPENS, I'M GOING TO TURN TO VAPOR AND REFORM LIKE A PORCUPINE INSIDE YOUR GUTS.
MY NON-SENTIENT FRIENDS ARE GOING TO SWIM YOU AS FAR AWAY AS POSSIBLE AND RIGHT INTO S.H.I.E.L.D. CUSTODY.
I ALSO WANT TO SAY THANK YOU.
TODAY WAS A *REALLY* BAD DAY, AND PUNCHING YOU HELPED.
SO, THANKS. I OWE YOU A SODA OR SOMETHING.
BYEEEEEEEE.

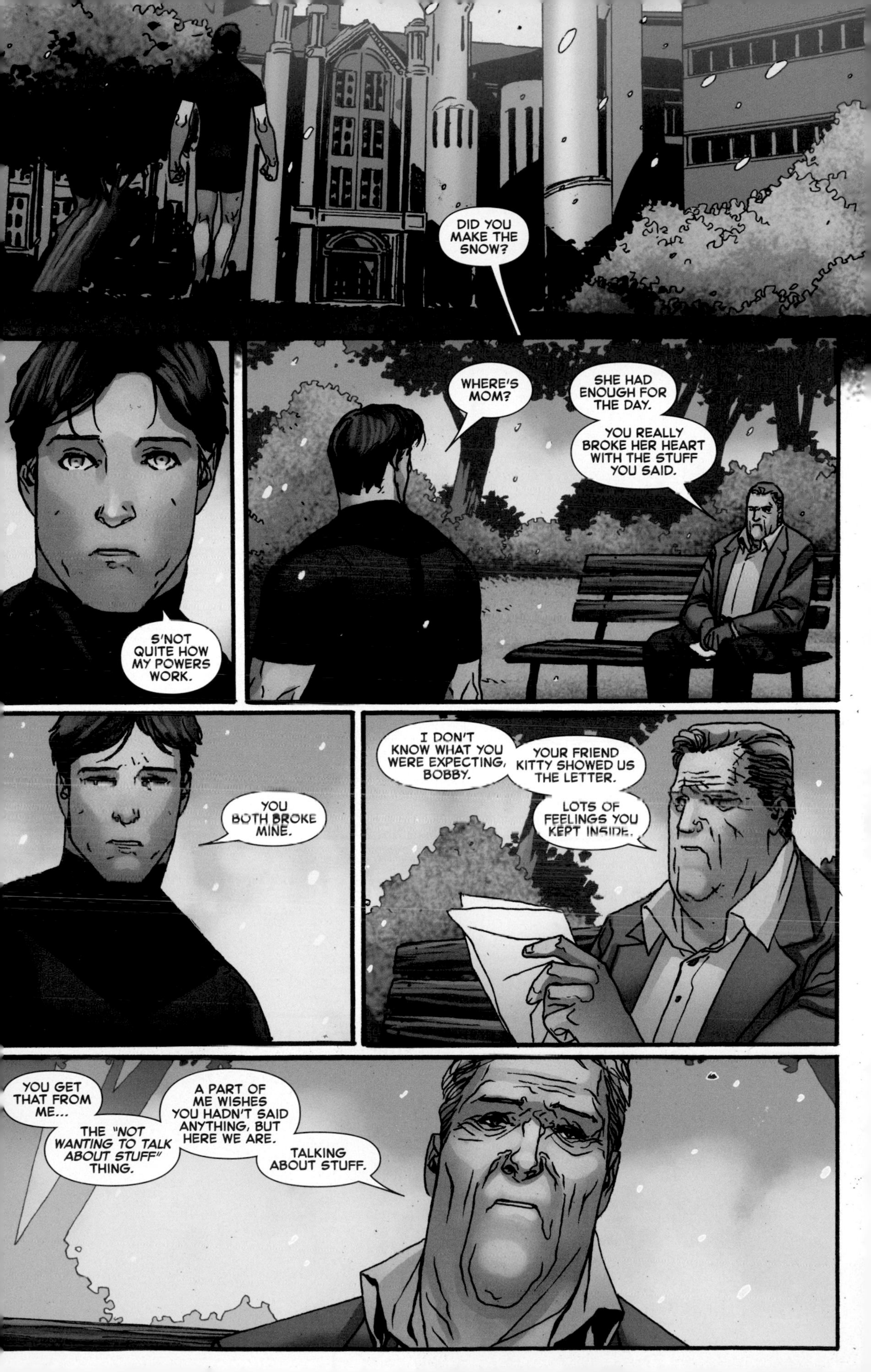

DID YOU MAKE THE SNOW?
S'NOT QUITE HOW MY POWERS WORK.
WHERE'S MOM?
SHE HAD ENOUGH FOR THE DAY.
YOU REALLY BROKE HER HEART WITH THE STUFF YOU SAID.
YOU BOTH BROKE MINE.
I DON'T KNOW WHAT YOU WERE EXPECTING, BOBBY.
YOUR FRIEND KITTY SHOWED US THE LETTER.
LOTS OF FEELINGS YOU KEPT INSIDE.
YOU GET THAT FROM ME...
THE "NOT WANTING TO TALK ABOUT STUFF" THING.
A PART OF ME WISHES YOU HADN'T SAID ANYTHING, BUT HERE WE ARE.
TALKING ABOUT STUFF.

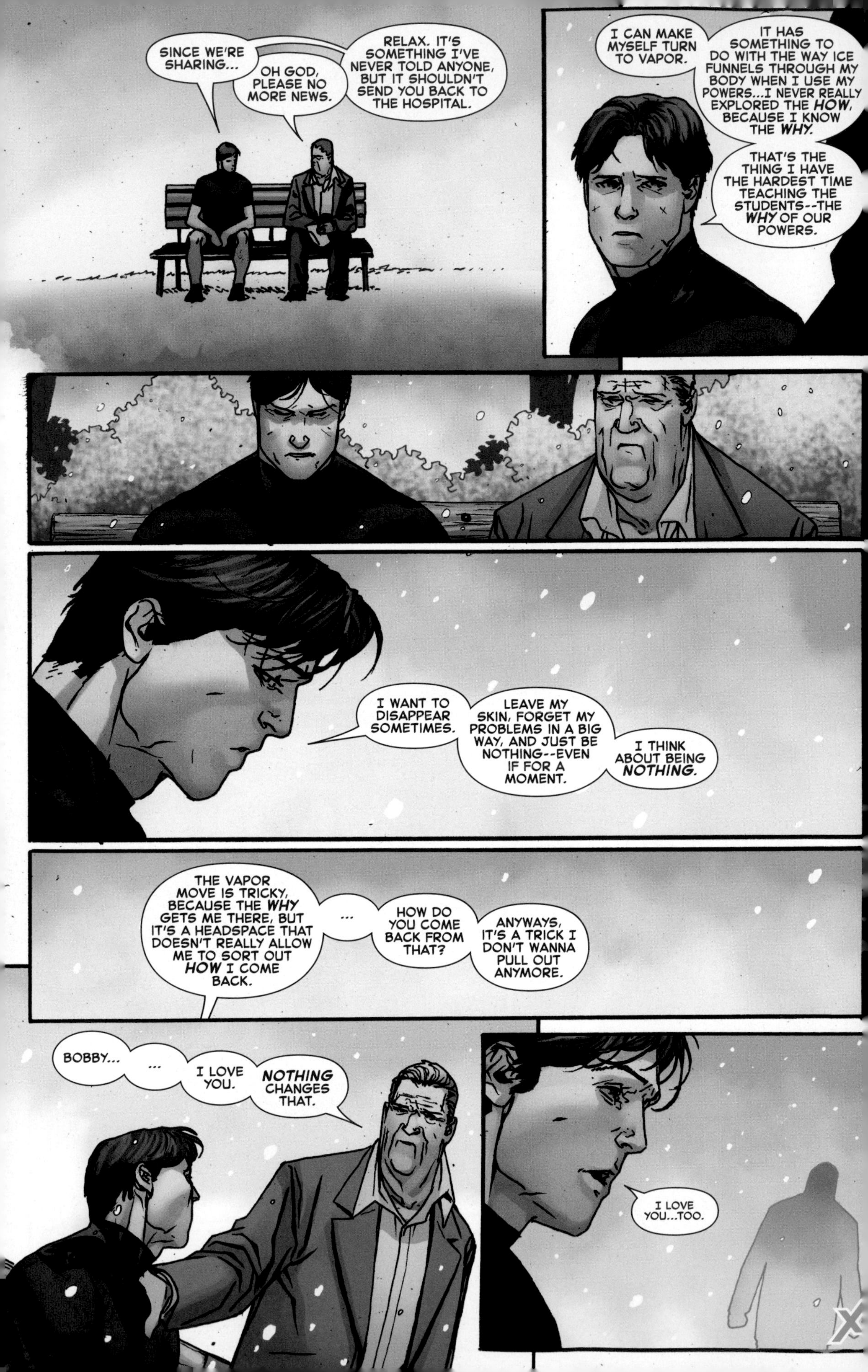
SINCE WE'RE SHARING...
OH GOD, PLEASE NO MORE NEWS.
RELAX. IT'S SOMETHING I'VE NEVER TOLD ANYONE, BUT IT SHOULDN'T SEND YOU BACK TO THE HOSPITAL.
I CAN MAKE MYSELF TURN TO VAPOR.
IT HAS SOMETHING TO DO WITH THE WAY ICE FUNNELS THROUGH MY BODY WHEN I USE MY POWERS...I NEVER REALLY EXPLORED THE *HOW*, BECAUSE I KNOW THE *WHY*.
THAT'S THE THING I HAVE THE HARDEST TIME TEACHING THE STUDENTS--THE *WHY* OF OUR POWERS.
I WANT TO DISAPPEAR SOMETIMES.
LEAVE MY SKIN, FORGET MY PROBLEMS IN A BIG WAY, AND JUST BE NOTHING--EVEN IF FOR A MOMENT.
I THINK ABOUT BEING *NOTHING.*
THE VAPOR MOVE IS TRICKY, BECAUSE THE *WHY* GETS ME THERE, BUT IT'S A HEADSPACE THAT DOESN'T REALLY ALLOW ME TO SORT OUT *HOW* I COME BACK.
...
HOW DO YOU COME BACK FROM THAT?
ANYWAYS, IT'S A TRICK I DON'T WANNA PULL OUT ANYMORE.
BOBBY...
...
I LOVE YOU.
NOTHING CHANGES THAT.
I LOVE YOU...TOO.

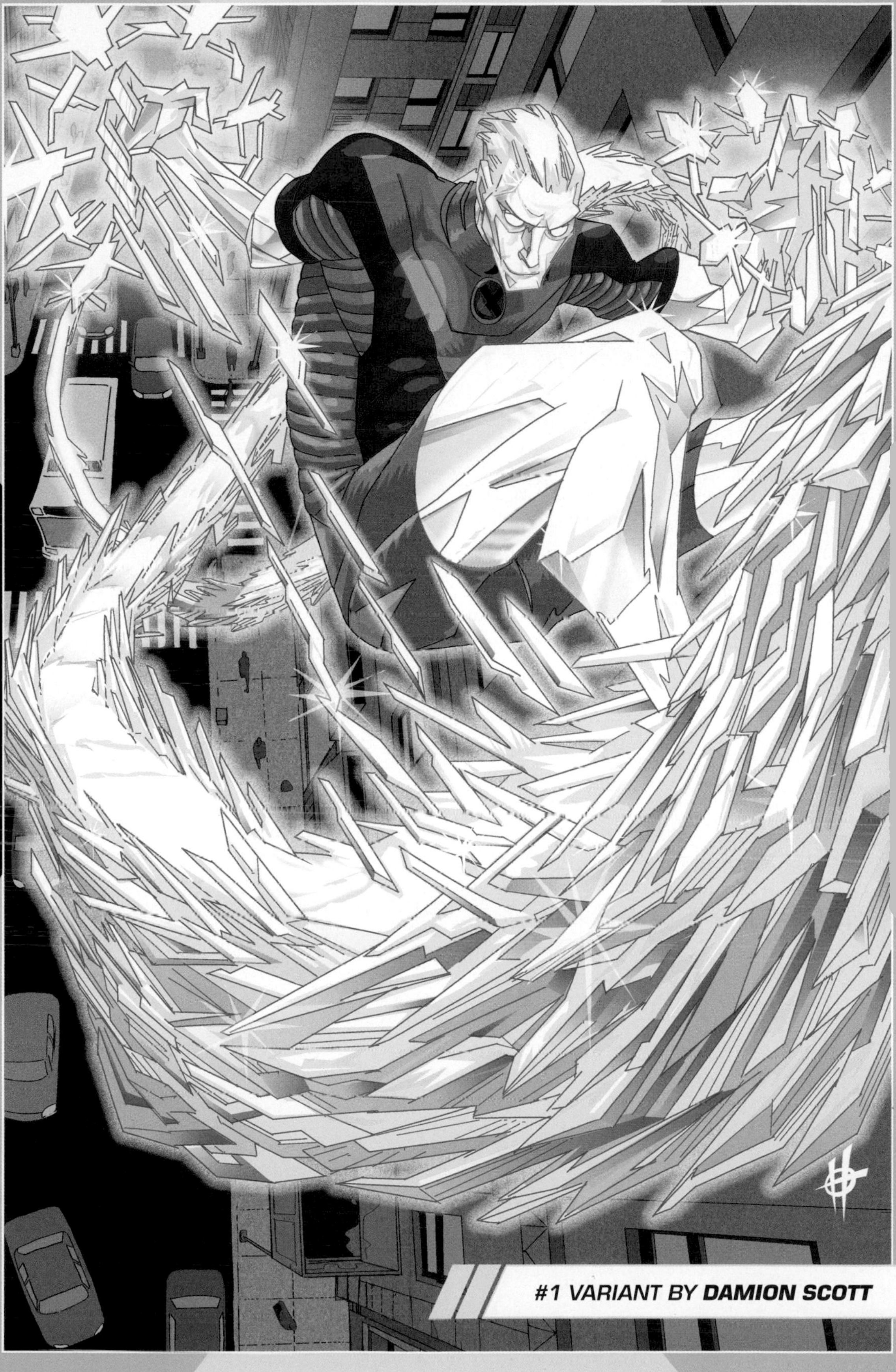

#1 VARIANT BY **DAMION SCOTT**

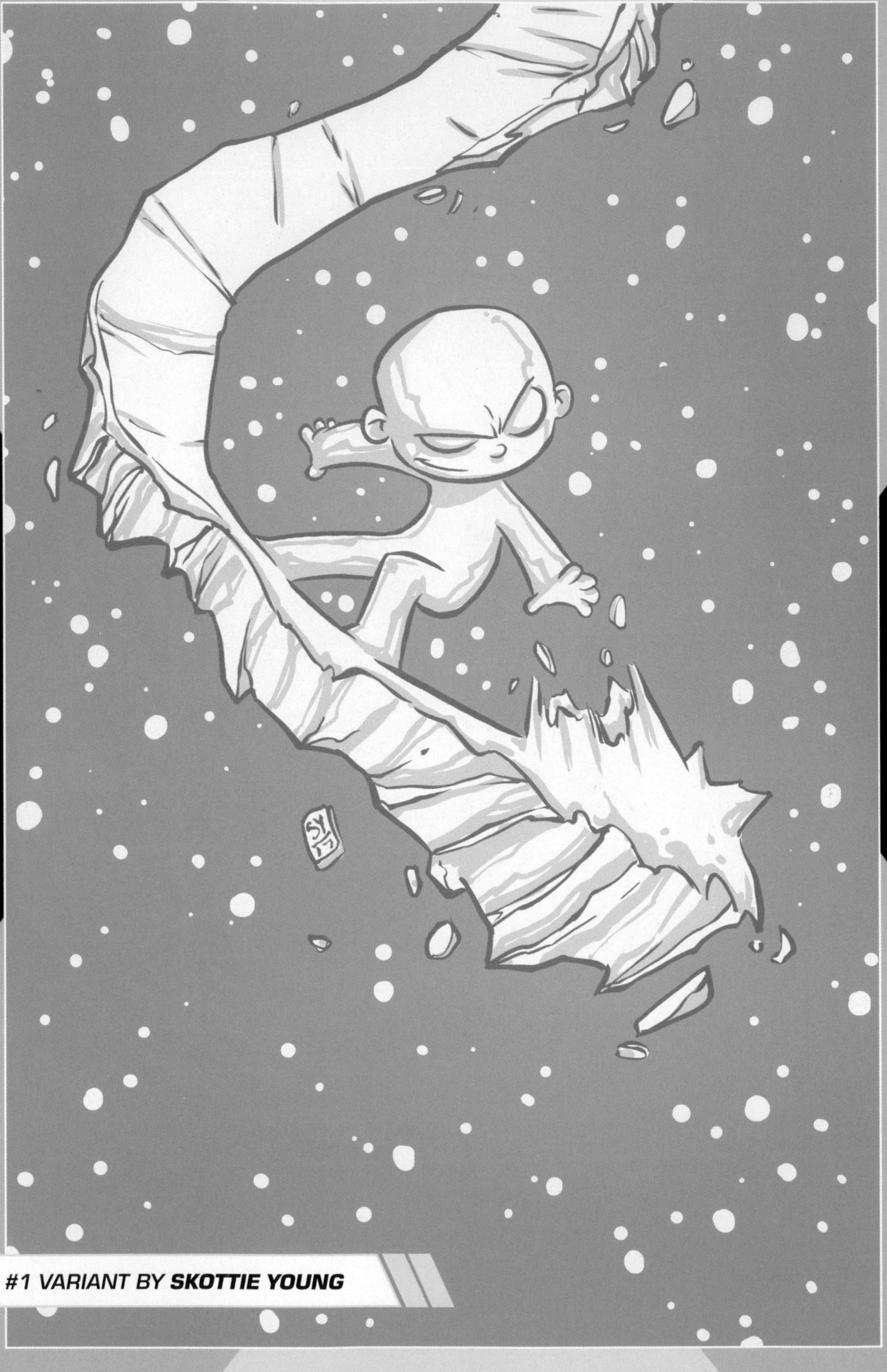

#1 VARIANT BY **SKOTTIE YOUNG**

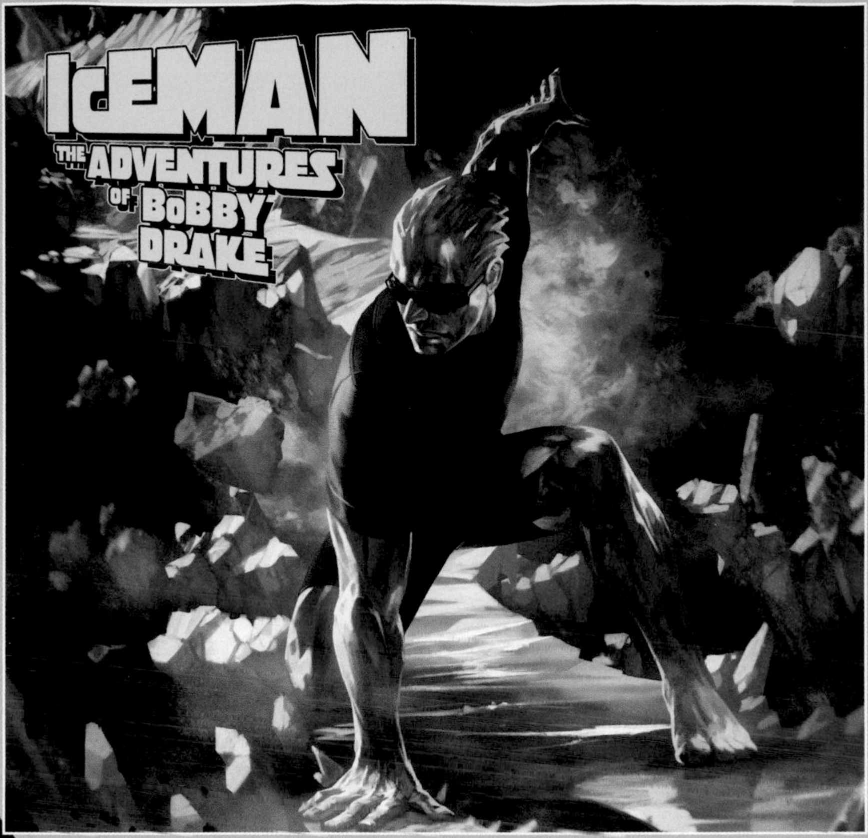
ICEMAN
THE ADVENTURES OF BOBBY DRAKE

#1 HIP-HOP VARIANT
BY ***SKAN***

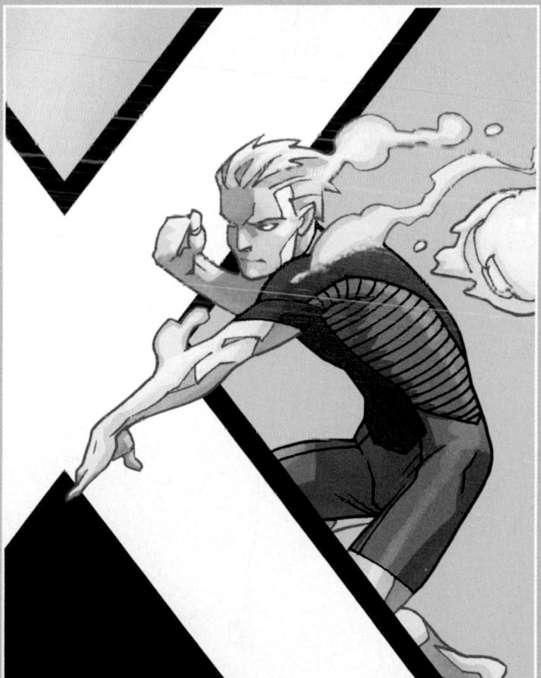

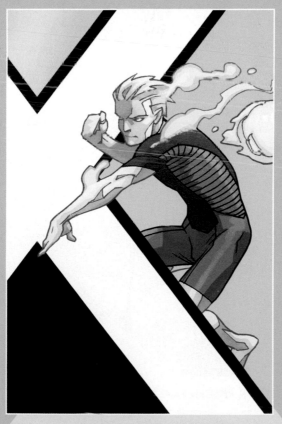

#1 CORNER BOX VARIANT
BY ***LEONARD KIRK***
& ***MICHAEL GARLAND***

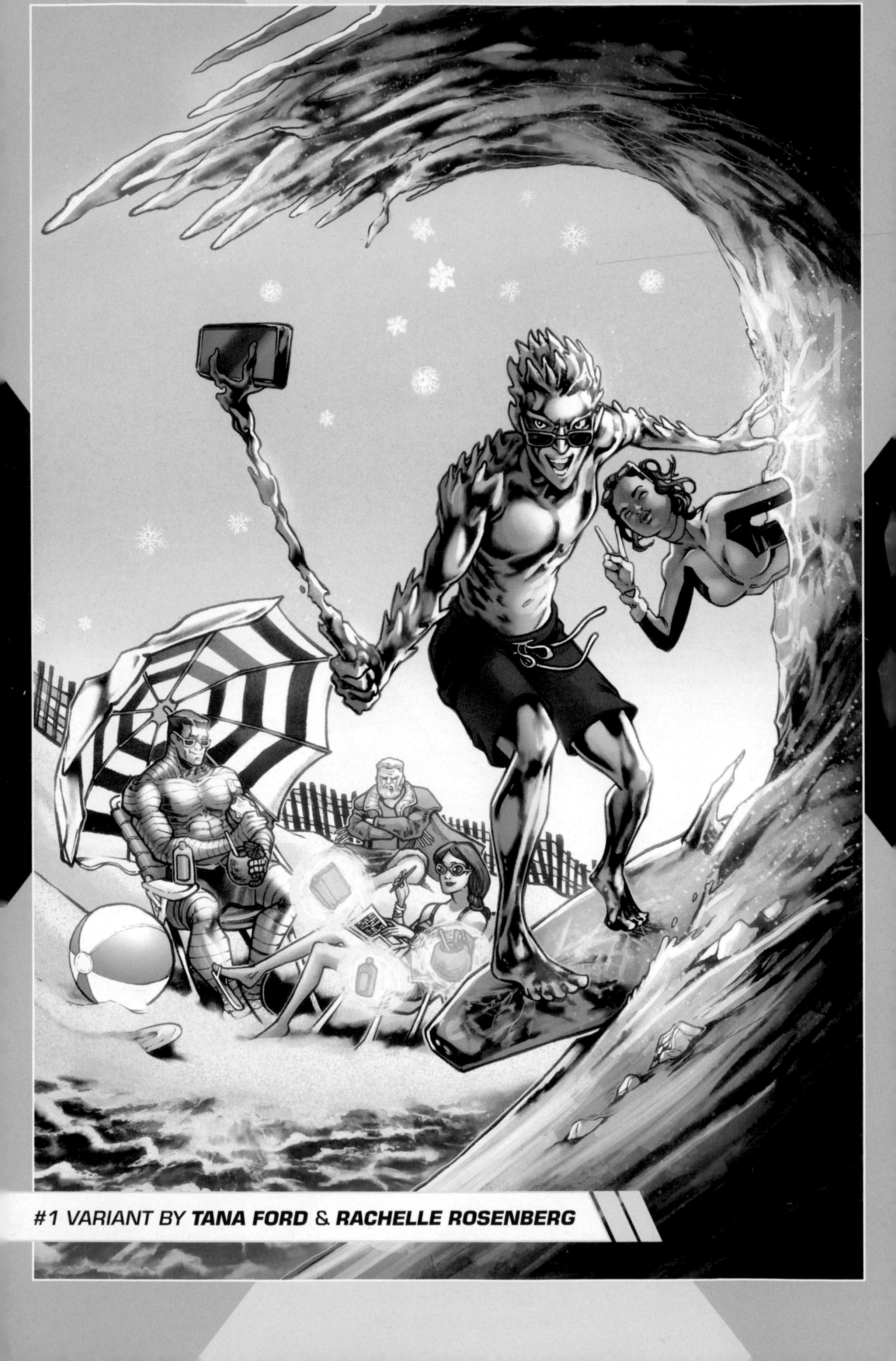

#1 VARIANT BY ***TANA FORD*** & ***RACHELLE ROSENBERG***